Early Childhood Educational Research

This book provides an introduction to research in early childhood education which will appeal to a large audience of early years policy-makers, professionals and practitioners. It offers an overview of recent history and the development of research in the field, how conceptions and methodologies have changed and what key issues and dilemmas have emerged.

The authors:

- identify key topics, perspectives and controversies in the field
- raise important issues – theoretical, methodological and practical
- examine and illustrate different research traditions
- include the consideration of a range of political and ethical issues.

Early Childhood Educational Research: Issues in Methodology and Ethics is written in an extremely accessible manner with no special knowledge presupposed. This is an ideal introduction to research in the field of early childhood education research.

Early Childhood Educational Research
Issues in methodology and ethics

Carol Aubrey, Tricia David,
Ray Godfrey and Linda Thompson

 RoutledgeFalmer
Taylor & Francis Group

LONDON AND NEW YORK

M1055l9 3wks.

First published 2000 by RoutledgeFalmer
11 New Fetter Lane, London EC4P 4EE

Simultaneously published in the USA and Canada
by RoutledgeFalmer
29 West 35th Street, New York, NY 10001

Transferred to Digital Printing 2004

RoutledgeFalmer is an imprint of the Taylor & Francis Group

Typeset in Galliard by
HWA Text and Data Management, Tunbridge Wells
Printed and bound in Great Britain by
TJI Digital, Padstow, Cornwall

British Library Cataloguing in Publication Data
A catalogue record for this book is available from the British Library

Library of Congress Cataloging in Publication Data
Early childhood educational research : issues in methodology and
ethics / Carol Aubrey … [et al.]
        p. cm.
    Includes bibliographical references and index.
        1. Early childhood education–Research–Methodology. 2. Early
    childhood education–Research–Moral and ethical aspects. I.
Aubrey, Carol.

    LB1139.225 . E37 2000
    372.21´072–dc21   00-021337

ISBN 0-750-70746-1 (hbk)
ISBN 0-750-70745-3 (pbk)

Contents

PART IV
Current policy, perspectives and practice in the field   **141**

Tables

Figures

Abbreviations

BERA	British Education Research Association
BSE	bovine spongiform encephalopathy
CJD	Creutzfeldt-Jakob disease
DAP	developmentally appropriate practice
DES	Department of Education and Science
DfEE	Department for Education and Employment
DHSS	Department of Health and Social Security
EARLI	European Association for Research on Learning and Instruction
ECER	European Conference for Educational Research
EEL	Effective Early Learning
EPPE	Effective Provision for Preschool Education
ERIC	Educational Resources Information Center
ESL	English as a second language
ESRC	Economic and Social Research Council
EU	European Union
FE	further education
FSM	free school meals
GCSE	General Certificate of Secondary Education
HE	higher education
HEFC	Higher Education Funding Council
HEFCE	Higher Education Funding Council for England
HM	Her Majesty's
IEA	International Association for Evaluation of Achievement
IES	Institute for Employment Studies
IQ	intelligence quotient
KS1	Key Stage 1
LEA	Local Education Authorities
MPG	main professional grade
NC	National Curriculum
NFER	National Foundation for Educational Research
NNEB	Nursery Nursing Examination Board
OECD	Organisation for Economic Cooperation and Development
OFSTED	Office for Standards in Education

OMEP	L'Organisation Mondiale pour l'Éducation Préscolaire
PCFC	Polytechnics and Colleges Funding Council
PE	physical education
PIPS	Performance Indicators in Primary Schools
PNP	Primary Needs Programme
QCA	Qualifications and Curriculum Authority
QR	quality-related research
RAE	research assessment exercise
SAT	standard assessment task
SCAA	Schools Curriculum and Assessment Authority
SEN	special educational needs
SSRC	Social Science Research Council
TIMSS	Third International Mathematics and Science Study
TSE	transmissible spongiform encephalopathies
TTA	Teacher Training Agency
UFC	Universities Funding Council
UGC	University Grants Committee
UN	United Nations
UNESCO	United Nations Educational, Scientific and Cultural Organisation

Preface

Educational research in general and early years educational research in particular has never before been higher on the agenda of policy-makers. According to Charles Clarke, Schools Minister (1999), he perceived: *Shirly Assigned.*

> a discontinuity between research and what the Government is doing and a widespread ignorance on what works and what doesn't in education as well as an effective database that could provide answers to questions about schools, teaching and learning.
>
> (Clarke 1999, p.1)

At the same time he explained that he would welcome views on the way educational research could better serve the needs of the educational system and help to raise standards.

This may sound a little harsh but perhaps as researchers we should recognise that educational research *is* still in the earliest stages of theoretical development. Murray (1989) stated that the development of educational practice has not gained much credence by relying on education theory:

> In the educational world and explanations market ordinary words and neologisms are bought and sold to help us understand educational issues and problems. What possible sense do these make?
>
> (Murray 1989, p.1)

In his view the proper definition of an education concept was not stated in terms of its presumed properties but instead should be stated in relation to the procedure or operation used to *measure* the concept in question. In other words the researcher's hypotheses (or yet-to-be-proven statements) needed to be operationally defined and tested and eventually needed to fulfil all the assumptions that everything is measurable and obeys the vital principle of parsimony – the simplest explanation with the fewest assumptions. According to Murray, definitions can be examined at a number of levels:

- At level 1, the definition states merely what the researcher does. In the case of a Piagetian task, for instance, the researcher might roll out one of two balls of plasticene into a sausage shape and ask the child which piece of plasticene is bigger.

- At level 2, the definition includes what the child does in response. In this case, the child might say either that the two pieces of plasticene remain the same or that the rolled-out ball is now bigger.
- At level 3, the phenomenon described at level 2 is attributed with cause by stating exactly *what* the cause is – in the case being considered, conservation, or that the pupil can or cannot conserve, as the case may be.
- At level 4, the nature of the cause is specified.
- At level 5, sets of level-4 concepts are integrated into a coherent theory. That is, the theory accounts for the way discrete facts, based on observations of children, their actions and summaries of these, fit together through structural and causal relationships.

In Murray's (1989) view even Piagetian theory does not reach level 4 and 5. He concluded that educational practice cannot be guaranteed by theory and that principles derived from practice will be a safer bet! Suffice it to say at this point that early years practitioners are advised to adopt a healthy scepticism towards educational theories and concede that the schools minister may well be right in recognising that we are, so to speak, in *our* infancy in respect of our knowledge and understanding of learning and teaching in general and theories of child development specifically.

More worrying in this regard for us to note is that our own Chief Inspector of Schools is still working at a level formulated on assumption, that is, he accepts certain beliefs as self-evident. For example, the Office for Standards in Education (OFSTED) report (1999) states:

> The achievement of a more consistent, high quality programme of nursery education has not been helped, however, by a rather sterile debate which has pre-occupied this phase of education for far too long. At the heart of this debate is a tension that needs to be resolved, between those who believe nursery education should be shaped around play-based 'child-directed' learning, and those who believe young children benefit from rather more structured learning involving some direct teaching, which ensures, for example, that they make a good start on such important things, as reading, writing and early mathematical work.
>
> (OFSTED 1999, p.3)

It is made clear in the following paragraph that those who favour structured teaching and who have the 'most effective and ... the most improved settings' support the latter view and that some unspecified and, presumably, misguided early years professionals, whether they be providers, practitioners or so-called pre-school educational 'experts', seek to reduce rather than retain or increase – in other words oppose – the degree of challenge provided within specific areas of learning.

Interestingly, in the same month, a report from an all-party inquiry into the work of the Office for Standards in Education was concluding that there was a danger of the Chief Inspector being seen simply as a 'pundit or polemicist' unless his publicly-expressed views were more clearly based on evidence from inspection reports. He should restrain his 'intemperate approach'.

In this climate it behoves us all to examine critically our current early childhood education knowledge base – its theories and its research. In fact a primary goal for this book is to identify and describe changing views and accumulated research findings in order to avoid precisely what Woodhead's oversimplified polarisation between child-directed play and structured learning represents – which is a deep misunderstanding about what is developmentally appropriate. To take just one example, a detailed knowledge of children's early and informal conceptual knowledge in an area of learning such as numerical cognition and a careful analysis of its component skills will allow early practitioners both to identify those children *without* this early numerical competence and to ensure that this is imparted to such vulnerable or 'at risk' children as exist. Simply providing all children with an early formal numeracy curriculum ignores the fact that certain numerical skills play a crucial role in children's ability to benefit from formal schooling (Aubrey 1999). Perhaps at the true heart of the debate is a recognition that just giving children direct teaching at an early age will *not* help them to make a 'good start' to formal schooling and that a child-focused specification of the necessary component skills in number knowledge that individual children possess and coordinate *must* be obtained if they are to be helped to develop a real number sense and become successful at early mathematics in school. Direct teaching in itself will *not* ensure early progress and a child-centred way is essential.

The writers of this book do not intend to provide an exhaustive account of any one particular theory of early childhood nor, for that matter, support the adherence to any single approach to early childhood education research. There exist already a huge range of methodological texts which set out to identify and describe the vast range of strategies and techniques which are available for collecting, analysing and interpreting data and which can be applied to early childhood education contexts. We cannot attempt to represent this field in its entirety, review how far we have come or predict where, in time, we shall be. Instead we aim to offer a brief discussion of the recent history and development of early childhood education, how conceptions and methodologies used in early childhood have changed and to identify some of the key issues and dilemmas. Denzin and Lincoln (1994) have referred to a 'quiet methodological revolution' which has been taking place in the social sciences in general so that

> where only statistics, experimental design and survey research once stood, researchers have opened up to ethnography ... experimenting with the boundaries of interpretation, linking research to social change ... to understand more fully the relationship of the researcher to the research.
> (Denzin and Lincoln 1994, p.ix)

We do not ourselves feel that 'tensions', competing definitions or redefinitions should be a matter for concern or attempted resolution. In fact we should be surprised *not* to find essential paradigmatic differences, contradictory styles and types of research. Most important, as noted by Denzin and Lincoln, is to locate ourselves within this cultural context. Other writers would construct a book of this type in different ways.

In terms of movement, the early chapters (1 to 4) locate the field, examining changing constructions, paradigms and methods of investigation. Chapters 5 and 6 trace the development of early childhood education research from past to present. Chapters 7 and 8 provide two exemplars from contemporary research case inquiries – one in the quantitative research tradition and one in the ethnographic and interpretive research tradition. We do not attempt to represent the current field in its entirety but rather to identify and illustrate different traditions – one from social anthropology and one from educational research. Chapters 9 to 13 turn to the politics and ethics of the field and end by considering current theoretical perspectives and future directions.

We have attempted to identify some of the key topics, perspectives and controversies though have found that as one person has completed a chapter, another has called for revisions. No doubt the process could continue endlessly so we have to accept the book's shortcomings in the hope that at least we have shown that research in early childhood education, if still in its infancy, nevertheless constitutes a field worthy of serious study in its own right and that interested readers may pursue for themselves some of the issues – theoretical, methodological or practical – this text has raised and for which it can only provide a starting point and a signpost.

Carol Aubrey
October 1999.

Part I

Changing concepts and methods in early years education research

1 Researching early childhood education

What's the use of research?

It is an interesting paradox that as the certainty of research evidence is called more and more into question (for example following the bovine spongiform encephalopathy – BSE – controversy and other similar debates which have made press headlines), there is an increasing demand for practitioners in every field of service to the public to develop 'evidence-based practice'. Moreover, the Treasury is calling for the 'best evidence possible'. It is ironic that it took the BSE crisis to produce an effective regulatory system for animal foodstuffs and it is now illegal to feed lifestock on meat and bones from feedmills and farms in Britain. Slaughter houses are required to ensure that animal body parts are not resold and used in feed. Meanwhile in other parts of Europe recycling of insects, algae, used fat and cooking oils, besides the carcasses of all kinds of animals – including dogs, cats and rats – is still permitted, although scientists have discovered a link between transmissible spongiform encephalopathies (TSE) in cats and dogs and Creutzfeldt-Jakob disease (CJD) in humans. Professor Mac Johnson of the Royal Veterinary College and an adviser to the Economic Union Scientific Committee in *The Sunday Telegraph* (31 October 1999, p.20) was reported as saying 'you should not recycle animals in feed ... if you do, then you are risking an epidemic like the one we have just experienced'. It seems that the risks uncovered by research go unheeded as 'the European Commission appears doomed to shut the stable doors after diseased animals have already bolted into the food chain'.

Meanwhile teachers, doctors and social workers are all urged to improve the quality of research, evaluate it more carefully and publicise it more widely. For those in education in England and Wales, the Teacher Training Agency (TTA) is urging evidence-based practice as a central tenet of its aims to create a climate of greater professionalism in schools, and funding for small-scale research projects and for teachers who have findings to disseminate from research conducted for higher degrees is also on offer. However, while the TTA does not expect every teacher to begin conducting research, it is expected that teachers will read research reports, make informed judgements about them and then apply, if appropriate, the findings to their own work.

A recent evaluative report (Hillage *et al.* 1998) criticised the failure in uptake of the findings of educational research in the UK. Not only the researchers themselves were censured for failing to disseminate findings effectively, but policy-makers (for failing to wait for and use findings before leaping on to make new policies, such as the *National Numeracy* or *Literacy Strategies*) and practitioners too were criticised. The latter were, according to this research team, simply not accessing research knowledge, although they were forgiven because their lack of time to scour research journals, to reflect and discuss findings with colleagues, was given as an excuse.

In the field of early childhood education, much is in fact already done on two fronts: through dissemination of existing research and through the sponsoring of new work. Practitioners can gain access to research findings through conferences at which researchers are invited to speak and through the pages of 'popular journals' with a wide circulation in schools and nurseries, such as *Nursery World* and *Child Education*. This is not to say that more could not be done! Many early years advisers have lamented the poor or nonexistent budget for seminars, conferences and continuing professional development, especially for those working in the voluntary and private sector nurseries. However, with the new Early Years Development and Care Partnerships with funding through the government's Standards Fund there is the chance for inter-agency professional development with improved training opportunities.

In terms of new knowledge production, indeed, it seems that worldwide there is interest in the earliest years of life and their importance for lifelong education. The Organisation for Economic Cooperation and Development (OECD), whose main focus is *economic* as its name suggests, is currently conducting a survey of the Early Childhood Education and Care provision in thirteen member states – the UK being one of these. Publishers seem more eager than ever to contract books about learning during the first years of life. In other words, there is finally, after a century of (mainly women's) calls for the importance of early learning to be recognised and appropriately funded, a 'window of opportunity' which those of us working in this area of study cannot afford to miss.

So, what is research and how will it help us during this time of unprecedented interest and development? What is the use of educational research? Research was defined by Lawrence Stenhouse (1975) as systematic inquiry whose results are placed in the public domain. In relation to research on child development, Schaffer (1990) went further to distinguish five characteristics of the scientific method as:

- empirical, that is, based on direct and verifiable observation of relevant phenomena
- systematic, that is, executed according to an explicit plan designed in advance and followed exactly
- controlled, in order to isolate the important factors and possible patterns of relationships among them as well as control of extraneous factors so that associations between particular factors can be identified

- quantitative descriptions, which allow greater rigour and exactness in theory construction and in testing of theory whatever the nature of the original data collected (photographs, tape-recorded discourse, video-recording or more traditional numerical data)
- public scrutiny by others working in the same field in order that all aspects of the research process are subjected to criticism, according to agreed and legitimate criteria.

There are many different ways of conducting research, as we shall explain in later chapters of this book, but the main point is that research must be scientific and provide as reliable a knowledge as possible. The researcher should know why certain methods and procedures have been selected as fittest for the purpose and an awareness of the limitations should be acknowledged. This makes it vital to recognise the ways in which different parts of the process are all integral to the research to make a coherent whole. Moreover this is the reason that before publication research studies are critically reviewed and, hence, accepted as legitimate by the research community.

One of us worked with the late Corinne Hutt as a researcher in the 1970s. One day someone came to see Corinne, knowing that she was an expert in observational techniques and that she had used film for research purposes (this was before the days of video). Corinne was told in triumphant tones that this person had collected 'sixty hours of film' on her research topic. Corinne was unimpressed. 'So what? It's easy to do that – it's what you now do with it that counts.' What Corinne meant was that the recording of 'real life' was only part of the process. How you systematically and logically draw together data from the raw processes, how you analyse the data, the rigour in your analysis, the interpretation of those data, and the subsequent dissemination of the research results are vital elements of the research process, demanding many research skills as well as integrity. The process also demands the ability to be both reflective and reflexive. A researcher needs to engage in reflection throughout to ensure that the research is appropriately conducted, in order that the experience and understanding brought to the research is fully exploited and with proper attention to ethical considerations. Reflexivity means that one is aware of one's own potential influence on the research process, as a result of one's standpoint and assumptions. It means taking account of the advantages of the principal enquirer's common human experience whilst remaining alert to potential sources of bias.

Additionally, studies which monitor the progress or quality of what is happening in a school or nursery are thought of as educational evaluation and sometimes not regarded as true research. This seems a pity because often evaluations of policy and/or practice provide just as much that is new or useful as original research projects and it is at times difficult to see where the boundaries between the two actually are. However defined, the evaluation process is intimately related to research, whether external and accountability-oriented or more democratically-oriented, self-evaluated and concerned with needs, values, costs or effectiveness.

Unlike some of our European Union (EU) partner countries, the UK has not had a tradition of government-funded and sponsored small-scale practitioner research projects. However, evaluations of education programmes, processes and outcomes are often carried out in early childhood contexts using controlled research procedures.

Perhaps the most compelling reason for conducting and understanding research is that we are human and human beings are by nature curious, born to try to 'make sense' of any situation in which we find ourselves. The research process by its very nature attempts to generate reliable knowledge which can justify its cost in terms of time and money. The latest twist in the BSE controversy suggests that reliable knowledge may lead to an effective regulatory system in one member state of the EU which is not automatically pursued by others as the global agricultural economy develops. More and more we need high-quality research to promote new knowledge because the world is ever-changing. This provides a sound knowledge base upon which to respond to change. In fact society today is probably changing at a faster rate than at any earlier time. Further, we are more aware of the ways in which citizens need to make informed decisions about their own lives and those of their children. Those decisions need to be informed by research, as far as research is able to provide answers in what Beck (1992) has called 'the risk society'. Early years professionals, moreover, will be stimulated to increased skill in enhancing the development and learning of young children and, hence, their effectiveness through reading and incorporating sound research findings in their practice.

In this book we are focusing on issues related to educational research concerned with the period of life internationally recognised as early childhood – birth to eight years. In the UK 'early years' or 'early childhood' has recently been used in official documents to mean the years before statutory schooling and in some cases it means only children aged three and four. But because the longer view is taken internationally and because we wish to reiterate the importance of continuity across this age span, we ask readers to take this longer perspective.

In Chapter 2 we discuss the ways in which societies think about young children, the assumptions they make and the consequences for both the children themselves and for those who educate them. The consequences of seeing three- and four-year-olds as a homogeneous group and as different from two- or six-year-olds are far-reaching. A teacher known to us, highly respected by colleagues and parents alike, who was carefully providing for the individual needs of the children in her reception class of four- and five-year-olds was taken to task by an OFSTED inspector who said he could not see how her curriculum changed on the child's fifth birthday (statutory school starting-age) to take account of the statutory nature of the UK National Curriculum. Examples of this kind cause one to wonder about the misunderstandings between the two people involved. Perhaps we should not too hastily jump to conclusions about an inspector who had no early years background. It is possible that all he was signalling to the teacher was the statutory nature of the National Curriculum (although it is generally agreed that the National Curriculum should not be applied until a child begins Year 1, the year the child becomes six, not immediately the child passes the fifth birthday). Further, a note in the teacher's planning might have sufficed, to show that as the child had now attained statutory school-age, a shift in planning from the areas of learning used by Schools' Curriculum and Assessment Authority (SCAA 1996) for children under five to the subjects of the National Curriculum would be demanded, even if what the child actually did would seem very much the same to that child. This example serves to illustrate the misunderstandings which can arise when examining early childhood education even with a detailed knowledge of the educational and socio-cultural context. Moreover, research is especially important when change is occurring or being contemplated so the following section provides a brief overview of the changing UK context.

Early childhood education and care: A brief history of the UK context

The provision of services for children under eight in the UK has a long and mixed history. Soon after the Education Act 1870 the elementary schools provided almost exclusively for the children of the working classes. They were intended to enrol children from the age of five, in order to ensure that a future workforce could learn to read, write and become numerate, as well as to become respectful and law-abiding citizens. In summary it was important that girls and boys acquired the kinds of skills which were then deemed necessary for the fulfilment of their future gendered positions in the home and workplace. That children younger than five were often found on the bottom benches or the steps of the galleried classrooms is evident from inspectors' reports from that time. In many areas this was the result of kind-heartedness, rather than some view of the potential of early schooling, for it usually happened in areas where children from poor families would roam the streets, a danger to themselves and others, if they were not brought into the schoolhouse. The choice of a compulsory admission age of five years was not decided upon as a result of any kind of educationally informed consultation. Compulsory school starting age was introduced in the Education Act 1870 as part of a wider parliamentary debate about establishing a national system of elementary education. It arose through pressure from industrialists who felt that if children were to be schooled for six years, then better to get it over with as quickly as possible. Young children had also long been cared for by local women running 'dame schools'. However, the women inspectors' report of 1905 argued that young children should be cared for and educated in a different way, through proper nursery schools. Sadly, their vision remains to be achieved almost one hundred years on and the outcome of their protest meant that most elementary and primary schools blocked the admission of children until at least the year in which they became five. The Education Act 1944 did place a duty on local authorities to provide nursery education for three- and four-year-olds but this was enacted through the opening of nursery schools and classes attached to primary schools in only a minority of areas, usually those in areas of traditional female employment, with a tendency to be Labour-controlled.

Further developments in the forms of provision for children under five were:

- publicly-funded day 'rescue' nurseries offering children time away from very ill or troubled parents
- fee-paying playgroups (now often known as preschools) – initiated in the 1960s by middle-class parents in areas where there were no public nursery schools
- private nurseries – which offered either early education and/or childcare to cover parents' working hours, again charging fees
- childminding in minders' own homes
- nannies and *au pairs* in children's own homes
- a range of other provision – such as parent and toddler clubs, community groups and workplace creches (for further information about this period and the developments see David 1990)

What this ad hoc development has meant is that we are left with a very different situation from that of many of our neighbour countries in the EU. Where we have a miscellany of different services, with differently trained staff, countries such as France and Belgium cater for high proportions of their young children in publicly-funded nursery school classes. These are now making further developments in order to offer more comprehensive facilities such that parents' hours of work are covered, the children usually remaining in the setting with which they are familiar. Similarly, in the Scandinavian countries, provision which began as a response to women's needs for childcare is now being refined in order to attend to the educational potential of that provision (see David 1993 and 1998).

The UK is at present alone among EU countries in offering only part-time publicly-funded nursery provision. Children in the UK are often required to attend several different settings over their first five years, some even attending two or more settings within one week or one day. This type of discontinuity hardly bodes well for children's learning. The reforms set up by the last government which put in place a comprehensive programme of policies and initiatives to raise standards from preschool to adulthood were unlikely to solve this kind of problem and it will require considerable effort on the part of those involved in enacting developments resulting from the current government's policies to overcome the muddle and fragmentation inherent in the system (for a fuller discussion of some of the issues see, for example, Moss and Penn 1996; Nutbrown 1996b).

Young children's early education does not take place in a vacuum. Having examined the changing education and care context of young children it is necessary to consider the earliest and most intimate influences on the young child's development. Most importantly, this development begins in the family and parents are the primary educators. Thus what has happened to parents before the child was born and what is happening to those parents now is of utmost importance to a young child. One important aspect of studying early childhood is the need to explore the 'ecological niche' in which the child is living. The characteristics of the person (child) at a given time in his or her life are a joint function of the characteristics of the person (child) and of the environment over the course of that person's (child's) life up to that time (see Bronfenbrenner 1989, p.190). This so-called person-context model allows development to be studied in context, that is, in its 'ecological niche'. Furthermore it allows the identification of regions of the environment that are especially favourable or unfavourable to the development of individuals with particular personal characteristics.

Within one country, each child's ecological niche will be influenced by the ways in which policies for children relate to policies for families. In the UK, family policy has traditionally been *laissez faire*. Parents have been expected to bear the responsibility for children under statutory school age without government support or interference – unless as noted earlier the children needed 'rescuing' by public services. This has meant that if women (or single fathers) need to, or wish to, go out to work in the UK, it has been up to them to sort out their own childcare arrangements. Generally speaking, countries which have a 'loose' approach to family policy, neither overtly encouraging women to work nor forbidding them from doing so, tend to have 'loose' regulation of childcare facilities though there is no good reason why this should be so. In other words, for the most part, nursery provision has been created in response to terms of women's capacity to be involved in the labour market (or not), rather than as a form of education in its own right, with agreed guidelines, to which a young child, like children aged between five and sixteen to eighteen, have an entitlement. This is particularly the case for children under three.

Additionally, fathers of young children in the UK, when they are in employment, work more hours per week than their counterparts in other European countries. Similarly grandmothers, who for generations traditionally provided backup care, are now either too distant geographically or are themselves employed full time, as is the case for two of this book's authors. Meanwhile, the number of mothers of young children in the workforce in the UK is increasing (Central Statistics Office 1994). So while in the past other family members, often fathers, had been relied upon to provide care while a mother of a young child worked, these support systems have become less readily available.

In recognition of the need for further development in services, both for children themselves, so that they may begin the process of lifelong learning, and for parents, so that they may participate less stressfully in the workforce, the current government has set in place a number of initiatives. Their intent was signalled soon after they came into office in 1997, in the document *Excellence in Schools* (Department for Education and Employment [DfEE] 1997). Subsequently they have published various documents concerning the need for all nursery providers to be members of a local authority nursery partnership – a mechanism causing the creation of a collaborative network of those involved in provision for children under five. The initial focus of and funding for Early Years Development Partnerships and Plans has been the four-year-olds. The partnerships must be multi-professional and multi-agency, they must pay attention to the levels of provision, its quality and the training of the staff in the settings. The partnerships must also create plans for the encouragement of new developments, so that parents of three-year-olds wanting nursery education and care can access this. There must be an increase in the number of high-quality early childhood education and care places for children under three and in some areas it is the Early Years Partnerships which have taken on the additional role of fostering the growth in out-of-hours care facilities for school-age children.

At present the definitions of quality tend to be inspection-led, the inspections for all preschool settings except those in maintained and some private schools being the responsibility of social services, nationally under the Department of Health. (For further details about nursery partnerships see, for example, DfEE 1998a). Settings for four-year-olds are also inspected by OFSTED teams, if the children are in primary school, or by Registered Nursery Inspectors trained by OFSTED if the children are in voluntary or private nursery groups. As noted in the preface, research has a strong role to play here in ensuring that policy-makers are provided with the best possible evidence.

Other supportive initiatives include the new Sure Start strategy (1999) to help children under four and their families in more than 250 programmes established in areas of deprivation throughout the country. The government's commitment to such young children and their families is a response to the evidence showing that early intervention and support can help to reduce family breakdown, strengthen parent–child bonds and enhance school readiness. The longer-term goal is to prevent social exclusion, regenerating communities and reducing crime (Blunkett and Jowell in the Foreward to DfEE 1999 *Sure Start: A Guide for Trailblazers*).

A range of other initiatives are linked to this new strategy, such as Education Action Zones and the New Deal for Lone Parents. Also relevant are family literacy and numeracy, lifelong learning and the government's consultation paper *Supporting Families* (Home Office 1998). These are further examples of the fast-changing, multidimensional nature of the field in which early childhood education is embedded.

Although the statutory school admission age in the UK is five, most children begin to attend primary school at age four. For this age group the provision of places, at least during school hours, is not the issue, though whether each child is being appropriately educated might well be on the agenda. In terms of overall provision itself, for these young, school-aged children it is their need for out-of-hours care which is an urgent priority. Who should work in such a setting, where it should be, what should happen there, and how this connects with both the school day and home are questions as yet unanswered.

Thus the main problems with the history of the development of education and care services for young children in the UK have been their inadequacy in terms of the number of available places and the costs to most parents; their lack of coordination; their bases in different government departments (both centrally and locally); the differentiated training requirements and conditions of service, to name but a few.

A number of local authorities have, particularly during the last ten years, tried to integrate their preschool services. 'Centres of excellence', associated with the government's *Early Excellence Centres* initiative, have been nominated including several nursery settings which combine care and education facilities, because children need continuity in order to make sense of their lives as whole people. Further, as the European Childcare Network argued, the best services should combine 'reliable care with a pedagogical approach' (Moss 1996, p.48).

It seems likely that we, as a nation, have for a long time underestimated the learning capacity of children in these first years of life, because of our assumptions and accepted notions about young children. Received wisdom about very young children in UK society, or established 'régimes of truth' (Foucault 1977), have resulted in our having one of the worst records of nursery provision in the European Union and even 'lifelong education' plans propose the start at three years of age. The White Paper *Excellence in Schools* (DfEE 1997) which set out the government plans to raise standards in education over five years devotes a whole chapter to 'A sound beginning' yet does not seem to stress the importance, in learning terms, of what happens during the years before three. The idea of babies and young children as people with the capacity to learn and the need to relate to others in meaningful ways, not as objects or possessions who should be mainly restricted to their own homes with only their own mothers for company, remains largely unrecognised.

What research can tell us about early childhood education

In spite of a great flowering of large-scale, early years research in the late 1970s and early 1980s funded by government agencies, it is probably true to say that there has been *less* research of this nature sponsored in the period between the mid-1980s and mid-1990s. In the light of American and other evidence (Andersson 1992; Barnett and Escobar 1990; Sylva 1994), such as that from the High/Scope longitudinal study (Schweinhart *et al.* 1993), we need to recognise what other countries already seem to know: that spending on the early years is an investment. This most rigorous study of the long-term benefits of a high-quality, cognitively-oriented nursery education programme with adult-guided play between the ages of three and five to six years showed that children who took part were doing better than peers who had not taken part, through school and in later functioning in society. It was concluded that, in this case, nursery education was an investment in terms of savings on education or in dealing with social problems later in life. It is significant that the High/Scope curriculum demanded not only good home–school liaison but also highly-educated, qualified early years teachers. The importance of investment in the training of those who work with young children is also emerging as a key factor in a number of other studies (see David 1996a) and support for parents as the primary educators of their children is only with these exciting reforms beginning to take shape.

The research on the impact of daycare on children's later development presents a more mixed picture but supports the view that good quality care can enhance development whilst, unsurprisingly, poor quality care does not. Osborn and Milbank (1987) compared social and educational outcomes for daycare children with those receiving half-day programmes or staying at home. Towards the end of primary school the daycare children showed more educational and behavioural problems. McGuire and Richman (1986) also found children attending London local-authority daycare nurseries had ten times the amount of emotional and behavioural problems that playgroup children did. These findings, however, reflect the lack of high-quality, publicly funded daycare in the UK and the high evidence of multiple problems in families receiving such care. By contrast, in Sweden, for instance, where high-quality daycare is widely available to families from varying social strata, Andersson (1992) found local-authority daycare in Gothenburg provided children with a better start to formal schooling. Howe (1990), moreover, demonstrated different social and educational outcomes according to the quality of care received. These results clearly indicate the impact of high-quality daycare on children's later development in terms of adequate numbers of stable and well-trained staff, which reflect sound social policies.

Research has shown that if we want children's early experiences to have beneficial effects in terms of their emotional stability, present contentment and later achievements, we need to pay attention to certain key factors (Field 1991). Those key ingredients include:

- the development of self-esteem in young children
- investment in young children
- stable childcare arrangements ensuring children interact with a limited number of familiar carers each day
- low staff turnover
- good training
- low adult–child ratios.

Research suggests that high-quality early childhood care and education services can contribute to young children's early learning and future social and academic outcomes, particularly so for less-advantaged nursery-aged children, though there is some evidence for benefits to children from a variety of backgrounds and aged below three years.

This brief review of learning before school demonstrates the complexity and, hence, the cost of conducting research into early learning. Research concerning young children and their families is extensive and is closely intertwined in broader societal trends – for instance, the growth of divorce and increase in non-traditional family structures. Learning takes place in a variety of environments for young children and has to be examined in different settings, in relation to costs and benefits in terms of later social and education achievement, and in comparison with other countries.

The above discussion may suggest that research in early childhood education has focused solely on the social organisation of preschool and early schooling settings within the broader macro-social context of socioeconomic forms and their change. As well as investigations of face-to-face interactions between children and caregivers in situated activity in a variety of educare settings, developmental characteristics of children in the cognitive, affective, social, psychomotor or self-help and adaptive areas have been studied as well as broader issues related to gender, diversity and multiculturalism. More recently (see for instance, Aubrey 1994) there has been a growing interest in children's subject-specific development in language and early literacy development, emergent mathematics and numeracy, children's conceptions and misconceptions in science as well as their thinking and problem-solving in other areas.

Much research evidence on early childhood development and learning comes from developmental psychology research, rather than from educational settings or work conducted by those who have themselves worked in the field as educators. Some may be difficult to use directly in the improvement of early childhood education and the theories on which much of the research is based may never have been meant to be applied to educational settings.

Theories of development which attempt to identify and describe the nature of change over time in areas such as language, memory, cognition and intelligence, emotion or perception have adopted one of two approaches: cross-sectional or longitudinal. The first method of recording change over time is to observe children of different age groups. Harris (1989), for instance, put forward tentative claims about children's emotional development on the basis of their response to 'emotion words' at different ages. One of the writers of this book has investigated the development of children's arithmetic and mental calculation from six to eleven years, using related but different assessment tasks for different year groups. The cross-sectional method has the advantage that the researcher does not have to wait five years for a cohort of children to develop, in this case, arithmetic and calculation strategies. This carries the assumption, however, that existing eleven-year-olds represent what today's six-year-olds will become. Since the researcher's interest may well be in current sociocultural and educational conditions and their impact on learning, this may well be defensible, but it does not justify an assumption that tomorrow's eleven-year-olds will perform like those of today, particularly in view of the relentless reforms in the teaching of numeracy.

By contrast, longitudinal methods repeat observations on the same subjects at different points in time. The Basic Skills Agency (1998) has recently reported the results of a study of the influences on basic skills, from birth to thirty-seven years, in a sample of 1,700 people born in 1958 as part of the National Child Development Study. Poverty and disadvantaged circumstances were more evident in the childhood of adults with low levels of numeracy and literacy and, in fact, tests at seven years showed them struggling from the start of formal schooling. The technical problems – never mind the financial implications – of describing change over such a period, are beyond the scope of most researchers but such work does illustrate the need to identify associations between change in children over time and associated changes, or otherwise, in other factors. In such cases the researchers may be justified in constructing a theory of not only what, but how, development takes place. Furthermore, such research raises important questions about who conducts research on young children and who pays for it.

The nature of early childhood education research

Large amounts of research are carried out by people engaged in MPhil and PhD research degrees, most of which will be lodged in University or College libraries without being published unless the holders move on to an academic career. In the latter case an active research and publication record would be a professional and academic requirement. Moreover, in the field of early childhood education, the number of academics themselves engaged in PhD study is increasing. In fact at whatever stage of their career academics will be required to demonstrate a serious and ongoing record of research and scholarship which in many cases is 'pump-primed' by their own institutions. More senior academics, together with research teams which include both junior and contract researchers, are likely to be engaged in more extensive research projects externally funded by government bodies such as the Economic and Social Research Council (ESRC), agencies such as the TTA or charitable organisations such as the Nuffield Foundation, the Rowntree Foundation or the Leverhume Trust. Noteworthy in the area of early childhood education has been the Esmée Fairbairn Foundation which has been particularly generous in its support to such work. Externally funded grants are much sought after and applicants submit competitive proposals which attempt to appeal to the particular areas or issues that specific funding bodies support. The proposals are typically assessed by outside referees, then judged by review panels or charity board meetings and some few, highly-rated research proposals may gain financial support. The TTA, with its role in developing teaching as a research-based profession, encourages:

- improvements in the accessibility of the existing stock of knowledge, scientific investigation and evaluation as well as disciplined enquiry and comparative studies
- higher quality and more relevant research which can have an impact on day-to-day practice
- a more active role for teachers in conceiving, implementing, evaluating and disseminating research projects.

Research funding from external sources, however, is relatively modest by comparison with the educational research funding held by the Higher Education Funding Council for England (HEFCE).

At the time of writing – in 1999 – there has been some deep questioning of educational research in general with educational researchers now being urged to give the 'intellectual and moral support' to the government's radical new approach to commissioning, reviewing and disseminating research which is intended to mirror that used by the medical profession. The move towards improving the quality of research, to evaluating it more carefully and publicising it more widely, was marked by the Chief Inspector of Schools commissioning an independent researcher to investigate the foci of work reported in four 'elite' academic journals, largely as an element in discussions about the relevance, or otherwise, of educational research (Tooley 1998). A second review, by the Institute for Employment Studies and commissioned by the DfEE (Hillage *et al.* 1998), asked those in the field to respond to a number of questions, such as: what constitutes research, and does the right balance exist between different forms? This project also asked about the research process; review and evaluation; dissemination; and implementation. Meanwhile, Professor Michael Barber, adviser to the government on standards in education, is said to have indicated that educational research is going to change appreciably. Whether this means a move away from reflective (critical or analytical research) to more empirical or creative research (inventing new systems), or whether researchers' ability to challenge governmental edicts will be limited by future policy changes, remains to be seen. The British Educational Research Association's (1998) submitted response to the DfEE project argues that all types of research are vital in a democracy. Research which focused only on children's learning in classrooms would be very narrow and would fail to bring to bear many of the factors which impact on a child's ability to take advantage of what the teacher in the classroom has to offer. This is even more starkly apparent when the learner is a very young child.

In this respect the role of the research community in early childhood education as well as a number of relevant profession organisations, national and international, will be important in helping to shape future policy and practice as well as influence the direction of future research. To take one example, the OECD definition of educational research and development suggests that a broad view of the field should indeed be taken:

> ... educational research and development is systematic, original investigation or inquiry and associated development activities concerning the social, cultural, economic and political contexts within which education systems operate and learning takes place; the purposes of education; the processes of teaching, learning and personal development of children, youth and adults; the work of educators; the resources and organisational arrangements to support educational work; the policies and strategies to

achieve educational objectives; and the social, cultural, political and economic outcomes of education.

(OECD 1995, p.37)

As the OECD (*op. cit.*) report points out, there can be a danger in making the definition of 'educational research' too wide or too narrow but, as they argue, much research that is useful to the field of education actually goes on in departments in institutions of higher education focusing on other disciplines, such as sociology, psychology or economics, and that to make the definition allow for, say, a narrow research base in classrooms would exclude much that is important to our understanding of learners and their lives.

A further point made by this OECD report relevant to our early years research overview – and echoing the preface to this book – is the relative youth of educational research. It argued that in fact the first tradition or paradigm to emerge in educational research was the approach associated with hermeneutics and critical philosophy, which sought to understand such general questions as 'what should be in education?' (OECD 1995, p.33). The experimental, quantitative or 'positivist' paradigm, with its roots in natural sciences, it opined, emerged towards the end of the nineteenth century. Certainly, the field of educational research seems to have been dominated by natural science assumptions and methods during this century, but it may be that developmental psychology has been a greater influence on early childhood education research.

During the last twenty years both educational research and developmental psychology have been wrestling with the challenges thrown up by different approaches and models or paradigms of 'how the world works' and therefore how to conduct research. A related issue which must be addressed by the educational research field as a whole, including those in early years research settings, is the questioning of 'certainty'. For example, in the USA the Committee on the Federal Role of Education Research (1992) rejected the so-called 'scientific' model based on the expectation that research could deduce a hypothesis or deduction from a theoretical model in order to test experimentally whether associations between variables are causual ones, leading to 'improvements' and, hence, solve problems quite simply. However, the Committee came to the conclusion that it was still important to invest substantial sums in educational research, particularly in the founding of 'learning communities ... partnerships among researchers, practitioners and policy-makers, in which each becomes involved in disciplined inquiry and each contributes to the learning of the others' (US National Academy of Science 1992, p.17). The OECD report concludes that educational research has much to offer the field; the weakness seems to be that this research has not been sufficiently exploited. According to the Institute for Employment Studies (IES), research review funders, researchers, policy-makers, teachers and publishers have a joint responsibility to create a more effective research system in which educational research informs policy and practice. Perhaps we should be exploring a wider range of routes for dissemination, as well as different modes – such as video and television. In Denmark, for example, the preschool teachers' union plays a very active role in encouraging and disseminating research findings. In fact the DfEE (1998b) research action plan has advocated that:

- policy-makers and teachers become more involved in commissioning, steering and disseminating research
- local education authorities make more use of research evidence in planning
- research findings be made available in more accessible forms
- researchers on DfEE-funded projects release interim findings and discuss them with focus groups to encourage earlier 'user-involvement'.

While the OECD report seems to favour greater sharing of knowledge among researchers, practitioners and policy-makers, and this is to be welcomed, there is also a need to ask to what extent all the parties involved require the same type of information about particular issues or different aspects of findings concerning the issues. Parents and carers too should be provided with research briefings and they might need yet another form and style of dissemination. It may be only when parents have access to key research information that they will feel sufficiently confident and knowledgeable to challenge some of the mistaken interpretations of educational practice provided by the press.

If we wish to generate debate about what early childhood is, what it means to be a young child in a particular society and what educational services should be provided as a result, we, the researchers, need to make our debate more accessible to a wider audience, we need to befriend the press, parents and politicians alike. Further, we need to encourage our teacher and educator colleagues to become involved in research projects, to share in the excitement of exploring, thinking and writing – activities which, certainly in Britain, are rarely recognised as real work requiring sufficient time to carry out properly.

Accessing recent and relevant early childhood education research

Although early childhood education research forms only a fraction of the remit in the OECD (1995) report, this is a growing field of interest. Each time we, as early years educators and researchers, meet at national and international seminars and conferences, there is much to discuss and much to learn from colleagues representing other countries. The authors of this book, based as we are in Singapore and the UK, bear testimony to the ways in which the Internet and the fax machine have improved our ability to collaborate over long distances and across boundaries. After all, when a group of early years researchers meet together, they usually find they have far more in common than differences between them. The linguistic and geographical boundaries which have separated us seem more easily surmountable. Disciplinary boundaries form a different kind of challenge, for we recognise the ways in which the deliberate confluence of different perspectives and knowledge bases can bring new insights.

Much has been made of the dissemination of research in more user-friendly forms but producers of research are themselves key users of research, bibliographic research constituting a critical element in the research process by providing the conceptual framework as well as the basis for serious research reviews in a specific area. Early childhood education sources include archival collections which are accessible in the form of published books and journals in academic libraries, while unpublished research reports and technical papers, theses and conference papers are also available, if less easy to locate. The papers from the European Conference for Education Research (1998), for instance, have been placed on the internet, electronic sources becoming another and rapidly-growing site for locating research papers, researchers and research topics on an international scale. Whilst e-journal articles are widely available, printed journals – national and international – remain the biggest primary archival source for research projects. Whilst particular journals – such as the *European Early Childhood Education Research Journal*, the *International Journal of Early Years Education*, *Early Years*, *Education 3 to 13*, *Early Childhood Research* and the *International Journal of Early Childhood* (the journal of l'Organisation pour l'Éducation Préscolaire – OMEP) – spring immediately to mind, almost all educational research journals carry papers on early childhood education.

Abstracts and indexes such as the *Child Development Abstracts and Bibliography,* the *Current Index to Journals in Education, Education Index* and, in fact, *Resources in Education* published by the Educational Resources Information Center (ERIC) which has a specific clearinghouse for elementary and early childhood education, provide a valuable starting point in accessing what is already available in print and relevant to research in the area. Other 'abstracting' journals which include *Psychological Abstracts* and *Sociological Abstracts* also reveal rich and relevant material which is currently in print. All of these sources attest to the growing importance of this field. As noted by Goodwin and Goodwin (1996) in relation to primary and secondary sources for research in early childhood education – or for that matter in respect of *any* education journal – 'almost all of them' might be consulted for early childhood education topics (p.12). Perhaps it should also be added that one would need to consult a large education library such as can be found at the University of London Institute of Education in order to find a wide range of such sources under one roof.

The maintenance and development of greater international links in early years research may prove both a safeguard and a catalyst in seeking to understand our own societies and their expectations of young children. We must be aware that Western/Northern models of early childhood generate similar societal expectations, with the concomitant limits this may put on future generations. What comparative early childhood research demonstrates above all is that early childhood is constructed by its society, according to the needs and position of that social group. Sally Lubeck (1986) showed this to be true in her qualitative study of two preschool groups in two very different neighbourhoods in an American city. The young children in one group were learning to be competitive individualists, while in the other they were learning to be cooperative group members. What we really need is for children to grow with the capacity to be both interdependent and cooperative as well as brave individuals. Once the underpinning ideologies and research assumptions are problematized, what we can learn from research in other countries can create our greatest challenge. For example, soon after the Berlin Wall fell in 1989, some Eastern European and Western European early childhood researchers and practitioners were exploring the idea of democracy in relation to the education of young children. 'You will have to teach us all you know,' said the Eastern European seminar members. 'But maybe you know more about membership of groups, of society, about working together,' said a Western delegate, 'maybe all we know about is individualism and the young child'.

In a similar way, a Nigerian colleague issued an invitation to visit her, adding that in her country they really know how to live with young children, many adults sharing the joys and the effort of childrearing in the compounds, reinforcing the sentiments of the African proverb 'It takes a village to raise a child'.

In this book our aim is to engage readers in reflection on the areas of methodology and ethics in early childhood research. To this end we offer some chapters which provide an historical and contextual background; some which provide detailed accounts of the main features of qualitative and quantitative research, methods and analysis as well as examples of projects conducted which exemplify the quantitative and qualitative approaches; while the remainder of the book focuses on those specific ethical and methodological issues which confront a researcher in the field of early childhood education.

2   Constructing childhoods

In this chapter we explore some of the underlying assumptions made about young children and the implications for research processes, as a result of social constructions of children and childhood in particular societies at particular times. Images of childhood and beliefs about young children are related in intimate ways to cultural, economic and historical factors. Similarly, changing theories of child development are reflected in expectations and even social policies about what is developmentally appropriate at particular periods of time.

Ways of seeing

Dominant views of babies and young children in the UK, often based on limited and outdated theories, have had a perennial influence on beliefs about child care and education. Ideas about attachment and maternal deprivation, for instance, of John Bowlby (1953) or later, of Ainsworth *et al.*, (1974), and children's emotional needs and relationships of Klein (1932), with others, have been used as arguments against the provision of nurseries in the postwar period. Psychodynamic theory and later, notions of attachment and bonding, derived from ethological studies on nonhuman species, had a profound influence on childrearing views, stressing both the critical importance of early experience and the potential harm done to young children if their emotional needs, wishes and drives were not met. Piagetian theory (1954), by contrast, focused on the child's cognitive development and gave little attention to the effect of social dimensions of the environment on the child's thinking. In this respect it has been argued that his *lack* of regard for the social and contextual dynamic in the child's development of space, number, time and so on has served to limit some of the experiences thought relevant by teachers in primary classes according to the so-called 'Three Wise Men' report of Alexander Rose and Woodhead (1992). The idea that young children are active learners capable of co-constructing their own view of the world with caring, familiar others, participating in the creation of knowledge from the moment of birth, it is thought, has not been used to inform a coherent policy for our youngest children. In fact it is probably true to say that, on the one hand, theory construction in developmental psychology is diverse and wide-ranging and, on the other, the nature and extent of its relevance and popular appeal to a wider public is, similarly, varied and pervasive. Our purpose here is to indicate that theories – formal and informal – influence images of children and childhood and hence, affect adults' behaviour, psychological research and social policy.

Recent research (for example, Bruner and Haste 1987; Trevarthen 1992) indicates that babies and children live 'up' or 'down' to societal expectations, that they will try to please those around them, both adults and older children, in order to become part of their social group, to be valued, loved and accepted. Far from being a biological bundle, babies come into the world 'programmed' to make sense of the context in which they are growing (Trevarthen 1992). Many theories have been advanced to account for the developmental changes that occur over life and, in particular, in the early period of development. Given the recently uncovered and surprisingly sophisticated abilities that infants appear to have in terms of thinking, feeling and motivation (Nash 1997) there is a need to incorporate notions of 'innate preparedness' in relation to language, number and social skills but most of all, responsiveness to the environment and significant others. This points to the critical importance of the young child's social environment in fostering early development. In turn this generates the need for investigation of reciprocal and transactional effects as well as biological variables and indicates powerful interrelationships among biological and environmental influences in human development which, in turn, demand revision and expansion of existing theories.

Biology, culture and theories of child development

In the past decades the majority of early childhood development and education research has been conducted by developmental psychologists. Compared with the natural sciences child psychology is a relatively new science and it is barely one hundred years since it was founded as a separate discipline. The philosophical roots of the main theories, however, are considerably older with origins which can be traced back to Locke (1632–1904) and Rousseau (1712–1778) and beyond.

'That children have certain characteristics, that adults have others, and that it is natural to grow from one to the other, are messages that we receive from all forms of mass communication' (Morss 1996, p.29). In each of his challenging studies John Morss (1990 and 1996) questions the taken-for-granted nature of developmentalism or the stage assumption in its analogy with biological if not embryological development in Western/Northern thinking about children. He cites Rom Harré's (1983, 1986) argument that

> stage-based accounts of childhood make the pretence that a sequence of stages unfolds through some natural process ... The world or worlds of the child, Harré argued, have to be described not as if biologically determined but more as forms of culture.
>
> (Morss 1996, pp.33–4)

Just over a decade ago Harré and others (for example, Ingleby 1986) were challenging the roots of developmental psychology and its biological basis. Before this the so-called 'social construction' movement, which was especially strong in Britain, with its foundations in sociology, had been ushered in by the publication of Berger and Luckmann's (1966) *The Social Construction of Reality*. Yet even this book propounded a view of babies as part of their mothers and as largely biological beings, who *become* human through socialisation in the culture. Theories of childhood would appear to be largely a matter of ideology, that is, determined by the needs of society. Furthermore, as noted in the preface, it is essential that they are consistent with a body of facts and, hence, robust enough to be tested – or found wanting.

It was probably the ground-breaking paper *The American Child and Other Cultural Inventions* by William Kessen (1979) which really caused many researchers in a range of disciplines to begin to recognise that although children's bodies may respond to some extent to a 'biological clock', their minds were being influenced by the context in which they found themselves. Kessen could see that childhood was defined by a particular society at a particular time in a particular way.

According to studies such as those by Ariès (1962), childhood did not exist at certain times in the history of Western Europe, and in fact it was Postman's (1985) view that childhood was invented with the printing press, since children then required a period of time in which to become literate. However, a number of historical researchers have challenged both these writers (for example, see Hilton *et al.* 1997). The important point being made is that economical and philosophical values or ideologies underpin attitudes towards and beliefs concerning children and work, for example. Our images of children are social constructions which, whether we are aware of it or not, serve particular purposes.

It is not much longer than a century ago that legislation was first introduced to protect children. What we have achieved so far is open to debate if childhood is seen as a preparation to take part in society. It is not surprising that our constructions of childhood have changed as society has become more complex or that huge differences exist among societies with differing sociocultural and economic circumstances.

What Kessen (1975) highlighted in the mid-1970s, when he led a delegation visiting educational settings for children in communist China, was the question of why different societies construct childhood in particular ways and why certain childhoods are assigned to particular children. By claiming that one version of childhood is a correct or true version and by demanding conformity, Western developmental psychologists and early years practitioners appear to have operated in a culture- or context-blind fashion. 'Developmentalism' may be hegemonic according to Morss (1996), for we must ask if, in defining stages in development and in some of the arguments we use about protecting young children, we also limit our expectations for their achievements.

Concluding that we end up with 'the children we deserve', Ros Miles (1994) argues for greater attention to children's rights and personhood. From a historical perspective, if the concept of childhood has only lately been recognized, as has also been the case for women, it should scarcely surprise us that the notion of children's rights – independent of adults in general and parents in particular – is so recent an issue for debate.

What has been especially powerful about many Western academic studies of child development has been the assumption that findings can be generalised and applied to other societies. The impact of cultural context and the beliefs about young children permeating the shared meanings in any one social group, never mind nursery, have been largely ignored. Psychologists such as the Newsons (1963, 1968) were attempting, as early as the 1960s, to show how parents and small children together create their own meanings and family culture. And in America Bronfenbrenner (1975 and 1979) – another member with Kessen in the delegation to China – attempted to bring together context and biology in his ecological theory of child development. He proposed that each child's 'ecological niche' is unique because each will experience the relationships and processes of interaction between home, nursery, the wider world and the ideology in which all these are embedded. He also argued that children themselves, like the others around them, actively influence their 'ecological niche'. Since that time the idea that members of a group or society co-construct particular childhoods and that children are active participants in that construction has provided a powerful challenge to decontextualised theories of child development.

Yet despite these challenges, most research about young children and their learning has continued to be dominated by assumptions and approaches derived from the natural sciences. The risk is that such approaches underestimate children's potential and capabilities (Deloache and Brown 1987). Morss (1990) shows how even Piaget ignored his own evidence when it did not fit contemporary preconceptions about young children's thinking. It would be fair to note at this point, however, that even theories of child development change. Writers may not be appreciated in the full context of their work over time, especially if they are considered in the context only of their early work. In this respect Mussen (1989) presented Bandura's (1989) later work in the area of social cognition which built upon and revised his earlier social learning theory and Bronfenbrenner's later extensions to his own ecological approach to human development, with a new emphasis on personality rather than environmental dimensions. In fact Beilins' (1985) survey of Piaget's later work, not generally available in English, posits the view that in order to extract the full legacy of Piaget's work, following Piaget's own model for change, one should 'delete from the theory that which does not adequately account for the research evidence, substitute other models for those that are non-functional and augment and modify them as psychological reality dictates' (Beilin 1989, p.127).

Neo-Piagetians such as Mugny, de Paolis and Carugati (1984) meanwhile have been concerned with those aspects of research neglected by Piaget – social relations, cultural influences, the effect as well as applications to education.

Watching two-and-half-year-old Arthur helping the eighteen-month-old granddaughter of one of the writers onto a garden bench, where he had never been before nor seen an adult model this behaviour, she was spurred to reflect on Piaget's lack of attention to the social milieu in which young children are reared and the development of their social reasoning. As the work of Dunn (1988) has shown, there is much evidence to support a model of the growth of social understanding in which development starts from the child's interest in and responsiveness to the behaviour and feelings of others from a very early age – in fact, from eighteen months onwards. This model incorporates both cognitive changes that lead to the child's developing sense of self and affective significance to the tension between this self-concern and the child's relationships with others, particularly with family members.

An exhibit[1] from the Reggio Emilia nurseries of Northern Italy, where staff are encouraged to see themselves as researchers exploring children's learning and constructing their own theories of development from their documented observations, consisted of a series of photographs of eight-month-old Laura. The photographs had been taken as part of the documentation process. In the first photo Laura is looking at a catalogue with an educator. The catalogue is shown open at a page displaying a range of watches. Laura is then photographed looking at the worker's watch, which by chance (we are told) is the type of watch which ticks. The worker puts her watch to Laura's ear and one can see Laura's intent expression, listening. In the final photo Laura has laid her ear on the page of watches, exploring the watches in the display as if asking 'Do these tick too?' This example attests the early competence infants possess. It also demonstrates that through this early period of development, relations with others will be fundamental to the development of thought. It would appear that young children have dispositions to learn different things, that they are not simply bundles of biological urges slowly being transformed as they pass through universal preset stages of development, until they become fully-formed humans as adults. Matching the social environment to the young infant's developmental state may be the critical element. As noted above recent research suggests that children come into this world 'programmed' to make sense of the situations in which they find themselves and to communicate with other human beings (Trevarthen 1992) and that they learn more in their first five years than in all the other years of their lives. We need to throw out limiting old assumptions and respect what Howard Gardner (1993) has called 'the most remarkable features of the young mind – its adventurousness, its generativity, its resourcefulness, and its flashes of flexibility and creativity' (Gardner 1993, p.111).

Constructions of childhood and societal values

Once we become aware of the ways in which childhood itself is constructed in different societies or at different times, we also begin to ask ourselves why children are treated in certain ways, what is considered an appropriate education for children at different stages in their lives and what all this tells us about that society. For while new research demonstrates children's amazing capacity for learning in their earliest years (e.g. Bruner and Haste 1987; Trevarthen 1992), the effects of what Eileen Byrne calls the *Snark Syndrome* (Byrne 1993) mean that policies and practices often lag behind, failing to adjust to the new knowledge. Byrne argues that old understandings are embedded in practices to such an extent they are difficult to overcome. She uses Lewis Carroll's poem, *The Hunting of the Snark*, with the lines 'Just the place for a Snark! I have said it thrice:/ What I tell you three times is true'. Byrne's Snark Syndrome, about the constraints which can arise out of cultural assumptions and 'norms', is similar to the idea of 'regimes of truth' theorised by Foucault (1977). Being told repeatedly that babies and young children cannot understand or do very much becomes a self-fulfilling prophecy.

Collective responsibility for young children

Once it has been recognised that images and theories of childhood influence adult behaviour, issues relating to childrearing policies and practices are raised and, hence, the rights of children. As a nation, the UK has signed up to the UN Convention on the Rights of the Child (United Nations 1989). Furthermore, we have the Children Act 1989, which requires we act in the best interests of the child, heed the child's views, support parents in their role as responsible carers and, as professionals involved with children and their families, work together effectively to these ends.

For the first time in British legal history, parents are portrayed as having *responsibilities for*, rather than *rights over*, their children. For child liberationists, the Children Act 1989 was only a beginning, a small move towards some sort of representation for children. As Louise Sylwander, Children's Ombudsman for Sweden, has pointed out, 'the Convention is something which has to be lived' (Sylwander 1996, p. 49). The way we think of and, as a result, treat children, especially those in their earliest years, has consequences. In the end, we get the children we deserve. *The Child as Citizen* (Council of Europe 1996) reminds readers that children form one of the largest groups in society but they do not form a lobby and are rarely represented in decision-making processes. Valuing children, the inheritance of a 'civic covenant' which includes a moral responsibility for the generations which follow us, is John O'Neill's (1994) argument in *The Missing Child in Liberal Theory*. He suggests that the power of the global market must be restrained, that capitalism has always been dependent upon moral and political restraints to keep it from destroying itself. In other words, if we do not have government which pays attention to the needs of its least powerful members and we allow individualism free reign, ignoring social responsibility, we risk a total collapse of society. We cannot disembed the economy from the polity.

When one traces the history of 'child politics' in the global as opposed to nation-state context, many of the advances in awareness of children and their position in different societies have been due to the work of international non-governmental organisations, in particular the breakthroughs of child politics and child policy of the 1960s and 1970s. This was in part due to the impact of the rise of feminism in making children more visible in society worldwide (Therborn 1996) through women's recognition that children's position in society paralleled their own. In many ways early childhood research too can be seen as having been marginal to the main body of educational research and most of those researching in this field are, again, women. There have been a few notable exceptions, men who recently have been key UK research figures in recognising that early childhood is one of the most important phases in life However, most have not also had experience as early childhood educators or carers in the field like the practitioner workforce, early years researchers tend to be women.

Constructions of childhood and the challenges for research

The current emphasis of policy-makers on lifelong learning and the interest of bodies such as the OECD (1996) in the earliest years as the foundation for that lifelong learning, means that the spotlight is on young children and what constitutes the most appropriate education for them, within the parameters of their own cultural heritage. Rather than encouraging the export of irrelevant curricula from one culture to another, researchers need to assist policy-makers and practitioners in defining what it is they want children to learn and why, and then to help them evaluate whether their decisions and their practices are effective.

The constant reminders by policy-makers and the media that our education system, and now educational research, are failing our children always seem to omit the fact that we do not, as a society, pay enough attention to the very earliest years. Perhaps our current malaise is in part due to our lack of attention to the 'needs' and rhythms of young children (David 1996b) and to those who know them most intimately – their parents, carers and educators. If we accept that babies and young children are people, social beings who are trying to participate in and make sense of their world – whatever their age – then we need to ask ourselves some important questions about the *assumptions* we are making when we embark on a research project and about the way children are treated during the process of the research. Researchers have a responsibility to question their own constructions of childhood, so that they are aware of the way in which that construction impacts on their research conceptions, design and decision-making. They also have a responsibility to the children involved from the point of view of the power differential between children and adults in early years settings. As Fine and Sandstrom (1988) noted:

> All of us study children ... it could hardly be otherwise ... ideology, proximity, concern and, of course, memory all contribute to what we make of our daily experience with children. While such practical theorising about children rarely hardens into a formal sort, it does seem the case that most of us probably share the conceit that we understand children at least as well as they understand themselves ... the cultural worlds created by children are often as inventive, rule-governed, nuanced and guarded as those created by adults.
>
> (Fine and Sandstrom 1988, p.7)

In *Acts of Meaning*, Jerome Bruner (1990) showed that he questioned the assumptions of some of his own and others' earlier work in its ability to provide 'the whole picture'. One must consider whether observing children from the researcher's perspective, or at least the adult perspective alone, means that there needs to be a rethink of how one accesses children's understandings of the world around them and how their understandings have been shaped by 'living and learning' in a specific social context.

At the same time as the challenge to the orthodoxy of natural science approaches in research, in which children's behaviour was observed and interpreted without any reference to this inner life and meaning, there has been a challenge in relation to the assumptions about children and about the possibility that such research methods can transcend social and cultural bias or personal opinion.

Qvortrup *et al.* (1994) have raised awareness of children's personhood and the importance of multilevel factors in shaping children's life experiences. Their *Childhood Matters* project, for example, did not attempt to:

> prove any direct casuality between particular economic, political or societal phomena or interests, on the one hand, and on the other specific express-ions in the life world of children ... *but to* indicate that the common and general condition of children cannot be explained by reference to merely the level of the family or any other micro-level; it must in addition be understood in terms of the development of societal macro-parameters, which otherwise are only availed of in connection with adults' life conditions.
>
> (Qvortrup 1994, p.11, our italics).

This raises important concerns about the possibility of scientific methods providing valid answers to social and political questions with practical impli-cations for schools and nurseries.

What is important to remember is that images of childhood *and* theories of child development have an ideological as well as philosophical and economic base.

Challenging constructions

In our own research, then, it is necessary to ask ourselves what assumptions we are making about both young children and about the research process. How do we do this?

There are a number of strategies we can employ to help us 'see in a different way'. One is by linking and sharing ideas with researchers in other societies (see Chapter 10). Another is to attend seminars and conferences where our thinking will be challenged by researchers who do not share our views about appropriate research models or approaches (see Chapter 3). One can be similarly challenged by reading research reports in journals which make us attempt to stand in another's shoes and ask critical questions about one's own research assumptions and assumptions about early childhood.

A fundamental principle of early childhood research is that it should not be 'ethnocentric' – that is, it should not take for granted the dominant model or theory of childhood and childrearing in any one culture as a measure against which to judge others. This means, furthermore, that some reflection and self-interrogation on the part of the researcher will be necessary in order to examine what assumptions, beliefs and attitudes about child development are being brought to the research process. At the same time, our research – whether bibliographic, conceptual or empirical – will, ultimately, contribute to our understanding of, empathy towards and respect for young children in the context of early care and development.

Note

1 The British Association of Early Childhood was funded by the Esmee Fairbairn foundation to stage an exhibition by the Reggio Emilia nurseries at the Bethnal Green Museum of Childhood in the Summer of 1997.

3 Research paradigms

Ways of seeing

The ways in which researchers carry out their work convey messages about their beliefs concerning research methodology, their theoretical pre-suppositions and also their views of 'how the world works'. These messages, however, are often implicit rather than explicit. Perhaps because we are aware of the limited word length of journals, manuscripts required of contributors, research articles rarely include extended explanations of the paradigm, or model, underpinning the research process, the assumptions underlying particular concepts being used, or the implicit view about the place and role of theory, though they may tell us the techniques used to gather data. Of course, we are keen to know about the focus, content, results, conclusions and implications of a piece of research and, during our reading, judgements are made about the methods used in the research, but usually this means we assess whether the techniques were appropriate and whether the researcher used them in a 'rigorous' way. As Robson (1993) has noted, however, whilst systematic enquiry calls for a set of skills in observing and interviewing, designing, analysing, interpreting and reporting, the development of these skills takes time. Psychology and the related social sciences also have a substantive content of theories, models and findings with which it is essential that the researcher is, at the very least, familiar.

In a recent conference paper, Professor Kathy Sylva (1995) called for deliberation rather than debate on research methodology. She quoted Professor Lilian Katz who stated that in a debate there is one winner. However, it really depends on which definition of 'debate' one selects and a 'winner' mentality seems to be a macho, Western construct. Our intention here is to describe the research process by examining quantitative and qualitative methods. Some have construed these two general methodologies as opposing approaches. Our hope is to present them as complementary and encourage their joint use to investigate fully a particular topic or area. Studies of the ways in which women use language should encourage us to see that we can hold debates in which we seek affiliation, not confrontation (Tannen 1990). Perhaps we in Western societies need to develop our ability to find solutions in which no-one 'loses face', a point supported by Professor Charles Handy (1994), the business guru.

In this chapter we wish to encourage further this early years debate/deliberation. Firstly, we may need to think about the extent to which one research paradigm – one view of the construction of knowledge and how we find out about it – has dominated thinking in the field so that we may find difficulty in conceiving ways of seeing and thinking about the world, society and children, other than by the so-called 'scientific' method. Secondly, we will outline some other models and methodologies of the research process, used in the early years research field. There is no overall consensus on ways to conceptualise research. Some emphasise distinctions between 'basic' research, which is concerned to test and develop theory without much regard to practice and 'applied' research, which will use the same set of research tools or procedures but is likely to be generated by specific problems or issues in the field which it is intended to address. One could argue that early childhood education is an applied field which draws upon a number of disciplines, such as sociology, psychology and economics, rather than a distinctive discipline of knowledge. Ransom (1996) has questioned what kind of knowledge educational studies does constitute and acknowledged it has become too isolated from key theoretical debates of the period. To the extent that early childhood education focuses on the teaching–learning process, it is applied. It is generally accepted, however, that different views about the role of theory, the sequence and significance of the research procedures involved, cluster around two main traditions – the positivist, quantitative and 'scientific' model, and the qualitative, ethnographic or interpretative model.

In summary, early childhood education research is diverse in form and function. This chapter will consider how the dominant quantitative paradigm has been increasingly challenged by qualitative methodology which has, correspondingly, increased in prominence. Whilst this distinction is useful to deliberation on methodology, in practice it may underplay a variety in philosophical stances which are held and the range of methodologies espoused. Finally the chapter will move on from principles to the consideration of the research process.

Early development of quantitative methods

The positivist, natural-science-based paradigm has held sway in Western/ Northern societies for around three hundred years, since its inception in the 'Age of Enlightenment'. In this model of the world and the way it works, human beings (until recently only white, adult, male human beings) are considered capable of rational thought such that the natural world may be conquered and reason is seen as superior to and separate from emotion. Above all, knowledge – 'the truth' – is 'out there' to be discovered if only one asks the right questions in a rigorous manner. Researchers are expected to be capable of behaving objectively, uninfluenced by their own histories and cultures. Further, as a result of their research, they produce knowledge whose validity is absolutely certain, applying to all human beings, in all places, at all times.

This paradigm began largely as an antidote to the power of organised religion. What was not recognised about the positivist paradigm until about a century ago is the doctrinal nature of this view of the world and of knowledge.

The resultant impact on the creation of knowledge has meant not only that other ways of knowing and seeing have remained unacknowledged but also that certain groups in our global society have been refused acceptance as creators of knowledge. This view of the world has influenced attitudes to and treatment of the environment, animals and other life forms with which we share the globe as well as people originating from African and Asian cultures, women, and children.

Although educational research can take many forms, serving different purposes, it has been most commonly located within social sciences, specifically psychology and sociology. Similarly, a diversity of methods has been used in the laboratory, nursery school or classroom, including surveys of attitudes of teachers, evaluations of different programmes and investigations of particular settings, qualitative and quantitative.

Quantitative approaches

The roots of early educational research lay in nineteenth-century psychology, itself a new discipline and, not surprisingly, this influenced what was investigated and the methods used. Adherence to the 'scientific' approach led to quantitative measurement of the characteristics of learners and teachers with the aim of providing a theoretical base to the process of learning and teaching. A significant feature of 'scientific' work of the early twentieth century was the construction of mental testing, not only intelligence tests but personality tests and a wide range of attitude and achievement tests which were adminis-tered to pupils of all ages including those most young. These, it was thought, provided a scientific base to educational and special educational decision-making as well as an objective base to educational planning, particularly after the Education Act 1944 established a tripartite system of grammar, secondary modern and technical schools. The 'eleven-plus' assessment, which included intelligence tests, examinations and teacher recommendations, were used to apportion grammar-school places which, inevitably, disadvantaged working-class children and, at the same time, created the impetus for sociological research of the 1960s and 1970s, which examined if and how the new comprehensive system could redress these inequalities.

Research of this period was significant for its focus on family and background factors as the source for differences in achievement. This sociological research, although not experimental, nevertheless employed the same measurement techniques of pupils' intelligence and achievement, as well as broader survey data from questionnaires and analyses of official statistics. Furthermore, it carried out statistical analyses which identified causal relationships through manipulation of variables much in the manner of psychological research (see Reynolds 1985 for a critique of the psychological basis to educational research of this period).

A noteworthy example, already mentioned in Chapter 1, was the longitudinal National Child Development Study (Bynner and Steedman 1995; Bynner and Parsons 1997) of influences on the development of basic skills acquisition of people born in one week in 1958. This focused on family and home circumstances, early education and schooling to seven and eleven years, as well as transition from school to work and adult working life. The variables examined, however, inevitably reflected the dominant concerns of the late 1960s and early 1970s, which emphasised relationships between educational achievement and social class differences, manifest in both parental attitude and the home circumstances – for example, financial factors, housing and lifestyle. In this respect it is interesting to note the current resurgence of interest in such work with the present government's focus on the raising of standards.

By the late 1970s, however, measurement of school effects in educational research was being introduced. This led to the development of more sophisticated techniques which attempted to include classroom processes, organisational arrangements and school climate. Noteworthy was the Rutter *et al.* (1979) secondary school study and the later, Mortimore *et al.* (1988) primary school study, both of which reported significant school effects associated with a clear set of characteristics (again, Reynolds 1985 has provided a useful review of this area). Of a similar period and with a focus on early years education, Tizard *et al.* (1988) followed the educational progress of London inner-city pupils through the early years of schooling, with follow-up studies of achievement at the end of primary school more recently reported by Blatchford and Plewis (1990). Lately yet more sophisticated statistical methods of multi-level modelling (Goldstein 1987; 1995) have allowed the examination of individual pupil progress, nested within classes, within schools and in relation to different educational regimes.

A third strand of the quantitative approach can be traced through educational evaluation of both primary and secondary programmes. In the 1960s, large-scale evaluation projects of curriculum development in the area of, for instance, primary French, mathematics and science were commissioned by the Schools Council as well as by private funding agencies such as the Nuffield Foundation. Like other educational research of the period this focused on the identification of aims and objectives and the measurement of pupils' attitudes and attainments. This short and selective account gives some indication of the power of the 'positivist' approach in setting the educational research agenda for younger as well older pupils, which was experimental in nature and scientific in methodology.

The growth of qualitative approaches

To a large extent the rise of qualitative methods has been associated with an increasing unease about the validity of quantitative methods which relied heavily upon educational and psychological testing. Mehan (1973), for instance, drew attention to the fact that interpretation of test results depended for validity upon a shared frame of reference amongst test constructor, test administrator and the testee. Mehan pointed out that the way children interpreted test questions could differ from those intended by the researcher, resulting in test items failing to measure what they were designed to do. Moreover this potential mismatch in tester-testee interpretation was not simply a technical problem which could be removed by improved test administration but a more fundamental product of the interactive and interpretative processes which were mutually constructed in the testing situation. Test-taking attitudes and assumptions could not be eliminated, hence, close correspondence between the views of tester and tested could not be guaranteed. The same criticism was levelled at a wide range of techniques in the social sciences in general and educational research in particular.

Probably best known in relation to such measurement problems in child development research was the critique by Donaldson (1978) in respect of classic Piagetian tasks which purported to indicate a child's stage or level of logical reasoning. Donaldson suggested that replication of the tasks findings demonstrated not only the child's level of reasoning but also the extent to which the experimenter's requirements were understood. Like Mehan, she drew attention to the influence of the social context of the testing situation in which interactions took place and in which misunderstandings might arise either from the language and explanations provided or from the requirements of the task being carried out.

These criticisms, however, pointed to a more fundamental disquiet at the logical-positivist position which claimed a single, objective and value-free reality that could be deduced through experimental methods. Concerns, however, were not only about research methods and hypothetico-deductive procedures which seek to determine causal relationships through manipulation – physical or statistical – but also about the very nature of social life. Human behaviour is complex and thus open to negotiation and alternative interpretation. This stance amounted to an alternative philosophical position that posits the view that multiple realities exist and, hence, personal constructions of reality must be recognised. The approach described as 'naturalistic', 'phenomenological' or 'interpretative' emphasises the manner in which personal perspectives on the world may influence behaviour and, therefore, the importance to the researcher of understanding these. The researcher will attempt to make sense of these, working inductively to explore the natural context, social processes and constructions of meaning, suspending personal value systems so far as possible to gain access to others' view points.

Deliberation on quantitative and qualitative distinctions

Whilst the criticisms of quantitative research are justified it is equally fair to note, as discussed earlier, that quantitative research is now capable of handling complex and multi-level relationships, and if human responses and behaviour were as unpredictable and singular as some might argue the search for patterns and commonalities would be in vain. Further, whilst qualitative analysis may also seek causal relationships (see Strauss and Corbin 1990), they will inevitably be in a weaker position when dealing with counter-explanations. Rather than seeing the debate in terms of contrasting paradigms or opposing methodologies, however, it may be more helpful to regard the two approaches as complementary or even reflecting different stages of the same scientific process. To reject totally the quantitative perspective is to lose all right to claim factuality for one's results; to reject totally the qualitative may lose one the right to claim meaning.

Early, open-ended and exploratory work or 'naturalistic' observation may, for instance, lead to the identification of key variables and interrelationships, to more refined research questions, prediction and, thence, more systematic investigation. There is also another branch of quantitative work outside the laboratory which attempts to bring the rigour of experimentation to the real world – the survey strategy. Venturing out into real-world situations of nursery and classroom contexts may preclude 'experiment' in the technical sense but this may provide the opportunity for a case-study strategy which involves an empirical investigation of a particular real-life context, group, institution or innovation, using multiple sources of evidence, typically qualitative and quantitative data. Such an approach bridges the qualitative–quantitative divide and supports the view of Bryman (1988) and Robson (1993) that, in practice, there is 'considerable underlying unity of purpose' (Robson 1993, p.6).

A similar shift from quantitative towards 'mixed' and qualitative methods has been seen in curriculum evaluation (see Hamilton *et al* 1977) in order to document the processes which led to measured outcomes, as well as identifying unintended yet possibly significant outcomes. Furthermore, self-evaluation was developed, together with alternative approaches such as 'teacher-as-researcher' (Stenhouse 1975) and educational action research, in which evaluation is based on the detailed examination of evidence collected and evaluated whilst the action is underway in order that the next action can be planned and so on (see, for instance, Hopkins 1985; Walker 1985).

This brief review is sufficient to indicate some of the wide range of qualitative and quantitative approaches being employed. It also serves to show that many researchers have combined the two approaches and maintained a scientific commitment to the testing of claims. Whilst the call in education from the TTA is for evidence-based research, recent philosophy of science has argued, however, that it is not possible to gather a body of data by direct observation whose validity is independent of all theoretical suppositions. From this position it may be asserted that educational research cannot test claims against evidence if it depends upon shifting theoretical constructions of researchers. Postmodern philosophies (see Usher and Edwards 1994) in fact reject a scientific understanding of the world since there are only multiple and shifting interpretations, and imposition of meaning exposes the power of the scientific community (Foucault in Ball 1990).

This section has considered some elements of the debate and deliberation which has focused on quantitative and qualitative research as well as the relationship between the two. It leaves unexamined the generation of educational research to serve policy-making and, hence, to influence practice. Here, as one of us described in relation effective mathematics teaching (Aubrey 1997b), a similar pattern of development of applied educational theory and/

or method can be traced. This was the case for educational research in general, with an earlier tradition of philosophical/normative practice preceding scientific, empirical or 'engineering' models (Finch 1986) which sought to assess teaching effectiveness (Dunkin and Biddle 1974) or provide curriculum evaluation. The engineering model, being positivist and quantitative in character, tended to operationalise education objectives in order to measure effectiveness in terms of outcomes or seek relationships between teacher characteristics and pupil attainments but was criticised for failing to take sufficient account of teaching processes. Whilst 'systematic observation' was used – and widely so in the case of large-scale preschool research in the late 1970s and early 1980s – this was later criticised for overreliance on the observable and measurable at the cost of failing to capture the complex and multiple realities of the adults and children concerned. Similarly, in the area of curriculum evaluation, quantitative approaches were found wanting (see, for instance, Parlett and Hamilton 1972) since prespecified educational objectives and observable indicators used to measure effectiveness and cost-effectiveness provided, at best, a crude evaluation of the operation of programmes in complex and shifting contexts. Reconceptualisations of professional practice emphasised 'reflection-in-action' (see Schon 1987) which sought to account for the development of professional skill and practitioner wisdom, for which notions of technical knowledge application were regarded as inadequate models to deal with professional thinking and decision-making. Models of reflective practice have been extremely influential in recent reconceptualisations of the practice of teaching, as school-based training has replaced traditional forms of teacher preparation (see Zeicher, Liston, Mahlios and Gomez 1987) with its rational and technical methods.

The engineering model has been contrasted more generally with the 'enlightenment' model which, as the name suggests, aims to provide insight into practical situations for practitioners and policy-makers through description and analysis, from which theoretical concepts emerge. Again a wide range of applications can be discerned, including inquiry into teachers' subject knowledge (Aubrey 1997b) and so-called 'critical' research which provides ideological critique of schooling and its recapitulation of existing educational inequalities of class, sex and race. A nice example of such a study from early childhood is Steadman's research, which used stories written by eight-year-old girls to show how they revealed themselves

> to be concerned with a female future that they saw fraught with irritation and confinement – that they had no difficulty in presenting in a bad light – they both understood women's language and used language themselves, as a system of power, capable of the transformation of reality.
>
> (Steadman 1982, p.39)

A wide range of reactions to the engineering model in the area of evaluation arose in the form of 'illuminative' and 'democratic' evaluations (see Hamilton's

1976 account). These collectively have been grouped under the title of anthropological evaluation since the methods used are qualitative or ethnographic, to illuminate practices through the interpretation and construction of individuals and groups in particular situations. A well-used approach has been 'democratic' evaluation which attempts to represent a plurality of interests through extensive negotiation of roles and relationships with sponsors and education programme participants. A noteworthy example of this in the early childhood education field has been the Effective Early Learning (EEL) Project (Pascal 1993) in which many local education authorities have been involved in evaluation and improvement of early years provision. Its commitment to avoid defining quality as a value-laden, subjective and dynamic concept is a recognition of value-pluralism and suggests a political and ethical stance which has not gained unanimous support (such issues have been examined by Elliott 1977). Educational action research has been mentioned briefly above. Its employment by teachers to stimulate a more active role in conceiving, implementing, evaluating and disseminating research which focuses on classroom teaching has been much encouraged by the TTA as already noted and a number of such evaluations have been carried out in early years classrooms.

This account of educational evaluation has focused on methodological changes rather than the relationship between policy-makers and practice. Matters concerning the role and relationship of the researcher to the sponsors or stakeholders are subject to delicate negotiation and, finally, the contract specification.

The influence of power and vested interest on the process and outcome of research should perhaps not be underestimated. This raises ethical issues which will be returned to later in the book. In the meantime it is important to take a closer look at the research process before the more detailed examination of early childhood research is attempted.

The research process

Typical classifications and methods of researching may not, in practice, very closely match with what the researcher actually does but whilst the research process is in fact a messier business than textbook reports would have us believe it is important nevertheless that a research plan has been prepared. Whether or not the series of steps or 'stages' of the process are closely adhered to by researchers they provide a framework or structure from which to work which will be continuously open to revision and refinement. This chapter will conclude by examining some general design issues.

When critically reading research papers related to early years education a number of questions spring to mind:

- what is the area or focus?
- where is this located in the existing literature?
- what methods were used?

- what claims were put forward?
- how well supported by evidence were they?
- what conclusions were drawn and how solid do these appear?

Design, in fact, is concerned with turning research questions into project essence Robson (1993). The six stages or steps in the research process may be described as follows.

Conceptualising the topic or area to study

The area of research may have been generated in any number of ways. It may arise from current educational issues – for instance, how effective the new numeracy strategy is in enhancing young children's mental calculation – or it may be stimulated by the need to evaluate a new curriculum initiative, such as the new foundation curriculum for three- to five-year-olds. The focus may well be provided for contract researchers and result from a formal tender to an agency such as the TTA – for example, to evaluate existing induction programmes for new headteachers. Certainly for a small-scale project which is part of an award-bearing degree, personal interest is central to the choice of topic area. In this situation researchers will select their own focus. Similarly for a teacher's small-scale action research project an issue or problem in profess-ional practice may serve as the catalyst. In this case evaluating, changing and monitoring change in some aspect of practice will offer the opportunity to examine what is being done in the classroom or nursery setting armed with new knowledge or with the results of an investigation and evaluation. This suggests the inquiry should be grounded in a thorough knowledge of the literature. It is equally possible that the study is stimulated by background reading and with so much educational change in the UK over the last decade or so this has provided a rich source for potential evaluations. Whilst the range of topics available is almost unlimited, the choice will be limited by available resources – human, material or time, access to sites and cooperation of others, as well as the availability of suitable measures for data collection.

Whilst deciding the focus or problem, formulation is the first essential step in the process. The researcher will know considerably more about this at the end of the project than the beginning and, moreover, it is not at all uncommon for the focus to be adapted – if not entirely changed – as a result of experience in the field, which may constrain the investigation or, in the case of funded research, restrictions may result from the wishes or views of the sponsor.

Reviewing the background literature

The existing research literature or underpinning theory will have been thoroughly reviewed. This will provide not only a foundation upon which to build a new project but also an overview of measures and procedures already available in the area – that is, methodology already being used. A sound grasp of what is established knowledge in the field is fundamental and it may be that existing researchers in the topic area can provide useful leads and starting points and even identify key texts.

As outlined in Chapter 1, 'abstracting' sources have been invaluable to researchers as well as their computerised equivalents on CD-ROM. This may speed up the process of 'key word' searches. Citation indices are particularly helpful to the reader who will also be able to track forward in time a particular researcher through the work of later researchers who have cited the original work. Gash (1989) has provided useful and detailed accounts of computer/on-line searches. It is probably true to say that bibliographic researching continues through the life of a research project as the knowledge-base becomes more refined. Equally important, however, is reference to research methodology texts in order to review carefully procedures available and to clarify strengths and limitations of different approaches. Just as the research topic must be realistic in terms of its scale and resources available, so too it is essential for the researcher to identify the appropriate research strategy which takes account of existing practicalities.

Designing the procedures

From the review of the literature in conjunction with the researcher's initial ideas the details of the research in context will begin to emerge. Especially in the case of funded research, sponsors will need convincing that a plan covering all stages of the project have been carefully prepared which identify:

- a clearly formulated problem
- how the work will build on existing research and make a new contribution
- what aims and clearly attainable objectives are established
- a carefully-prepared design using an appropriate approach and relevant methodology
- arrangement for collection of data which are of high quality, validity, reliability and relevance, using a suitable sampling strategy and systematic analysis
- sensitive issues and possible problems (ethical, methodological and practical) which may need addressing in order to complete the work satisfactorily within a sensible time-scale.

First, the general focus will need refining by the researcher into the research questions. There is no single way in which this process is carried out, in fact, a mixture of effort and intuition is likely to be involved in the context of immersion in the theory and practice of the field. This process leads to hunches about events and processes, tentative hypotheses about what is happening (in the case of qualitative research) or more formal hypotheses which will be tested by experiment (in the case of quantitative research). Such hypotheses or informed guesses help set up the structure for the investigation and should lead to the selection of specific methods and procedures.

Robson (1993) has classified enquiries in terms of their purposes as well as research strategy as follows:

- exploratory purposes, which are usually qualitative, to uncover what is happening and to shed fresh light
- descriptive (or descriptive-analytical) purposes, which may be quantitative or qualitative and seek to provide an accurate record, exhaustive account or evaluation of persons, processes or events
- explanatory purposes, which are again quantitative or qualitative, usually seeking explanations and relationships but not always causal and, hence, predictive.

Purposes may, of course, be theoretical in which case the distinction between deduction which draws upon theory and induction which generates theory needs to be appreciated. Finally, as will be appreciated from an earlier discussion of research models, purposes may be evaluative and, hence, prescriptive. These purposes influence strongly the kind of outcome or end-product as well as case selection and the number of cases to be studied. 'Cases' in this sense refers to the phenomena which will be studied. Once the research questions and purposes are established it is likely that the research strategy will emerge. Three main strategies can be discerned – the experiment, survey and case study – and these correspond, but only broadly, to purposes identified above, with case studies generating exploration, surveys providing description and experiments explanations.

The three approaches can also be distinguished by their sampling strategies and by the degree of control over the events or processes the researcher wishes to have. In experiments the researcher generates the cases which are studied by setting up the conditions under which it is attempted to test causal relationships between variables which are the focus of the research, whilst at the same time attempting to control extraneous influences so that competing explanations can be eliminated. In surveys, by contrast, large samples of naturally-occurring cases are selected for study which, whilst using 'probability' case sampling, do not experimentally create them. The case study involves a small number of naturally-occurring and nonrepresentative cases with 'purposive' sampling in which a potentially rich initial case (or cases) influences the selection of subsequent cases as each decision is based on what has been previously learned. The first two strategies are thus quantitative in approach. The third, by contrast, is qualitative.

These three main strategies offer particular advantages and shortcomings. The survey with its statistical sampling will provide a robust empirical generalisation whilst the case study will provide rich descriptions of individual cases. If these cases are selected to maximise variation then greater validity for the evidence is obtained. At the same time the experiment, by its objective determination of relationships through manipulation of variables, is highly artificial and may not allow many inferences about the behaviour of subjects under other and more 'natural' conditions. On the other hand, the case study approach allows for the meanings and perspectives of individual cases to be portrayed which, correspondingly, relies on higher levels of interpretation.

Whilst these three strategies represent different ways of collecting and qualifying evidence, in practice specific methods are not confined to particular strategies. Each strategy may be used for any purpose – descriptive, exploratory or explanatory – in any combination. In fact, the case study, for instance, is typically multi-method in design.

Collecting data

Once the procedures have been planned, and subjects and sites identified, the type and what quantity of data collected will depend upon the focus of the study, the methods used and time available. They may take any number of forms: interviews, questionnaires, observation, field notes, audiotape or video-recordings and transcriptions or document analysis. Furthermore they will be derived from a range of sources or informants, including the researcher 'as main instrument' who will also influence the quality or validity of these data. Finally these data will vary in the degree of their formality or structure, that is, the degree to which they render quantitative information. Structured observation schedules used in preschool settings may provide frequencies of particular behaviours and interactions which can be analysed in a quantitative manner, whilst unstructured field notes or transcriptions of discourse from the same setting will require lengthy and time-consuming processing before any analysis can be undertaken. Each method of collecting data has particular strengths and associated issues or drawbacks and, as already noted, qualitative and quantitative methods in combination are increasingly being used. It should be noted, however, that designing research involves selecting which weaknesses you are prepared to tolerate since weaknesses cannot be eliminated!

Analysing data

As will be very apparent from the discussion so far analysis techniques will depend upon the data collected which, in turn, will have been determined by the research focus and intended outcomes. Numerical data will require statistical procedures which are technically appropriate and reveal the likely patterns in the data. Although it is at this point that expert statistical advice will be most needed, it cannot be too strongly emphasised that the statistician should be involved at all stages from the initial planning and design stage throughout the research process to the report-writing phase.

For qualitative data, analysis may range from computer analysis to the perhaps more common process of identifying the themes and surprises which emerge and where categories thereby generated may be inter-related in ways which lead to the emergence of a clear conceptual story (Strauss and Corbin 1990). This final stage may be distinguished from the earlier generating stages where themes identified are exemplified with rich descriptions selected from the data.

Writing the research report

This stage involves disseminating the results of the research to a wider audience. Conventionally it has taken the form of a report with a standard structure or format in which the researcher specifies the research problem, hypotheses, the aims and the background literature, describes the procedures and results, and interprets and discusses these in the light of new knowledge generated, as well as shortcomings of the design. This format of research reporting has been commonly used for journal publication and conference presentations in the case of quantitative research. Qualitative research reports do not have the same established traditions, yet, for academic purposes, it is common that researchers will adopt a similar style which outlines the focus for the research, the research questions to be asked, the conceptual framework which locates the work in a specific literature, the methods to be used and the cases to be investigated, a presentation of the main claims and supporting evidence with a statement of the conclusions to be drawn in the light of evidence presented from the cases involved. It is at this stage that the quality of the research will be judged by the wider research community and, on the basis of this, decisions will be made regarding its worth and whether it warrants publications. Research reports, conference papers and proposals for research projects to external funding bodies are all subjected to critical review by other researchers who, similarly, will be evaluating the stages in the research process from problem formulation, through case selection and data production/analysis, to the statement of main claims and conclusions.

The objective of the scrutiny will be to examine the claims made in relation to the investigation carried out and, hence, the conclusions drawn, located within the broader context or field from which the focus or problem was first formulated. It constitutes an evaluation of the overall argument which includes definitions provided as well as descriptions and explanations of phenomena to be studied. Moreover it will consider the conclusions drawn in the light of theoretical inferences made in respect of experimental findings or, in the case of large-scale survey work, generalisation to the wider population from which the cases investigated were drawn, or 'empirical generalisation'. Suffice it to say that the notion of 'evidence' is a broad one grounded within the main argument which supports a variety of claims requiring different types of evidence.

This discussion rather suggests that one scientific report will be provided. The current government would like research findings to be made available in more accessible forms for policy-makers, teachers, as well as fellow researchers, indicating that publication in professional as well as academic outlets should be more firmly established by researchers. Clearly, not only will different audiences have different background knowledge but also they may have curiosity about different aspects of the research process. In summary, different audiences will require different levels of supporting argument and differing amounts of emphasis on practical inferences or implications.

Conclusion

This six-stage process suggests a greater degree of rationality and linearity in the research process than is likely to have been the case and the conventional form of report writing, similarly, implies a more straightforward and step-wise progression in operation than was probably the case for the researcher. The structure provided, however, gives a support to the research process and serves to reduce ambiguity and uncertainty as well as offer sign posts on the way. Moreover, in a chapter which has set out to examine some of the key issues in debates about research methodology, it is important to recognise that without a sound understanding of such processes it is impossible to begin to judge the quality of studies reported in research journals. This suggests that even the reader or user of research will need to have a fairly sophisticated appreciation of the diverse procedures available as well as approaches or methodologies used in order to understand the research endeavour. This chapter has focused on broad strategies of design but the specific methods – or tactics – will now need a closer examination before turning to early childhood research in practice.

4 Forms of observation
Measurement and analysis

The goal for this chapter will be to consider how particular research strategies relate to specific methods of investigation. The previous chapters have offered an introduction to some of the key theories, models and findings in the field of early childhood education. The intention of this chapter is to provide a brief account of systematic enquiry in this area in order for the reader without a social sciences background to:

- gain a deeper understanding of the skills of designing, observing, analysing and reporting
- develop a more critical approach to the substantive content of early childhood research to be outlined in the remainder of this text.

These methods or tactics tend to be associated with particular research approaches although this relationship is not in fact a close one. For instance, case study approaches are multi-method in strategy and may employ observation, questionnaires and interviews. Experiments too depend upon very precise forms of observation which involve sophisticated measurement techniques. Surveys can also be carried out using observation. In other words just as each research strategy, be it experiment, survey or case study, may be used for descriptive, exploratory or explanatory purposes, so too may any method or technique be used with any of the three traditional research strategies described in the last chapter. In respect of observation methods – central to the investigation of early childhood education – one *could* argue that these provide the basic ingredients of the research cycle, as Richardson (1995, p.11) has argued, with the following stages:

- A series of systematic observations (ranging from relatively 'unstructured' to 'structured') are carried out in which factors or variables (things which change or vary) and their interrelations are progressively identified.
- These variables and interrelations are expressed in a remarkable intellectual device called a 'scientific theory'.
- The theory is tested in 'controlled experiments'.

- The results of any of these investigations may suggest further observations or experiments and/or modifications to the theory.
- When the theory has been adequately tested it may be deemed safe to apply it in practical interventions with children.

The first step in uncovering cause-and-effect relationships, thus, takes place through the part of the cycle known as 'inductive research' which will employ less structured or naturalistic observations. This may lead to more focused observations of specific variables with the use of coding systems which lead, in turn, to observations involving manipulations of these variables or 'treatments'. At this point the research becomes 'hypothetico-deductive', deducing a hypothesis or prediction from a theory-generating phase which may be put to the test experimentally.

In presenting early childhood education research methods it is therefore essential to describe the scientific method – the principles of experimentation – as well as to examine some of the various theoretical perspectives and research techniques used and the ethical considerations to be made.

The scientific method of observation

The study of children has taken place over time with philosophers, religious leaders and early years educators all offering explanations for their behaviour and development based on informal observations and theorising.

With the emergence of psychology as a scientific discipline in the late nineteenth century the study of children became more systematic, controlled and, hence, more objective in nature. Chapter 1 has already outlined aspects of the scientific method which distinguish it from less formal and structured ways of investigating early childhood and these were developed further in Chapter 3. Suffice it to say that these aspects relate intimately to some general concepts and ideas – specifically, the notions of theory, objectivity, scientific explanation and testability.

From psychology has come the expectation that theories will provide statements – or claims – describing the relationship between behaviour/s and the factors – or variables – that are associated with or explain them. In fact one of the most fundamental concepts is the *theory*. Theory has an important role in guiding research by indicating further research questions which need addressing or suggesting additional data-collecting which is required. Whilst in respect of the natural sciences theories may have the status of *laws*, when supported by substantial empirical evidence, so long as there is little to support these ideas they can be no more than *hypotheses*. This process may support the hypotheses or lead to modification of the theory. Collection of scientific evidence in theory-testing has specific requirements: for instance, *objectivity* where observation of events can be generally agreed upon. This aspect of the scientific method is established by reference to criteria which can be related to comments made above in respect of observation.

- Behaviours or processes must be *observable* and based upon agreed and objective information-gathering procedures. In practice psychologists are frequently interested in hypothetical constructs such as intelligence or creativity which cannot be directly observed, in which case operational definitions will be prerequisite to further investigation. In other words, observable behaviours assumed to be related to, or resulting from, these constructs would be the focus of attention.
- These behaviours must be *measurable* or defined in such a way that they can be specified and, hence, recorded.

These two criteria define what is – or is not – appropriate to include in an experimental analysis. Furthermore, as noted in Chapter 3, the study of young children may have the objective to explore, describe or *explain* their behaviour. Explanations require *prediction*, which may be based on prior exploration, description and *control*, which implies testing the researcher's ideas or hypotheses. To complicate matters further a young child's observed behaviour may have been determined already by prior learning, reflect current biological or physiological states, such as hunger, tiredness or irritability, as much as current contextual variables, such as people, processes or events in the setting. This brief discussion should illustrate the complexities involved in observation for descriptive purposes, never mind the rigour required for explanatory purposes. The scientific method, thus, requires that a hypothesis or theory be testable. In other words, it must be stated in such a way that specific predictions can be made and tested. Moreover, since the scientific method is far from exact it is accepted that predictions will *not* be proved but examined in terms of levels of certainty. Hence the child psychologist or educational researcher may be in a position to claim empirical support for the hypothesis or state that the results were consistent with the theory being tested. Usually, however, findings are not clear cut and, at most, will support the researcher's ideas. This means that procedures are required which determine whether or not the evidence is substantial enough to allow acceptance or rejection of the prediction. These procedures are referred to as *inferential* statistical methods.

The experimental process

The previous section has shown how behaviour may be explained by identifying its determinants, usually in a previous exploratory or descriptive phase, and then using prediction and control procedures. The experiment is then designed to establish *functional relationships* between environmental variables or events and behaviour. The events in this context serve as *independent variables* in the sense that the researchers are free to vary their levels or values along a scale or combine their levels in the experimental situation. This planned variation is described as *experimental manipulation* of the independent variable. One example of this could, for instance, be the planned variation of infant diet for two groups of young children – normal or enriched. The behaviour being studied in this context becomes the *dependent variable*, its 'variability' or levels of occurrence being studied in relation to levels – amount, type or form – of the independent variable. In the example chosen, infant weight and observed health would constitute the dependent variables. Differing levels of behaviour elicited by each level of environmental event reveal the strength of relationship between the two variables. Different types of diet would be presumed to be the cause of variations observed in infant groups receiving the normal or enriched diet in terms of weight and health. The identification of functional relationships between independent variables and behaviours is described as a *functional analysis of behaviour*. This means simply that as an independent variable varies (in this case diet), related dependent variables (weight and health) change in a predictable manner. Experiments are always designed to study differences or changes among events or behaviours. There is an *experimental hypothesis* which predicts differences in specific behaviour as a result of changes in the independent variable. Commonly the analysis considers the hypothesis that there are no real differences or changes. This is called the *null hypothesis*. The data are examined to see whether they are compatible with the null hypothesis. If not the experiment is taken as evidence for the alternative view, that the experimental hypothesis is correct and that real differences in behaviour are observed, corresponding to different levels of the independent variable. Where substantial differences are not observed, statistical methods are designed to allow only rejection of the experimental hypothesis (prediction of differences). The null hypothesis (prediction of no differences), however, can only be rejected. No conclusions regarding the null hypothesis can be made. In other words we never accept the hypothesis that a behaviour and an independent variable are unrelated. This means that whilst the experimental hypothesis can be either accepted or rejected the null hypothesis can only be rejected.

An important requirement of the experimental method is that the children – or subjects – of the experiment exposed to the experimental treatment – or level of independent variable – are in some sense equivalent at the start so that any change brought by the manipulation may be attributed to the effects of the different levels of independent variables. In the example chosen the researcher will attempt to ensure that subjects in each condition are equivalent in relevant characteristics – age, height and weight – at the start so that later differences in weight and height can be attributed to the effects of different levels of the independent variable (diet).

A popular procedure for assigning subjects to treatments is by *randomly* placing each subject in each condition on the assumption that different characteristics of the subjects have an equal chance to be spread or balanced across a group. Another procedure – matching – is based upon selection of subjects so that they are equal or *matched* on a number of characteristics. This provides another method for ensuring the subjects are alike at the beginning of the experiment.

There are exceptions to these procedures – for example, when the researcher is particularly interested in a subject characteristic and this, in itself, constitutes the independent variable of interest. A researcher may, for instance, be interested in high or low attainers in mathematics and, in this case, the particular subject and the level of variable are inseparable, that is, *nonmanipulable* independent variables. Although studies involving nonmanipulable independent variables are often carried out in the same way as other experiments, Campbell and Stanley (1966) have referred to them as *quasi-experimental designs*. Since subjects cannot be assigned to a condition randomly there is a greater likelihood that treatment groups may differ systematically in other respects as well. Higher attainers in a mathematics test, for instance, may have higher measured cognitive functioning in other areas.

Whether we use true or quasi-experimental designs, however, it is possible that other and uncontrolled factors have contributed to the observed findings. Just because the evidence seems to support the experimental hypothesis that there are real differences in behaviour corresponding to different levels of the independent variable, this does not mean we can be absolutely sure that the differences are actually caused by the differences in the independent variable which is under investigation. There may be other factors which are responsible. Factors which potentially have such an effect are called *nuisance factors*. As far as possible differences in nuisance factors need to be eliminated or the study needs to be organised to take full account of them as well as the variables of real interest.

Most experiments are of interest only because they allow us to draw conclusions which relate to a larger population of cases on the basis of the sample used in the experiment. This makes sample selection very important. The best known but, in practice, seldom-used method of selecting a sample is *simple random sampling*. This means that in principle each person in the population has an equal chance of being selected. Some *randomisation* can also be carried out within the experimental sample, by allocating the selected people randomly to the different treatments that are going to be applied.

For most purposes random sampling will eliminate *sampling bias*, which means that, on average, figures calculated for the sample will be the same as the average for the whole population. However, it will not eliminate *sampling error* which means that each sample will give rise to figures which are slightly different from the population average – or sometimes very different indeed.

An alternative approach to sampling attempts to reduce sampling error by *representative sampling*. This involves trying to choose a sample which on balance has the same sort of composition as the overall population. Once the sample is selected, if it is necessary to split people into groups for different treatment, the same principle can be extended by *matching* the members of each group so that, as far as possible, the composition of each group is the same.

Even if subjects are selected appropriately there is a possibility of bias in the experimental procedures through subject *reactivity*. The subjects' behaviour change may not simply result from the experimental manipulation but from a reaction to being observed, as a result of repeated assessment or, indeed, in response to almost any other uncontrolled environment variable. The most obvious way of dealing with the first type of reaction is to use methods which are as unobtrusive as possible and, in response to the second, to repeat the procedure until it is routine to the subject. The problem with the latter method is that the researcher ends up observing improvement through practice rather than initial performance. Another strategy would be to use different but equivalent procedures or forms of measurement of the dependent variable.

A third type of reactivity is commonly known as the *Hawthorne effect* where changes in the subjects' behaviour result simply from introduction of change per se rather than from the particular manipulation under consideration. This is a common problem when people are involved in experiments. One solution is to include a group of control subjects who receive only the attention of the researchers rather than receiving the independent variable of interest. It may be that simply extending the period of observation is sufficient to deal with such reactivity. Characteristics and behaviour of the researcher may also introduce bias – *experimenter* bias. The age, gender or race of the researcher may influence response as well as unintentional and more fine changes in experimenter behaviour which may increase the chances of certain findings.

Another problem, particularly acute when observing young children, is the *maturation* which takes place between pre- and post-testing and may account for changes observed rather than the intervention. Sometimes non-maturational events occur and have an unplanned influence on results. Two of the writers, engaged in a limited longitudinal study of children's early numeracy competence, have been confronted with a 'day of the week' effect on the second of three measurement phases which, it has been playfully suggested by the statistical adviser, may relate to late television watching of the World Cup on the evening preceding measurement! This may indicate a possible social and cultural influence on the observed behaviour, calling for further investigation and perhaps even replication of the study. Another important possibility is that this is simply a fluke. Even if the sampling is not biased, sampling error can still produce interesting but meaningless fluke results. The usual way of eliminating such fluke effects is to estimate the expected extent of sampling error and to reject the importance of any effect which is likely to occur simply by this chance variation. The standard test is to say that any difference in behaviour which might be found, purely by chance, more than one time in twenty is not significant. (This is just a rule of thumb and strictly speaking we ought to say that it is 'not significant at the 5-per-cent level'.)

Qualitative, interpretative or ethological methods of observation

Not all research is carried out to test a theory or hypothesis or even to investigate a particular functional relationship. Even so research which is exploratory is usually carried out with a view to investigating a particular area of interest which leads to the identification of potential relations between independent and dependent variables or the influence of a particular independent variable on behaviour. The purpose of such studies may be to determine teaching variables, for instance, influencing children's mental calculation strategies. Here the dependent variable (mental calculation) provides the basis for the exploratory studies: in other words, it is *theory-generating*.

Reference has already been made to Bronfenbrenner's (1989) 'ecological niche' and the ecological approach rests on the assumption that when the young child is removed from its natural setting valuable information relating to the determinants of its behaviour will be lost. As will be considered later in more detail, children's behaviour is most usefully examined in the context of the physical and social environment, which includes physical characteristics of the setting as well as reciprocal relationships between young children and significant adults in this environment. Characteristic of this approach are unobtrusive and nonmanipulative observations of behaviour in relation to aspects of the physical and social environment. Whilst this type of observation may be termed descriptive or descriptive-analytical the researcher is still likely to be alert to, if not attempting to identify, functional relationships. The limitation of non-manipulative methods of course is that the researchers must be satisfied that they are recording those interactions which occur naturally rather than creating the conditions which generate the relationships of interest.

The *ethological* approach may be distinguished from the *ecological* by an interest in the origins of behaviour. Methods used are similar to those used by ecological researchers which emphasise observation in the natural setting. Whilst there are differences in types of qualitative research, terms like 'naturalistic', 'ethological' and 'participant observation' have much in common (Erickson 1986). Just as some ecological research does involve experimental manipulations in the natural setting, ethologists may return to the experimental method to test a hypothesis generated in the field. The progression in research may thus be one of exploration leading to a focus on particular, significant phenomena. Further investigation may lead to possible theoretical or hypothetical explanations which lead in turn to theory-testing either in the field or under more formal experiment conditions.

Measurement and analysis of data

Quantitative analysis

Whilst a number of statistical concepts will be described in this section these can only be treated at a very general level. The detailed analysis of experimental data is well beyond the scope of this text and can be obtained from any number of introductory texts. Goodwin and Goodwin's (1996) *Understanding Quantitative and Qualitative Research in Early Childhood Education*, for instance, gives a brief but comprehensive overview of types of research, as well as basic information on measurement and analysis. Meanwhile our purpose here is to introduce descriptions, rationales and key features of the experimental design characterising early years research which may be described in future chapters.

To return first to the experimental method, after data have been collected – usually in a numerical form – they will be analysed to determine their significance. To consider a very simple experiment, imagine the researcher wishes to study children's performance on a basic arithmetic task as a function of teaching regime. The researcher has reason to believe that subjects will perform better on a timed task of basic arithmetic where they have received a teaching module which has emphasised oral calculation strategies as compared with a teaching module which has concentrated on formal written methods. Only two groups of subjects will be used: one group taught by methods emphasising oral calculation and one group taught by methods stressing the formal written calculation. This represents one of the most straightforward and simple experimental designs. There is only one independent variable (type of teaching received) and it can assume only two different values (emphasis or lack of emphasis on oral/mental methods of calculation). In experimental research the dimension is also described as a *factor* and each value along that dimension, or factor, a *level*. This example could be described as a single-factor design with two levels of independent variable.

The sample

The first step for the researcher is to select the sample of subjects in order for the composition of the groups to be as similar as possible at the start. These procedures may or may not allow for the subjects to vary systematically on any characteristic before the experimental teaching programme. As noted above this is achieved most usually by randomisation or matching. Randomisation does not assign subjects according to their characteristics but assigns them randomly and assumes no systematic variation has occurred. The larger the sample of subjects involved the more reasonable is this assumption. By contrast, matching may be achieved by selecting the subjects to aim for equivalence on a number of variables. In the case of the arithmetic experiment we shall assume the subjects are to be matched by:

* age (in this case, range 8.7 years to 9.6 years with a mean age of 9.2 years)
* educational levels (similar results on standard assessment tasks at age 7 years)
* socioeconomic background (all pupils were selected from a mixed urban and rural educational authority with a mixed socioeconomic intake)
* sex (equal numbers of boys and girls were included so far as possible) and
* mathematical attainment (according to teacher report).

Data collection

Moving on to data collection, the basic principle is that each subject must be studied under as standard a set of conditions as possible to ensure that the differences observed among subjects are those which result from experimental manipulation. This 'standardisation' is achieved through systematic application of test administration, ideally by someone other than the researcher who is not aware of the actual experimental hypothesis under investigation (that teaching which emphasises oral/mental calculation will be more effective in developing children's arithmetic than written methods) and cannot, thus, introduce experimental bias. In the case of the study being described, it would be critical that the experimental groups received identical instructions, delivered in a common manner. The arithmetic test would need to be administered in groups with ten minutes allowed for completion of sixty calculations.

Data analysis

After the data have been collected they would be analysed in order to interpret them. Let us assume the scores for the group who received teaching which emphasised written calculation were as represented in Table 4.1.

The individual raw scores are difficult to compare, simply because there are too many of them and they appear too chaotic for the human mind to cope with all the detail. It is far easier for people to think about the data if they are represented either by a graph or by a few numbers which sum up the pattern. These numbers are *summary statistics*. Generally speaking the most useful things to know about a set of numbers are, first, what a typical number is in the set and, second, how typical it is. This information is commonly provided by the mean, which clearly gives some idea of a number which is typical of the set, and the standard deviation, which gives an idea of how far away from the mean the numbers tend to be. Once we move from simply summarising the data to testing hypotheses, the standard deviation is often taken as the basis for estimating the extent of sampling error to be expected.

In the case shown in Table 4.1 it is easy to see that the mean for the group whose teaching stressed written calculation is considerably lower than the mean for the group whose teaching stressed mental methods. It is also clear that the group whose teaching emphasis was on written calculation had a higher standard deviation and varied more widely around the mean. This suggests that teaching emphasis on mental methods is associated with greater competence in timed arithmetic tests. Before the data can be taken to support this hypothesis, however, it is necessary to check that it is not likely to be a fluke result. An inferential statistical test needs to be carried out to see whether the difference between the means for the two groups is significant at the 5-percent level. On the basis of the variation which was found within the groups (shown by the standard deviation), is the difference in means so large that it is likely to occur purely by chance – more than one time in twenty?

The best known test for use in this sort of situation is the *t test*. This tests the null hypothesis that in the wider population there is really no difference between people given one form of teaching and people given another. Even if this were true, sampling error would lead to a certain amount of difference

Table 4.1   Performance on a timed arithmetic test for the group whose teaching stressed written calculations (Group 1)

	Subject number	Sex	Reported attainment	Raw score
a) Raw score			(High/low)	(Total 60)
	37	m	L	12
	38	f	H	41
	39	f	L	9
	40	f	H	35
	41	m	L	21
	42	f	L	11
	43	f	H	48
	44	m	H	47
	45	f	L	18
	46	m	L	15
	47	m	H	45
	48	f	H	34
				Total 346
b) Mean (average) score				28.83 (42.58*)
c) Standard deviation				14.27 (9.17*)
d) t = 2.82 (a value of t less than 2.074 is significant at the 5% level so we can reject the null hypothesis)				

* scores for Group 2 receiving teaching which stressed oral/mental methods

between the group means. The name 't' is given to the ratio between the observed difference between group means and the estimated sampling error. This can be expressed as:

$$t = \frac{\text{difference between means}}{\text{estimated sampling error}}$$

The sampling error is estimated, partly on the basis of the variation within the groups, indicated by the standard deviation, and partly on the basis of the number of people in each group.

Larger values of t are more significant statistically. They are produced by larger differences between the group means or by smaller standard deviations within the groups or by larger samples. Even a small difference between means can be significant at the 5-percent level if it is based on a sufficiently large sample.

In our example with twelve subjects in each group the actual value of t in the data (t = 2.81) is greater than the value necessary to accept the experimental hypothesis (t values are provided by the statistical computer package used). It is established practice that when recording the results of such tests to include not only the t value and its statistical significance (in this case t =2.074 or greater is necessary for significance at the 5-percent level, leading us to reject the null hypothesis) but also the means and standard deviations of the two sets of scores as in Table 4.2.

Table 4.2 Using the t-test of significance.

Variable	Mean 1	Mean 2	t value	p
Timed arithmetic test score	42.58	28.83	2.81	0.05

This two-group example is the simplest type of single-factor experimental design, though studies involving three, four or more levels of the independent variable are also quite common. To continue with the worked example, if a third type of teaching regime were included which provided, for instance, a regime using a mixture of oral and written methods, then three levels of independent variable might be included with twelve subjects assigned to each. Again important summary statistics such as the mean scores for each group and their standard deviations would be calculated. To analyse the results of more than two groups an *F test* or *analysis of variance* is often used. This is similar to the t test in that the ratio of variability between group scores is compared with the estimated sampling error, expressed as:

$$F = \frac{\text{variability between groups}}{\text{estimated sampling error}}$$

Again, as the difference between group scores grows larger or the scores within groups becomes less variable, the value of F increases. High values of F lead to the rejection of the null hypothesis that there are no real differences between the groups. It is also possible to use a single-factor *repeated measures* design where the same subjects are studied under different conditions – that is, different levels of the independent variable are examined within subjects rather than between subjects. A modified F test is available to deal with such circumstances.

It is also possible to design experiments which examine more than one independent variable at a time. Returning to the first worked example, in addition to the differences in the two teaching regimes, their effect on two groups of subjects – high and low attainers in mathematics – could be investigated. Four different groups are now required. In the example provided there are now nineteen subjects in each group. This study would be described as a two-factor design with two levels of one variable (teaching regime) and two levels of the other (high and low attainers). An outline of this model is shown in Table 4.3

Here the raw scores are presented (under a). They have also been summarised as averages (under b) and variance at the two levels as well as combined (under c). At this point it appears that the experiment is being carried out as two separate investigations. Once again a functional relationship appears to be apparent, with emphasis on mental calculation in teaching strategy increasing scores for timed arithmetic. We can also examine the low and high attainers' manipulation independently of teaching regime. Unsurprisingly the scores indicate the superior scores of the high achievers.

Table 4.3   Performance on a timed arithmetic test for four groups: two levels of one variable (teaching regime) and two levels of a second variable (high/low attainers)

a) Raw scores	Teaching group 1		Teaching group 2	
	High attainers (HA)	Low attainers (LA)	High attainers	Low attainers
	43	46	32	29
	36	47	45	29
	45	41	31	12
	51	35	30	21
	40	37	30	19
	48	36	30	28
	51	47	37	28
	45	35	45	23
	47	44	38	20
	51	36	29	15
	49	25	48	17
	52	36	28	11
	50	35	30	27
	46	32	32	19
	52	42	29	23
	52	45	35	26
	47	51	35	23
	51	40	41	28
	51	41	31	18

Summary	Teaching group 1		
	HA	LA	Total
Sum	907	751	1658
b) Average	47.74	39.53	87.26
c) Variance	19.65	39.93	59.58

	Teaching group 2		
	HA	LA	Total
Sum	656	416	1072
b) Average	34.53	21.89	56.42
c) Variance	38.04	32.43	70.47

d)	F values
Sample	138.97
Column	63.46
Interaction	2.85

($F = 3.97$ or greater for significance at the 5 per cent level leading us to reject null hypothesis)

These data can be analysed using an analysis of variance that calculates separate F values for each of the variables. These values are greater than necessary to reject the null hypothesis, indicating a functional relationship between arithmetic scores and both mental methods of teaching and high achievement. Table 4.3 also shows an F value for the interaction. This means that the experimental design allows us to test whether the effects of the different types of teaching are significantly different for the different types of pupils. Given that children score higher if they are high-achieving and score higher if they are exposed to an emphasis on mental methods, is the advantage in this form teaching equally great for both high- and low-achieving pupils? In this case the answer seems to be no. The F value for the interaction is not significant at the 5-percent level.

Whilst the experimental method provides an apparent elegance, precision and rigour, assumptions made with respect to the nature of the population, the sampling strategy as well as decisions about the assignment of subjects to experimental conditions are less certain. More fundamental challenges to the role of such statistical methods are beginning to emerge; however, these problems are made worse not better if the experimental method is thrown away entirely.

Meanwhile there are also a number of different statistics which describe the type and extent of relationship between two variables, since much quantitative research concerns associations between two variables, or more simply-termed *correlation*. This is a statistical term meaning that two variables change or vary together in predictable ways but does not imply a causal relationship. A positive correlation means that two variables change in the same direction: that is, if one increases the other does or vice versa. A negative correlation by contrast means that the two vary in the opposite directions – when one increases the other decreases. Correlations are seldom perfect, however, and tend to be expressed in terms of strength or weakness. A perfect positive correlation is expressed as +1.00 and negative correlation as –1.00. In each case as the number reduces – or increases – to 0.00 the relationship becomes weaker. A common example provided is the strong positive relationship between a child's height and weight. Correlational findings are often useful for suggesting potential relationships in a longitudinal-correlation approach. In this case a researcher may be interested in a variety of measures – such as word matching, concepts about print, word reading, letter identification, handwriting and vocabulary – in relation to later reading ability. A distribution of scores would be obtained on various measures and the researcher would then follow subjects for the next two to six years. Again a distribution of scores would be expected on different measures. When more than one predictor variable is used to predict an outcome or dependent variable, a technique called *multiple regression* is used. In the example chosen, Blatchford and Plewis (1990) found that early literacy-related knowledge was a predictor of good reading at seven; by eleven years handwriting was a slightly better predictor than letter identification. Maclean, Bryant and Bradley's (1987) predictive correlational study examined the relationship between children's knowledge of, and skill in, reciting nursery rhymes at three years and the development of phonological skills over a fifteen-month period and found a significant statistical relationship. Furthermore, knowledge of nursery rhymes was predictive of reading but not early numerical competence.

Quantitative designs provide rigorous methods of investigating children's behaviour but to be of high quality the measures used must be reliable and valid. *Reliability* refers to the consistency and repeatability of the measure used whilst *validity* concerns the appropriateness and meaningfulness of inferences made on the basis of scores about the child or children. Also important though less so than reliability are *usability* characteristics which relate, for example, to technical features of the measures being used, the appropriateness of the test format – its administration, scoring and interpretation – as well as its cost.

In summary, descriptive data are commonly used to describe data in terms of central tendency (mean), variation (standard deviation) and relationship (correlation). Differences between sets of scores, values or observations may be explored using inferential statistics. These are commonly used to make estimations about the state of affairs in some 'population' as compared with the actual sample of scores or observations. Two common inferential procedures for comparing group means are the t test and analysis of variance. Researchers also strive to achieve high quality in the experiment: that is reliability, or consistency in measures, and validity, or meaningfulness of inferences made in the experimental situation.

When planning experiments it is useful to think in terms of how traditional significance tests can ultimately be used to analyse the data, but Royall (1997) argues that once the experiment is completed these techniques are of less value in representing and assessing the data. He refers to the traditional approach as a decision-making paradigm. It is concerned with controlling the number of errors you make in deciding whether or not to reject the null hypothesis. A significance test does not address the question of how well the specific data collected offer support to one hypothesis against another. If you use conventional significance tests to reject null hypotheses, only 5 percent of the rejections will be mistaken, but a close look at the evidence after a particular experiment might well show that this particular rejection is almost certainly one of 5 percent. Royall favours a likelihood paradigm. This interprets evidence in terms of how likely the data are under competing hypotheses. It answers the question: how far should this evidence cause a rational person to alter their opinion either towards or away from each of the hypotheses considered? One advantage of this approach (once initial problems of unfamiliarity are overcome) is to answer questions that people really want to ask. The answers in graphical or numerical form could well make better sense than reports of conventional significance tests.

Qualitative analysis

The methods described above exemplify the scientific approach in which the detached, or objective, researcher is distanced from the experimental subject through the formalised procedures and ritualised observation. An alternative criterion for this objectivity, according to Robson (1993), is inter-subjective agreement in which *objectivity* is taken to refer to what multiple observers agree to as a phenomenon involving people in social settings, in contrast to the subjective experience of the single individual. This perspective demands an *involved* rather than detached researcher and invokes notions of *triangulation* where accounts of participants with different roles are sought, combined with the researcher's own, in order to reach an agreed and negotiated case. Objectivity in the sense of detachment from the values and assumptions of the researcher have been claimed by both experimenteral and naturalistic enquirers. Lincoln and Guba (1985) make a strong case for research carried out in a natural setting where the enquirer is the main data-gathering instrument, using tacit as well as other kinds of knowledge. Qualitative methods – which will involve flexible observation, and possibly, interviews or questionnaires – are regarded as sensitive and adaptable. *Purposive* sampling is preferred to representative or random sampling as it increases the range of data disclosed, with inductive data analysis allowing a fuller description of the setting and theory grounded in the data. Outcomes are negotiated and interpreted in terms of the particular rather than the general; thus, application is tentative. In fact the focus emerges as the research proceeds and from this boundaries are set. Special *trustworthiness* measures (equivalent to reliability, validity and objectivity) have been devised through such techniques as *prolonged engagement* – that is, sufficient time to build trust and understand the culture of the context – *persistent observation*, in order to identify salient and pervasive features, *triangulating* evidence from different sources and *peer debriefing* to provide analysis from disinterested peers. *Thick description* provides a specification of the minimum elements needed and the range of information required in order to provide the database. Auditing the research process to check that acceptable standards have been maintained in the enquiry – that findings are consistent with these processes – are established through independent auditing, or examining the accuracy with which the account of the process and products have been kept. This will include scrutiny of raw data, data reduction and analysis, process notes and pilot instruments being designed. The purpose of the audit is to increase the probability that the findings and the interpretations will be found credible. Throughout the period of data collection, interpretation will be checked with those who have provided sources for the data and outcomes will be agreed. The coding and analysis requires *constant comparison* of incidents which leads to conceptual labels being placed on discrete happenings, events or instances of phenomena. *Concepts* are the basic building blocks of *grounded theory* and the basic analytic procedures by which concepts are generated are by the asking of questions about data, and the making of comparisons for similarities and differences between phenomena. Concepts are grouped together under a higher order or more abstract concept called a *category*. These categories and their properties emerge from the data and the inductive analysis involves the uncovering and making explicit of embedded information which can lead to relationships being established among categories as well as the clear specification of the conditions and consequences under which this occurs.

In terms of analysis, then, the main source of participant observation will be field notes, interviews and documents. Comprehensiveness in respect of data collection is urged – in other words, continuation of data collection until no new ideas emerge. Full transcription of early observations and interviews is advocated by Strauss and Corbin (1990) with increasing selectivity over time. Data analysis, in summary, follows an inductive process through data coding of topics and categories which are regrouped to form patterns of concepts, themes and surprises. The goal is understanding of these phenomena as well as their interrelationships, hence, a *conceptual story* will emerge.

Thus the typical experiment could be construed as one extreme form of controlled observation whilst the unstructured, participant observation of anthropologists is the polar opposite. The experimental method, however, is not part of a tradition associated with direct observation which, in any case, varies from qualitative to quantitative. In fact, as will be apparent from the previous discussion of naturalistic enquiry, perhaps the first questions to ask are:

- what will be observed?
- which behaviours?
- how will these be defined?

These questions are important to the researcher who will need to ensure they are reliably identifiable when more *structured* observation is being used. Furthermore, the behaviour of others in the child's environment will be important as well as the range of physical and social events and activities during the period of observation. Structured observation will be examined in more depth in the next section.

When, for how long and how many observations will be required

If observations take place within a small amount of time it is important to ensure a representative sample of information is acquired. Wells' 1972–1982 *Language at Home and at School* Study (Wells 1981a) recorded mothers and children at three-monthly intervals from eighteen months to forty-two months. Recorders were used for collecting ninety-second samples, irregularly at roughly twenty-minute intervals, but unknown to the family, between nine a.m. and six p.m. until a minimum of eighteen samples or one hundred utterances by the child had been collected. Observations at particular times of the day or on particular occasions may not accurately reflect the usual pattern of activity. Furthermore, initial observations are likely to cause reactivity and, hence, bias in the study. In the Wells study the researcher was not present and, in fact, played back recordings at night to the mother to collect valuable contextual information.

This leads to the critical question: which observational method will be used? In this respect it is important that the researcher is fully aware of different procedures available, including their strengths and weaknesses. Whilst video will provide a permanent observable record, it is intrusive and may well influence the behaviour of those observed in a more marked manner than hidden or unobtrusive measures. Moreover, considerable technical skill would be required as well as costly equipment.

The Wells study raises another question for researchers – how will the accuracy of the observations be verified? If the observations do not provide an accurate and reliable account of the actual events, processes and activities in the setting they will be of no value. If the observer is a participant, as has already been noted, perspectives of others can be elicited and recordings validated. For structured observation, issues of multiple observers and inter-observer reliability will be raised.

Informal observations which attempt to make free-hand field notes at unsystematic intervals are liable to distortion but, at the same time, if used at the first stage of a research process, may simply provide the means of identifying the focus for more systematic observation. Informal, 'naturalistic' observations reveal significant aspects of human behaviour which may, at a later stage, be subjected to more systematic enquiry.

Indirect observations through other sources, such as parent interviews or questionnaires (e.g. the Newsons' 1963 study of patterns of infant care), may inject rigour but are subject to a variety of response sets which may distort replies. Diaries, journals and interviews can, however, serve to illuminate other more direct and quantifiable methods, as well as triangulate the observations taking place.

Another form of unstructured observation involves collecting samples of the child's behaviours, as well as related aspects of the social and physical environment, as completely as possible and systematically – in terms of time, for example, one hour per day – which is then subjected to analysis and coding. Sometimes single subjects are observed over years to provide rich case accounts. Typically such approaches have involved the researchers' own children. An example of this would be Matthews' (1988) account of the young child's early representation in drawing or Buckham's (1994) case study account of one girl's drawing across her life span from birth to adolescence. Such approaches provide a richness and immediacy of the child's developing response such that the source material is unparalleled in completeness and in its unfolding over time.

Formal observations will constitute the extreme opposite to the naturalistic observations in their inclusion of systematic observation and recording procedures. Such approaches take account of the time, duration and frequency of the observation, and show rigour in specification of the behaviours to be observed – social context, activity and interaction – and the procedures used to record them. Examples of such formal observations, supported by schedules for recordings, are those of Clark and Cheyne (1979) and Sylva, Roy and

Painter (1980), both used in nursery settings. Reliability measures are also typically provided in such studies which involve multiple observers.

How the observed behaviour is sampled is another aspect to be considered. This can be a simple frequency count for behaviours of interest, provided they are defined with sufficient clarity for reliable identification of their occurrence. Where the observation periods are long and the behaviour has a high frequency this method may not be advisable. In fact, interval sampling or time sampling may provide an approach which leads to higher agreement between observers. Clark and Cheyne (1979), for instance, used a thirty-second observation interval in which to record the interaction involving the target child, note the social code and activity before moving to the next sample. An observation period of twenty minutes would provide forty samples, which would not necessarily focus on one child for the whole period. In time-sampling, some principle will be used to select the time intervals when coding does or does not take place and is critical in the extent to which this provides a representative picture (see Appendix 1).

In essence, coding sequences of behaviour depends upon the unit to be measured, as noted by Robson (1993), and this may be based on time or an event. Tallying events provides frequencies and adding a time-line gives information about the time-interval between similar events (see Appendix 2). State – or change-of-state – coding may also be used to record states of mind or mood, usually including time information, in other words, duration. Cross-classifying is another technique – or using the A-B-C chart – which allows the researcher to note significant behaviours, such as naughty behaviours in context, in terms of antecedents as well as consequences (see Appendix 3).

Problems arise when an observer's recordings show variations at different times or different observers' recording of the same phenomena vary from one another. For reliability purposes two observers each must observe the same subject at the same time. This need not occur on every recording session or even for the whole observation period. Data from the two observers are then compared for the same part of data collection. A comparison of the number of agreements of the *occurrence* of the behaviour with the total number of agreements plus disagreements of its occurrence is usual.

The formula is:

$$\text{Reliability} = \frac{A}{A+B+C} \times 100$$

where A means both observers recorded, B only one and C only the other observer (usually the reliability assessor).

The expectation here of course is that observations will generate quantitative records which, in turn, may be subjected to the sort of statistical analysis described earlier in this chapter.

Conclusion

As noted by Richardson (1995), as variables, properties and their associations emerge in the course of observational research, they provide an increasingly refined model or theory. This building of theories from observations is called the inductive aspect of science and it provides a device for describing causal relationships. The status of such theories in child development varies in refinement. Ideally the model induced should be such as to make possible predictions that can be tested experimentally. Inducing a new model is not an end in itself but simply a theory or hypothesis to be tested. In other words, informal to formal observations lead to structured observations which may involve treatments or manipulations. At some stage, researchers may feel confident to apply it in a practical context although this raises a number of further issues about gate-keeping to policy-makers and media which will be picked up later in the book. In the mean time it has been suggested that the relationship between inductive observation and hypothetico-deductive, structured observations is that they are in fact part of the same cycle.

It should be observed, however, that this simple introduction to conventional research leaves entirely *unexamined* the postmodern challenge to existing research theory and practice. Lacan (1977), for instance, has shown that meaning and truth are not individual but intersubjective matters. Meaning is not just an unproblematic 'read-out' of intention, nor intention of meaning. Because meanings are located in the intersubjective field, the notion of the individualistic researcher as 'one who knows' is based on the assumption of a self with self-transparent consciousnessness, who determinedly ignores his or her own unconscious.

Lacan's view is that the very presence of the unconscious poses a challenge to this sense of mastery. Two questionable assumptions in 'modernist' research are, thus, identified :

- the individual subject, as researcher, who can 'bestow' meaning on the researched
- the language of reporting research, which is a transparent template for the articulation of rational thought.

This brief analysis suggests that the distinction between the researcher and the researched may never be as clear-cut as is traditionally assumed and that the researcher may have less mastery of knowledge than is commonly supposed. Suffice it to say at this point that postmodern ideas have had considerably less impact than they deserve on educational research but in fact pose a considerable challenge to conventional theory and practice.

Meanwhile, as the current debate about early childhood education is showing, however, research is only one source of information in decision-making which is political, cultural and ethical. The next two chapters will describe research in action, for which the current and previous chapters have served mainly as preparation.

Part II

Early childhood education: changing research practice

5 Early childhood research prior to 1985

In the last two chapters we examined research methodologies which can serve to support the generation of reliable knowledge related to early childhood education. Broad distinctions were made between qualitative/inductive observation and quantitative/controlled observation which may involve treatments or manipulations as well as careful measurement of variables (hypothetico-deductive research).

This analysis led to the recognition that 'inductive' observation and structured or 'controlled' observation were, in fact, likely to reflect different stages of the *same* research process. Questions which arise from this analysis of the cycle of research are: what *methods* are being used to generate the observation – for example, naturalistic or structural observations – and does the observation involve treatments or manipulations? Between these two extremes lies the gradual induction of theory through the progressive teasing out of variables and the identification of relationship/s between variables which, at some stage, will require rigorous testing, with possible refinement and retesting (theory testing). The direction may be from unstructured to structured with progressive revision and replication, in other words from qualitative to quantitative, although it is also the case that quantitative findings can throw up whole new areas for qualitative enquiry.

In early childhood education the trend over time has been towards the greater use and development of qualitative and naturalistic observational techniques and away from structured and quantifiable observation. A major difficulty with the later approaches with non-manipulable observation has been that functional relationships have to be identified in a naturally-occurring setting in the physical and social environment. When precise control is absent the researcher must rely on observation of processes that naturally occur and relationships that emerge, rather than impose predetermined, quantifiable categories upon the observed phenomena. Whilst the sophistication of our knowledge of observation techniques has increased over the last twenty years, it is still far from precise and may not bear close scrutiny in terms of traditional criteria for objectivity (requiring data which are observable and measurable in predefined ways). In this chapter we outline some of the research models and processes used in early childhood education research in the 1970s to 1980s at a time when observation was still largely structured and quantifiable. This will then be followed by an overview of the research from the mid-1980s to the present day, which shows the wide variety of methods now being used – from large-scale and quantitative to small-scale and qualitative.

The context

In the economic recession which marked the early 1980s, when education authorities were drawing up contingency plans for spending cuts through that decade, a public expenditure White Paper was produced which envisaged cuts in education spending totalling some six per cent over a five-year period. As a response, to this Powys County Council, for instance, voiced plans to *abolish* nursery education over two years.

In the Plowden Report (Plowden Committee 1967) the Department of Education and Science (DES) set targets which were reiterated in the White Paper *Education: A Framework for Expansion*, (DES 1972): to provide without charge, within ten years, preschool education for all those children aged three to five years whose parents wished it. The Plowden Committee estimated that provision for ninety per cent of four-year-olds and fifty per cent of three-year-olds would be adequate to meet the demand.

By 1975, however, as Bruner (1980) indicated, only fifty-five per cent of the children projected in Plowden were actually in attendance in nursery schools or classes.

In spite of the increased demand for nursery provision and rapidly changing social circumstances of the time – the change in status of women and the increase of their number in work, the dispersal of the extended family network and increased pressures on the nuclear family, the increase in one-parent families and changing philosophies of infancy and child care – a government Survey (Bone 1977) showed that one-third of parents of preschool children were unable to find the preschool provision which they considered themselves to need. Planned expansion of nursery education in this country had been over-taken by economic crises and contraction.

In the early 1970s, when massive expansion of nursery education was proposed, a decision was made to establish a programme of research into services for under-fives. Funding was available from the DES and the Scottish Education Department as well as the Department of Health and Social Security (DHSS). The Social Science Research Council (SSRC) also commissioned research within the programme as did the Schools Council. Furthermore a committee was established by the DES with representatives from the various bodies which provided funding within the programme to explore ways of disseminating the findings. One of the works commissioned within the programme was the work of the Oxford Preschool Research Group which resulted in the three-year project under Professor Bruner. There were already a number of other researches with relevance to preschool education funded by these and other bodies during that time. The work of Smith and Connolly at Sheffield

University during the early 1970s was one example of such relevant studies. Theirs was undertaken to explore how the preschool environment influenced children's behaviour (see, for example, Smith and Connolly, 1980).

In Scotland, Clark, then based at the University of Strathclyde, with the support of the Scottish Education Department and the DES, began a series of nursery projects looking at the effects of nursery education, parental participation, and studies of the handicapped and exceptional child in preschool units (see Clark and Cheyne, 1979).

These various studies were published during 1979 and 1980, at a time when the government had been forced to shelve indefinitely projected changes in preschool, and future care seemed to be gaining impetus largely from the playgroup movement and from independent child-minders. At this time, perhaps more than ever, it seemed critical to take stock of existing nursery provision – its purposes and aims, and the effects these had on the preschool child.

Existing nursery provision

Nursery schools stemmed from two separate traditions. On the one hand, there was the 'welfare' nursery school, the original impetus having come from the need to prove daycare for children of the poor, and women mill workers, associated with figures like Margaret and Rachel McMillan (1930) and Maria Montessori (1936), whose express intention was to improve the conditions of the working-class child. On the other hand, the beginning of the twentieth century saw the rise of the 'progressive' nursery school movement in which the kindergarten was conceived as an opportunity to provide a stimulating environment in which to develop the child's 'potentiality', with a more directly-educational bias, informed by the work of Froebel (1826), Pestalozzi (1826), and later realised in the work of Susan Isaacs (1936).

To some extent this dichotomy was perpetuated still in the early 1980s by the division in responsibility between the DES, which was responsible for nursery education, and the DHSS, whose focus was to provide daycare. In many cases the latter was regarded as substitute care, the emphasis being on providing a stable, secure environment together with imparting some basic skills necessary for school.

Early childhood education research of the time

As Bruner (1980) noted when his Oxford Preschool Research Group was started in the 1970s, little seemed known about what constituted preschool care away from home. Moreover, he found little in the way of precise description about what went on and much in the way of assumption about what constituted good nursery practice. In general, he noted, literature on early human development had little to say about the effects of different kinds of preschool experience, and preschool practice seemed to follow the purposes of good parental care rather than seek informed use of tested knowledge.

Perhaps one of the first persons to make a systematic attempt at observation of child behaviour in the preschool was Susan Isaacs (1936) in the meticulous records of the Malting House School she kept during the 1920s, particularly in relation to children's interactions, both with one another and with an adult. This was very much an ideographic, case approach to preschool behaviour.

In contrast, and of much more recent time, came the large-scale test-train-retest American Head Start programmes with emphasis on educational products of the late 1960s which attempted to monitor a wide range of varying, compensatory preschool programmes and follow up with measurable results on entry into formal school in terms of intelligence quotient (IQ) or school achievement. The views of Bernstein (1960; 1962) on language influenced such figures as Hess and Shipman (1965) and led to a vast US research programme making the assumption that assumed deficits in early cognitive and linguistic skills could be ameliorated by improved preschool programmes relating to cognitive and linguistic skills (see, for instance, the work of Bereiter and Englemann 1966; and Blank and Solomon 1968).

In most of the Head Start projects, children on the programmes failed to retain early leads over peers who had not been exposed to the 'treatment'. Longer-term evaluation of intervention at the beginning of the 1980s showed less permanent success and the Westinghouse Report (Cicarelli, 1969) documented how, compared with controls, children showed some benefits at grade 1 (six years) but by grade 3 (eight years) this was largely lost. This, of course, was before the longer-term follow-up studies had been carried out, from which a different picture emerged.

Often the programmes were short and usually parents were not involved. Hence no reinforcement activities which might have aided maintenance of newly-required skills were implemented. Little concern was shown for observing actual day-to-day behaviour of the children involved. Since more attention was directed towards outcomes – or products – conceived in terms of school achievement rather than to actual interventions or interactions between staff and children involved, there was no objective means for determining what components of the programmes were maximally effective.

The failure of this 'deficit' model, using a pretest-posttest design, with tests of cognitive and linguistic achievement, led to renewed consideration of the value of different kinds of preschool experience.

Another strand which helped to direct more attention to process variables was the re-assessment of Bowlby's work (1953) by Rutter (1972). Rutter suggested the essential nature of the continuous, permanent mother figure of Bowlby was an overstatement, and this led to the more detailed research on mother–child interactions of, for instance, Ainsworth *et al.* (1974) on early attachment relationships.

Tizard *et al.* (1980), examining language and interactions of working-class and middle-class children at home and at nursery school, concluded that there were marked differences in language at home and school; working-class children did not engage in extended interactions with the teacher at school, and the teacher language had a heavy bias to questioning. Working-class children asked fewer questions and tended to gain assistance of adults for purposes of management rather than conversation or contact; middle-class children, by contrast, were asked fewer questions by the teacher and, correspondingly, initiated more extended dialogues, including asking more questions. Many of these differences were not maintained at home where both groups were as likely to engage in extended interaction.

Here attention to process variables highlighted the difference, both in interactions to working- and middle-class children by their teachers and to their different responses not being upheld in the home situation. Focus on process variables gave some indication of the limitations of models which paid too little attention to day-to-day happenings. It illustrated the danger of utilising models which imposed a rational system on what was being observed but which, correspondingly, reduced the degree to which the results could be generalisable to any social situation in the real world.

Galton, Simon and Croll (1980) discussed the problems of using models where too little attention was paid to actual interactions in the classroom. As McIntyre (1980) noted, the complexity of what happened in the classroom situation entailed consideration of a multiplicity of perspectives and definitions of the situation. In the typical nursery, this might involve one to three members of staff with between ten and twenty-five children.

Wragg *et al.* (1976) suggested that context variables and presage – or pre-existing – variables might also be chosen for investigation in addition to process and product variables (see Figure 5.1).

Some of the early models used in preschool research were clearly not sufficiently sensitive to process variables themselves or to the possible complex interactions between variables.

Researchers' concerns about observation in the late 1970s

As can be seen above, a major decision had to be made about which aspects of observable activity were relevant to the stated intentions of the researchers. Where the purpose was to look at the effect of setting on behaviour, the main problem was to decide how to conceptualise nursery life and on what to focus attention.

McIntyre (1980) stated this to be one aspect of systematic observation research most neglected in general, and least adequately theorised. In fact a number of other issues exercised researchers of the time as will now be examined.

Selection of variables for attention

A major problem in this type of study was seen to be the selection of variables for attention and the difficulty of taking full account of the complex interactions

CONTEXT VARIABLES

↓

(The classroom – or in this case,
nursery – environment)

PRESAGE VARIABLES ⟶   PROCESS VARIABLES ⟶   PRODUCT VARIABLES

(already present when learning   (describe actual behaviour   (learning outcomes:
commences: characteristics of   in the classroom)   changes in attitudes,
teachers and learners)   knowledge, skills, etc)

Figure 5.1   Variables for investigation

between variables in design and analysis. Paradoxically it was only through recognition that much that was occurring must be ignored, in order to focus on selected aspects of behaviour, that any degree of objectivity could be achieved. By selection and focus on what was hypothesised to be significant it was thought that areas of interest could be defined.

Category selection and controlling the degree of inference

An implicit assumption made by many of the researchers of the time was that behavioural events had an objective meaning, known to them, whilst not having direct access to the meanings which the individual participants attributed to them. As an example, the Bruner Oxford Preschool Research Group (Sylva, Roy and Painter, 1980) set out to study concentration of children at play and its relationship to play materials, events and social interactions. This led to the formation of high-inference categorisations of play in terms of cognitive complexity, focusing on 'contingent progression' or sequence of play activities. These might involve long-term planning or organisation and 'transformation' of materials or people, such as occurs in make-believe play. Already it is clear that some degree of interpretation of behaviour was involved in terms of inferred intentions on the part of the child as these two aspects of complexity would not necessarily be behaviourally explicit.

The fewer the inferences the observer made about what was happening in the setting, however, the more likely it was that his or her view would be seen as accurate. Low-inference behaviour categories were as explicitly described as possible and were to be preferred to high-inference categories which made more assumptions about observed events. The higher the inference the greater was the likelihood of distortion.

Another necessary condition was the selection of mutually-exclusive categories of behaviour whilst at the same time remaining alert to the use of over-simplified categorisation. For instance, Smith and Connolly (1980), whose activity categories for children were defined in terms of equipment used – for example, dolls, dressing-up clothes, table play, and so on – showed too little regard for the *use* made by individual children of the specified apparatus.

A balance had to be maintained between selecting sufficient categories to account for all aspects of relevant behaviour and over-proliferation of categories which would lead to difficulties in handling the sheer numbers of variables for analysis. The Sylva, Roy and Painter (1980) activity codes for preschoolers – thirty in all – showed some tendency to over-elaboration of, for instance, non-specific activity – 'watching staff', 'watching peers', 'watching events', 'waiting', 'cruising', and 'aimlessly standing around'. On the other hand the fine distinctions they made in tasks involving fine-hand skills did enable the researchers to make a detailed analysis of the child's specific activity, in terms of 'small-scale construction', 'art', 'manipulation', 'structured material' and 'scale version toys'.

One suggestion made by McIntyre (1980) was that better-directed research occurred where more than one observation schedule was used.

Observer effects

Another assumption made by the researcher, as noted already, was that the data collected were not affected by the relationship between the observer and the effects on the participants of the observation. In fact, interpretation of the data depended upon assumptions made about the relationship between the observed and the effects of the observation on the observed activities. The assumption made was that the observer's presence would be discounted by the staff and children. If time was allowed for the participants to become familiarised with the observer's presence and if the observer avoided any overt interaction, was unobtrusive and his or her behaviour or means of observing were predictable and non-fluctuating, then this might have been a fair assumption to make.

It could be assumed, for instance, that over time the familiar figure in the role of non-participant observer would be less likely to affect children's behaviour appreciably. Lack of contact, however, does not guarantee no effect of observer presence even if it strongly suggests this to be the case. Moreover the effect of observer on teacher behaviour might be more subtle and less easily defined. Whilst an observer could negotiate acceptance by offering a purpose not impinging on the interests of the participants, if he or she avoided any overt interaction with others present, it was noted by Galton, Simon and Croll (1980) that teachers will focus on meeting their own criteria, in relation to the function of the observation as they perceive it. This could have the effect of increasing the amount and kind of specific teacher–child interactions in a nursery setting; it might also not be reasonable to assume that different staff are affected to the same degree or in the same direction.

Furthermore, if the researcher was observing adult or teacher behaviour, it was recognised as essential not to ignore the teacher's own constructions of what she was doing, or trying to do. Taba and Elzey (1964) defined as 'strategy' a teacher's attempts to translate aims into practice, and Strasser (1967) distinguished between strategic decisions made before the lesson begins and the ongoing interactions between child and adult, through which strategies are implemented, which he called 'teaching tactics'. Within the context of preschool studies, this suggested that the strategic decisions of nursery staff informed organisation of the setting, the structure of the tasks set and how these were mediated, in terms of tactics. This suggested that supplementary data would need to be collected relating to the nursery teachers' aims and purposes, in the form of documentary evidence, in order that account could be taken of longer-term aims and purposes informing observed staff decision-making and, hence, behaviour.

Relating context variables to process variables

As noted by Wood, McMahon and Cranstoun (1980), the physical design of the preschool, too – by supporting or hindering the nursery teacher's aims – could exert an important influence on teacher style or child–adult interactions. They also noted how the number of adults available helped to influence the pattern of interactions.

Observed differences obtained in the behaviour of the children, or in the child–adult interactions, were, thus, seen to have been related to a range of variables – space, equipment, staff behaviour, number of children present, and so on. Whilst it was likely that context variables would exert a powerful influence on process variables there seemed to be no very precise means by which to measure the extent of the influence in a natural setting, or any very objective way to tease out the complex interactions likely to be operating within and between context and process variables.

Ultimately, however, the design of a study would be determined by its overall aims and purposes. Analysis of data would need to be consistent with the methods used and appropriate to the measurements taken. As Bennett (1981) noted at the time, however, the methods most potent for collecting data might lack techniques and procedures for assessing the strength of the evidence.

Time and resources available

Examining process variables at all was seen to involve detailed and time-consuming data collection. This could be a particularly acute problem for a small-scale study with significant time constraints. It was also thought to raise issues of sample size and representativeness where detailed information tended often to be gathered on a small number of subjects. It will be noted at this point that the assumptions being made at the time were that structured observation with observable and measurable categories would be employed.

Moreover, a major justification for mounting a well-designed, small-scale study in the end was the hope that the findings would synthesise with those of other investigations. As McIntyre (1980) noted, relationships found consistently over several investigations could be accepted as meaningful and as having high generality. This approach would lessen the chance that results had arisen by chance or had been situation-specific.

Background to observational studies of the time

The observational studies of preschools reviewed by Smith and Connolly (1972), in fact, went back as far as the 1920s and 1930s, mostly in the United States. Noteworthy was Mildred Parten's classification of social behaviour (1932; 1933) which comprised solitary, parallel and group activity – distinctions still regarded of value and used in the observational schedules of the 1970s period. By the 1940s, naturalistic observations declined in popularity in favour of the greater utilisation of standardised assessment – testing, interviews and questionnaires.

Smith and Connolly (1972) noted how the studies involved were imbued with prevailing attitudes to childhood. One reason for the postwar resurgence of interest in preschool may have been related to the increased interest in early experience, deriving from such traditions as Bowlby's (1953) views on maternal deprivation, raised in Chapter 2, and Hebb's (1949) *Organisation of Behaviour* studies which suggested plasticity in the central nervous system and development of cell assemblies in response to environmental stimuli. Also influential was the concern dating from the 1950s to provide equality of educational opportunity to all socioeconomic groups with the assumption that differential achievement of the lower classes was associated with deficient early experience, as noted above.

There was, however, a gradual reintroduction of naturalistic observational methods. Smilansky (1968), for instance, used direct observation of children's play in studies of fantasy and socio-dramatic play. In the 1960s there was also a rapid growth in ethological studies of primates carried out in order to examine social structure and communication. This was followed by the application of ethological techniques to the study of human beings and, in particular, preschoolers (see the work of Hutt and Hutt 1970; Smith 1974; and Blurton Jones 1967, 1972). In this work there was a strong bias towards categorisation of behaviour in physical terms – facial expression, vocal units and detailed breakdowns of locomotion (for example, skip, shuffle, walk, chase) and postural units. Use was also being made of systematic behaviour-sampling techniques.

From this basic approach, highly developed classroom observational techniques evolved (reviewed, for example, by Rosenshine and Furst 1973) with a shift to careful analyses of settings, as well as behaviour. Although, as Smith and Connolly (1980) noted, much research was carried out investigating the effects of space and crowding on nursery children (see also Smith 1974), little research was conducted on the physical environment or its effect on pre-school behaviour.

Themes in early childhood education research of the late 1970s

Scrutiny of early childhood education research of the late 1970s shows a number of preoccupying themes related to teaching style and interaction, play-tutoring, nursery teachers' aims and values, task structure, spatial design and layout, teacher–child ratios and use of equipment. These will be examined, in turn, in order to identify some of the substantive content and research findings of the time.

Teacher style and interaction

In the late 1970s, research into adult and child interactions had tended to focus on a narrow range of linguistic functions. As mentioned above, Tizard *et al.* (1980) had looked at language and interactions of working- and middle-class children at home and in the nursery school. Much research had been devoted to examining the nature of the relationship between nursery staff and preschool children, which among other things, seemed – according to researchers of the time – to reflect home background. Differences observed between children at school tended to be less apparent at home: see, for example, the work of Wells (1978). Turner (1977) observed that some children were managed more than others and that adults were more concerned to control than play with, talk to or instruct them. He found a relationship between the type of contact received by the child and measured language ability, the least competent appearing to receive most management contact.

From initial work on in-depth transcripts of practitioners' interactions, Wood, McMahon and Cranstoun (1980) described twenty-six functions of interaction, in terms of five main categories – management, conversation, instruction, play and rapport. Interestingly, when in-depth transcripts of practitioners were classified according to function, whilst there was a common thread of activities and roles between teachers, this accounted for only one-half of the interactions identified. There were styles frequently employed by all staff and others used only occasionally by them; in some areas there were marked differences between staff.

Two of the most frequent moves by the adult were within the category of 'rapport', which took the form of monitoring or repeating a child's utterance. This had the function of reassurance, without making any demand on the child in terms of provoking a response or action. It was the 'social oil' which Tizard *et al.* (1980) had identified as being used regularly by nursery-school teachers. It could have positive or negative connotations depending on the context: either to maintain a conversation or to function as a management device to avoid involvement.

In fact management was a category prominent in interaction analysed by Wood, McMahon and Cranstoun and, like rapport, depending on the particular style, it could be facilitative or inhibitory. Some management functions involved organising or initiating an activity, others involved crisis management, an inevitable feature of nursery life.

Other frequently used approaches were more specifically educational, relating to highlighting the environment, discussing the immediate activity by offering relevant information, or asking the child to offer some.

Wood, McMahon and Cranstoun (1980) found conversation, rapport and practical instructional moves shared eighty-four per cent of the interactions. A play style was the least popular accounting for six per cent of the interactions and direct management, ten per cent. Whilst rapport – monitoring and repetition – tended to permeate moves relating to play, conversation, instruction and management, staff were found to have quite distinctive preferences towards one of these four main categories of styles.

Play tutoring

It has been noted above that interactions relating to play appeared to constitute a small part of the nursery teacher's overall 'style' (six per cent). A 'play' style of working, however, could be characteristic of a particular practitioner's individual approach. Wood, McMahon and Cranstoun (1980) referred to the benefits to be derived from 'play tutoring'. Smilansky (1968) called it 'pump priming'. If the child does not pretend, for instance, the teacher might act as if she and the child were role playing.

Bandura and Walters (1963) suggested that this play had three functions. It provided a model which was:

* disinhibitory: the child feels free to play and responses are awakened
* imitative: the child has a voice or action of the adult to copy
* eliciting: the child is given ideas to stimulate his or her own, or a means to elaborate them.

Teacher aims and beliefs

As noted above when observing nursery teacher behaviour, it was also regarded as essential not to ignore the teacher's own constructions about what she was doing. This entailed distinguishing between tactics which could be observed in the setting and strategies which informed organisation and structure and which were guided by long-term aims.

A national sample of nursery teachers was questioned about their major aims and purposes in handling preschool children (Taylor, Exon and Holley 1972). They saw their main purpose as the social education of the young child but other purposes were regarded as only a little less important since the teacher was not involved in 'formal education', which was not seen as central to the provision made for nursery school children. Their list was in the following order of priority:

* socio-emotional development
* intellectual development
* creation of effective transition from home to school
* aesthetic development
* physical development.

These findings provide some explanation for the high proportion (eighty-four per cent) of preschool interactions shared by conversation, rapport and practical instructional moves found by Wood, McMahon and Cranstoun (1980). Another study by Turner (1977), cited by Wood, McMahon and Cranstoun, showed that play group leaders' attitudes were similar, though aesthetic and physical development were in reverse order.

Task structure

One way in which the preschool setting was thought likely to affect children's behaviour was its organisation. Garland and White (1980) showed how the nature of the organisation of the day nursery had a direct influence on the behaviour of the children inside it: for instance, adult directiveness affected both play and conversation. With increased directiveness, both conversation and make-believe play decreased. Sylva, Roy and Painter (1980) found it useful to distinguish between the nature of tasks given to children, and the regularity of the daily preschool programme.

They suggested positive benefits to be derived from some short, directed period of activity, within the context of free play. Centres with some structured activities had three times as much play with structured materials – claimed by Sylva, Roy and Painter (1980) to be 'rich' in cognitive challenge. Even when mandatory activity time was subtracted there was still more play with structured materials and, correspondingly, less in pretend and manipulative play – claimed to be 'moderately demanding'.

In spite of time spent on adult-led activity they found there was still actually less adult-led group work overall: such group work as was required was found to be well-planned and challenging and often followed by the children in their free time. For the younger children the structure in the programme seemed to encourage interaction with other children as opposed to parallel play, and for older children there was more interaction with adults. The shared experience of the structured activity seemed to provide a focus for conversation between child and adult.

Sylva, Roy and Painter (1980) contrasted this 'task specific' structure with 'fixed routine', which was neither educational, nor compulsory, but served to provide predictably similar daily activities. This could be comforting to young children but, for older ones, fixed routines tended to encourage more adult-led activities and correspondingly diminished the opportunities for conversation.

Smith and Connolly (1980) highlighted some of the less positive effects of too much structure. Here children spent more time interacting with adults and less with other children, that is, more time on fewer activities with increased attention span. Play, however, could become passive and decreased in the degree of complexity. Furthermore, there might be an increase in aggressive interaction but correspondingly less physical activity.

Spatial design and layout

As noted by Wood, McMahon and Cranstoun (1980) the physical design of the preschool could exert a strong influence on teacher style and child–adult interactions.

In a study lasting nine weeks Smith and Connolly (1980), using three spatial densities (twenty-five square feet, fifty square feet and seventy-five square feet) with a constant number of children (twenty-four), found the amount of space mainly affected the amount and kind of physical activity. In a large space there was more running, chasing and vigorous activity; in a smaller space there was more use made of a climbing frame and slide, more physical contact, but no change in social interaction or aggressive behaviour.

They also made a relatively short study comparing fifteen square feet and sixty square feet per child. Here physical activity, even walking, was inhibited, leading to a more static, parallel play in large groups, either at table, or in the sand, with less social and more aggressive behaviour.

Neill *et al* (1977) however, suggested that rather than the amount of space, per se, the play-room *openness* had the most significant effects on children's behaviour, and that the number of children had fewer effects if other aspects of design were satisfactory. A main conclusion of theirs into the psychological influences of spatial design factors was that openness led to higher noise levels, less educational talk by staff, more adjustment difficulties for new entrants, and less constructive behaviour (where children spent more time doing nothing, engaged in rough and tumble play, and high activity movement).

When considering the effects of space on social behaviour, it was critical to consider the amount and distribution of resources generally, not only space, and clearly, for children, the amount of play equipment provided was a very important resource. Smith and Green (1974) showed that most conflicts in preschool related to toy possession – a point noted, too, by Wood, McMahon and Cranstoun (1980).

Use of equipment

Smith and Connolly (1980), co-varying independently three space conditions and three equipment conditions, found the effects of the amount of play equipment were more wide-ranging. When more equipment was available, children played in smaller sub-groups or switched from large parallel sub-groups to solitary play. More popular items like bicycles and the Wendy house were used extensively while less popular toys were overlooked. There was less sharing, less aggressive behaviour and less physical activity, but little change in the levels of social interaction. Interestingly, in conditions of more equipment, there were fewer signs of stress (in terms of sucking or crying).

Another study of Smith and Connolly (1980) compared behaviour with one complete set of toy equipment with the availability of half a set. With little equipment, children occupied themselves with increased motor activity and running. A third study of theirs compared the effects of having access to large apparatus only with effects of having access mainly to manipulative toys. The large apparatus produced increased social and physical activity while small toys produced increase in manipulation and decrease in motor activity. This suggested that some of the effects noted by Sylva, Roy and Painter (1980) in their comparison of nursery school and class – that the small space of the nursery class was conducive to pretend play, manipulative activities and informal games, whilst the larger nursery school produced less social children who spent more time in gross motor activity, inside and out – might have been due to differential access to equipment rather than to overall spatial differences.

Teacher–child ratio

Whilst task structure was likely to affect the amount and kind of social interaction of children, staff–child ratio was also bound to be a critical factor. It was noted by Smith and Connolly (1980), on varying the ratio of staff–child ratio from 1:4 to 1:10, that with increase in incoming contacts, that is, more children to one adult, staff left more initiations unanswered, conversations grew shorter, and the children talked more to one another. Staff talk became more management-orientated in content and adults, themselves, rated the experience as more exhausting. Sylva, Roy and Painter (1980) found that children in centres with 'excellent ratios' were more prone to conversation, not to one another, but twice as much to staff members. Additionally, they found that 'excellent ratio' led to more small-scale construction, art and use of structured materials, and adult-led activity. In classifying according to size, Sylva, Roy and Painter (1980) found greater frequency of pretend play, no differences in the amount of structured play but more physical play in large centres. Since a 'large' group might be reasonably expected to be housed in a larger environment, the effects of greater amount of space, if not controlled for, might have accounted for this finding.

Conclusion

It is clear from this outline of early childhood education research that the late 1970s and early 1980s was a period rich in research, if not plentiful in relation to provision development. In terms of methods, the observation methods which predominated were structured as the shift can be discerned away from large-scale, product-orientated evaluations towards smaller-scale, process-oriented studies with a greater appreciation being shown for context variables – the setting or environment as well as the complex interactions between context and process variables. It was assumed, however, that 'strength of evidence' would be demonstrated through the use of observable and measurable categories still amenable to more conventional forms of statistical measurement.

6 Early childhood education research in a time of change

In this chapter, early childhood education research over the last ten or so years will be reviewed. The review will be located within the broader context of radical educational and higher educational change. In fact, in this period, few aspects of education – management, governance and funding, the curriculum and assessment, teaching and learning in schools, colleges and universities or the role of parents – have been left untouched by politicians or unexamined by educational researchers. Such unprecedented educational change has provided a huge stimulus to research on policy and practice.

As one of us has noted elsewhere (Aubrey 1997b), policy-makers and educational researchers alike have been perennially preoccupied with research on effectiveness in teaching and, predominantly, such enquiry has focused on causality, quantification and prediction of achievement. Never has this been more so than in the last decade as research on the effectiveness of schooling, teaching and learning has been supported by the application of new, multi-level modelling statistical techniques in which individual pupils at one level are nested at the next higher level of classes which are, themselves, grouped together in schools or centres to form another level of aggregation, in order to utilise regression techniques[1] which take account of the hierarchical structure of these data (Goldstein, 1987). Such methodological advances, undoubtedly the most significant of this period, have allowed the calculation of estimates of schools' effects upon children's educational outcomes after controlling for the impact of such background characteristics as sex, age, social class or ethnic origin and of prior attainment. More recent developments (Goldstein 1995) – and most pertinent to this chapter – have included cross-classified models which allow the simultaneous analysis of, for instance, preschool and primary (infant) school effects on achievement at the end of this phase, Key Stage 1 (at seven years), whilst at the same time controlling for relevant child-level, personal and background characteristics.

Over the same period, theoretically, there has been a growing appreciation that children's early cognitive achievements are embedded in social settings. Highlighted in this has been the role of one-to-one interaction between the child and a familiar adult. The studies of both Wells (1985) and Tizard and Hughes (1984) have shown how responsive and sensitive caregivers in the context of shared, social activities of the home can provide a challenge to the young child's cognitive growth. Wells (1981) and Wertsch *et al.* (1984) have indicated how the quality of the adult–child interaction will be influenced by the goals and intentions of the adult who structures the activity in the cultural setting involved. Wood, Bruner and Ross (1976) introduced the notion of adult 'scaffolding' which both structures and extends children's own aims and activities. This bears much resemblance to Vygotsky's 'zone of proximal development'. More recently Schaffer (1992) has described the way adults both secure attention to topics of mutual interest and, at the same time, introduce new areas of interest to the child. Such views of learning, commonly described as 'social constructivist', which replaced Piaget's earlier emphasis on construction with objects, have been appropriated by early childhood education researchers and, implicitly or explicitly, underpin assumptions and beliefs concerning teaching and development in the early years.

Having outlined the broad background to research over the last ten years, as well as specific methodological and theoretical advances, the next section will consider in more detail the impact of changes in higher education on research activity in general before turning to considering in more detail the particular case of early childhood education research.

The research context

The last ten years have seen a fundamental restructuring of the whole educational system and this has taken place against a backcloth of widespread economic decline. At the same time it has been a period of rapid technological change, in terms of telecommunications, transport and information technology. This socioeconomic climate has provided the context in which higher education (HE) has operated and has created the need for a flexible workforce with generic, transferable skills. Suffice it to say, at this point, that reform of the HE system was seen as a necessary part of creating an educational system which would make a stronger contribution to the nation's prosperity, responsive to the growing number of suitably qualified school-leavers, and in step with the rest of the world.

Reorganisation in HE has been as radical as any experienced in other phases of the education system. The landmark for change to the compulsory education stage was the Education Reform Act (DES 1988) to be discussed below. At the same time, and related to the HE sector, the University Grants Committee (UGC) was abolished, a Universities Funding Council (UFC) created as well as a separate funding council outside the local authority framework for the polytechnics and colleges (PCFC). The Education Act (DES 1992) provided similar funding arrangements for further education but, more significantly, unified the HE system, redistributing the funding councils on a regional basis – with separate councils for England, Wales and Scotland – at the same time granting degree-awarding powers to the polytechnics and large colleges and the right of polytechnics to be called 'universities'. This led to a dramatic expansion in HE with significant underfunding. As Trow (1998) has outlined, it created the problem for HE of maintaining high academic standards, completion rates and quality research as well as steady recruitment across subjects for a mass higher education system, at a time when resources were dwindling. As in other areas of education, HE was charged with making 'efficiency gains' as well as increasing its relevance to the changed economic and technological context. At the same time as cuts were being made in the state grant from the newly-formed Higher Education Funding Council (HEFC), standards of performance were being introduced through periodic assessment of research productivity – the research assessment exercise (RAE) – and quality of teaching: in other words, increased accountability.

Establishing recurrent reviews of research activity in every department of every university carried the risk of emphasis being placed on short-term research projects and rapid publication at the expense of more serious and sustained scholarship. Furthermore, as academic posts contracted, through a period of university cutbacks and constraints, time traditionally made available for writing and research diminished as staff–student ratios increased and teaching and administrative loads expanded. The mutual insistence by government and academics that, despite the cuts in per-capita support, standards had not fallen, and the acceptance of new 'standards' to describe academic activities in terms of the concept of 'efficiency gains', resulted, according to Trow (1998 p. 122), in the 'deformation of academic life flowing from attempts to measure research quality'. On the one hand this placed pressures on some staff with little inclination or training to become researchers. On the other hand, as Simons (1995) warned, established researchers might be tempted to shape proposals to suit sponsors' priorities or submit to contractual control over the design, the process of the research, dissemination and publication. She argued powerfully that such practices posed a threat to the quality of educational research, restricting its influence on educational policy-making and limiting the contribution it could make to the generation of public knowledge. The main danger, according to Stronach, Hustler and Edwards (1997, p. 123), of these times of 'orchestrated research busyness' in a 'publish or perish research economy' was that 'methodological and theoretical concerns (would) become parochial and inward-looking, and ... ways of addressing these concerns stale'. When change is rapid, they noted, the need to innovate grows in inverse proportion to the opportunity, and it cannot be assumed that the 'methodologies and cultures of research are exempt from obsolescence or attrition'. When the global and the local are connected in increasingly complex ways, how, they challenged, can a research tradition not look outwards in order to look inward? The particular challenges and pitfalls of international educational comparison, however, will be considered in more depth in a later chapter.

More worrying, perhaps, has been the decline in university research funding. A recent HEFC review of research funding in February 1997, reported by Gipps (1997), relegated educational research from the intermediate band to the lowest of three cost bands for quality-related research (QR) funding. This reduced the grant available for educational research across the university sector from 1997–8 by thirty per cent, or seven million pounds. A further three-and-a-half million pounds (or thirteen per cent) was removed by HEFC for a new initiative to support projects designed to improve the quality of teaching. This came at a time when Bassey (1997) had reported that the annual expenditure on educational research in the UK was around sixty-six million pounds or 0.17 per cent of the total education budget. He estimated that around forty-seven per cent of this income was derived from the HEFC, thirty-eight per cent from externally funded projects, thirteen per cent from research institutes (The National Foundation for Educational Research and the Scottish Council for Research in Education) and around two per cent from other agencies, such as local authorities. According to Brown (1997) the annual expenditure on educational research was much less than the average of three per cent in industry, much lower than our industrial competitors and a contrast to our own ten to twenty per cent spent on defence research.

Hegarty (1997) concluded that the expansion in higher education could not be accompanied by a corresponding increase in research. It was not affordable and, thus, a close alignment between higher education teaching and research activities could not be maintained. He went on to challenge the traditional assumption that research *was* a necessary feature of all HE teaching and supported the view that high quality research could not be carried out in every institution. In fact, the original impetus for the Dearing Report, *Report of the National Committee of Inquiry into Higher Education* (DfEE 1997e), was the financial crisis in HE of the early 1990s, precipitated by underfunded expansion. It remains to be seen, at this point in time, whether a hierachy of HE institutions will emerge – research-led, teaching only and mixed – with a cut-off point at the current level of 3(a) on the RAE scale – of 1 (lowest), 2, 3a plus 3b, 4, 5 plus 5* (highest) – to indicate at least some research of international significance.

Gipps (1997) noted changes taking place since 1992 within the context of research funding by the DfEE, the Qualifications and Curriculum Authority (QCA), previously Schools Curriculum Assessment Authority (SCAA), and the ESRC who are funding high-quality, policy-related research as well as research on short time-scales. The ESRC has a theme-directed programme with emphasis on users and impact which is supporting more strongly applied research. The TTA is funding small-scale teacher researchers from its budget, which for 1997–8 included case-study research projects as well as a scheme to set up school-based research consortia with universities and Local Education Authorities (LEAs). Furthermore, it will be involved in the HEFC initiative for 'pedagogical research' in education, targeting researchers and practitioners in further education (FE) and HE as well as schools. This provides the overall context of the major funding agencies and bodies setting specific priorities for applied research, which could continue the trend towards more short-term and focused research with fewer large-scale projects. The danger with this may be the increasing imposition of research questions (if not answers) which risk becoming narrowly useful to client need, as defined by the client, whereas the real problem may lie in the need for external definition of the problem. Ranson (1996) has stated the case for connecting educational research to the wider issues facing our changing society and, thus, argued for research which places more emphasis on theoretical construction of generalisable knowledge. This suggests the need to address educational issues by engaging directly with the theoretical discourse and discoveries being developed in other disciplines. Ball (1996, cited by Ranson (1996) p. 526) has argued forcefully that the isolation of educational studies from the major theoretical developments of the period has led to a state of 'intellectual stagnation and loss of cultural capital'.

In summary, whilst academics in both the old and new universities have seen teaching and administrative loads increasing, there has been an even greater pressure to engage in regularly-assessed, high-quality research activity at a time of diminishing research funding, increased competition and greater emphasis on practical utility. The long-term impact of this on research is yet to be seen.

The changing educational research context

Having examined the rapidly changing HE context in which the research and publications activities of professional researchers and academics in general have taken place, it is now necessary to consider how the equally radical changes to the school system impacted, in particular, on early childhood education.

The reform of the education system for six- to sixteen-year-olds was marked by the passing of the Education Reform Act (DES 1988). This Act introduced the National Curriculum, assessment and local (financial) management of schools, as well as mechanisms for schools to 'opt out' altogether from the local authority system. This reform generated an increased interest, as noted above, in the existing area of policy-oriented research. The ESRC programme *Innovation and Change in Education: The Quality of Teaching and Learning,* (Hughes, 1996), for example, was developed in this context of major educational reform in order to address some fundamental questions about learning and teaching. Whilst most of the projects were concerned with school-aged pupils, one project – of Munn and Schaffer (1993), to be described below – looked at the development of children's ideas about literacy and numeracy before they started school. Two other projects focused on the first stage of schooling, for five- to seven-year-olds (Key Stage 1). One of these projects, of Plewis and Veltman (1996) at the Thomas Coram Research Unit, which focused on Inner London infant schools, noted that whilst there was little change in the amount of time spent on the 'basics', young children spent more time on science and less time on art, craft and constructional activities than before the reforms were introduced. The other project, carried out by Hughes, Desforges and Holden (1994) at the University of Exeter, examined the relationships between schools and parents with the introduction of market forces into schooling. They found that teachers underestimated parents' wish for more knowledge about the assessment procedures as well as their desire for more involvement in the assessment process. In fact little evidence was found that schools *were* accommodating to parents' views or were even aware of what views were being held.

Introduction of the National Curriculum drew a particular attention to the 'boundaries' of schooling , as noted by Broadhead (1995). Specifically, it drew attention to the needs of four- to five-year-olds in reception classes ('Year R') who were not included in the National Curriculum. Cleave and Brown (1991), in their National Foundation for Educational Research (NFER) study of four-year-olds in infant classrooms, expressed some unease at the possibility that the impact of the National Curriculum would be felt in the early years curriculum. Suffice it to say that Osborne (1981) had already drawn attention to the growth in the numbers of under-fives in infant classes and, by the end of the decade, there were more under-fives in reception classes than there were in nursery classrooms attached to primary schools (HMSO 1990). Moreover, Bennett and Kell (1989), Tizard *et al.* (1988) as well as Cleave and Brown (1991) were all expressing their concern that overall provision for four-year-olds in school was inappropriate to their developmental needs. The consideration of provision for four- to five-year-olds, however, provides one example of a continuing interest in policy-oriented research in early childhood education which marked both the 1980s, before the Education Reform Act (DES 1988) was introduced, as well as the 1990s, in its aftermath. Provision for under-fives and parents continues to exercise the minds of researchers and policy-makers alike and attracts some very large research grants. The new legislation, thus, clearly served to highlight – if not exacerbate – some existing areas of concern in the educational system.

What *does* appear to have distinguished the 1980s from the early 1990s, in terms of research activity in the early years sector, has been the lack of large-scale, government-funded projects such as those of Margaret Clark, commissioned by the DES in the 1980s, and already described by us in the previous chapter. But as discussed above, raising standards in education has been an ongoing concern of policy-makers and large-scale research on effectiveness in provision is a recurrent theme of funded educational research. Early childhood education has been no exception to this and, in fact, Sylva, Melhuish, Sammons and Siraj-Blatchford (1996) have been carrying out a large-scale, DfEE-sponsored evaluation of effective provision of preschool education through a prospective study of 2,500 children from three to seven years of age, as they move through preschool education to the end of Key Stage 1 (KS1).

At the same time newer forms of enquiry in learning and teaching, however, have shifted attention in research toward an understanding of context and situation, requiring different theoretical and methodological approaches to access qualitative aspects of processes in 'real world' settings, and early childhood education research has provided a rich exemplificiation of this movement. Bassey (1992) has, in fact, described this in terms of two sorts of educa–

tional researcher which provide equally valid descriptions of the early childhood researcher: the first whose purpose is to understand some aspect of education; and the other whose purpose is to change it. The first category of research worker will explain or interpret what is happening without attempting to induce any change. The purpose here is to provide a descriptive-analytic account without interfering with the situation or disturbing the setting and the majority of early-education researchers fall into this category. The second category of researcher will have the purpose of trying to induce some change which is seen to be beneficial. To do this it is necessary, first, to carry out systematic and critical enquiry in order that ways in which to effect desirable change can be identified and second, to put these into operation, with monitoring, reviewing and adjustment carried out, in an iterative process, as necessary. This is commonly known as 'action research' and is a relatively recent development. Usually it is carried out by 'insiders': those people actually teaching in or managing the practice or setting under study, in other words, the 'teacher-as-researcher'. Similar research may constitute 'illuminative evaluation' where researchers seek to combine evaluation with professional development in order to improve the quality of early childhood education through the consideration of the processes of learning as well as setting and context (Pascal, 1993).

In this respect, as well as commissioning large-scale studies to inform policy, such small-scale teacher research projects have been funded by the TTA. In fact an overarching goal of the TTA (Cordingley 1998) has been to increase teacher interest in classroom evidence and promote teaching as a research and evidence-based profession. What marks out these newer forms of research is that they 'involve an empirical investigation of a particular contemporary phenomenon within its real-life context using multiple sources of evidence' (Robson 1993, p.5).

Interestingly, even before the radical reforms to the educational system which took place in 1988, Wragg (1986) was making reference to the particular difficulties of academic researchers working in a time of economic constraint. On launching his new journal *Research Papers in Education* he noted, however, that despite difficulty in finding sufficient time: 'there are still numerous examples of incisive and rigorous educational research being completed against the odds' (Wragg 1986, p.3).

He identified three features of educational research of this time. The first feature was the reduction in the amount of large-scale project work but with more small-scale inquiry, frequently undertaken by determined individuals or pairs. The second feature which he identified was the likelihood of such work to be policy-oriented rather than pure. As noted above, one drawback to this type of research can be the external definition of the research problem, another is the possibility of constraint in research design, process or dissemination. A third feature of contemporary educational research, he saw, was the welcome breadth of style. Whereas large-scale and multivariate statistical analysis dominated research in the 1960s, case studies of a single school or classroom and in-depth inquiry into the achievement of a relatively small group of children had attained a 'respectable place in the techniques of investigation of the 1980s' (p.4). This characterisation of research in the mid 1980s is, in fact, quite close to the one provided above for the late 1980s to early 1990s, suggesting perhaps, on a more optimistic note, that the range and quality of research may not have changed as much as feared.

The nature, scope and sponsors of early childhood education research

In terms of quantity, the number of studies carried out fluctuated from the late 1980s until 1992, and then rose. This coincided with the time when the new universities came on the scene and the last RAE began and reflected the keen interest of some of the new HE institutions in early childhood research, notably University College Worcester, Manchester Metropolitcan University and Roehampton College of High Education. The National Foundation for Educational Research (NFER) register, for instance, shows fifteen entries under early childhood education for 1987–9, eleven entries for 1989–91 and four entries for 1991–2. These then increased to thirty-one entries for 1993–5 and forty-three entries for 1995–7.

There are, inevitably, significant omissions from this register. May-Bowles (1998), Head of Library and Information Services at the NFER, has commented that one of the main problems in finding out about educational research in progress is the fact that the sources of data remain 'fragmented and it is necessary to look in several places to ensure that nothing has been over-looked … and … even after this one cannot be sure that coverage is com-prehensive' (May-Bowles 1988, p. 7). Nevertheless the register offers a useful – if self-reported – index of institutions, and even particular persons within them, engaged in early childhood education research, an outline of the studies concerned, as well as an indication of whether or not these attracted external funding. Of a total of one hundred and four projects recorded over this period, some forty-two were supported from a variety of sources: eleven by UK charities, six, notably, with the support of the Esmee Fairbairn Foundation; two by the Economic and Social Research Council;[2] two by central govern-ment, that is, the Department of Health; one by the European Commission; two by funding councils (one by the old UGC and one by HEFC); five by research bodies (four by the NFER and one by the now defunct Schools Council); four by local authority support; and a number internally funded, notably by University College Worcester, Roehampton College of Higher Education and one supported by the Open University). This information indicates some of the main external sponsors as well as the keenest supporters in HE institutions of early childhood studies. Research was being carried out by small groups, pairs and by lone researchers; a number of solo workers were members of staff carrying out supervised research for PhD degrees, in both the old and new universities. The type of research recorded varied from large-scale evaluation of preschool effectiveness to reviews of early years curricula, as well as work geared to the identification of training and support needs of adults working with children under three and including parents. There were policy studies related to provision for under-fives, the educational needs of four-year-olds (as mentioned above) and the study of parents' needs and expectations, as well as a linked study of local authority implementation of the Children Act (DES 1989) in England and Wales. There was also curriculum research (for instance, in the area of religion in the early years) and in-depth enquiries into the achievement of relatively small groups of children (for example, working with parents to promote early literacy) and classroom research, which investigated teachers' mathematical subject knowledge and processes of instruction in reception classrooms.

Another source of information on the field of early childhood studies was the Educational Resources Information Center (ERIC), a clearing-house data base on Elementary and Early Childhood Education. Its director, Lilian Katz (1993), emphasised that, of some three-quarters of a million documents on the database at the time, early childhood was only one part and that, as was the case for the NFER register, there were other sources for documents concerning young children in special categories: for instance, special needs, bilingual and other language-related topics. Her 'best guess' at 1993 was that 'something close to 80,000 of the documents in the collection related to the field of early childhood education' (Katz 1993, p.9).

In terms of the scale of early childhood studies in relation to the overall field of educational research, Bassey and Contable's (1997) analysis of the recent RAE for 1992–6 gives an indication. Some 11,613 papers from 2,800 research-active staff were sorted into nine fields of inquiry: curriculum issues; school, teacher and child issues; teaching/learning issues; governance; phase areas; overseas studies; disciplines in educational settings; methodology; and other. Curriculum issues with 3,496 papers accounted for more than any other group, dominated by the three, core National Curriculum subjects, and reflecting the extent of response to recent, national policy. Whilst the overall total for phase areas of 2,724 was high, 685 related to initial teacher training, and nursery education (for under-fives) – the nearest category to early childhood education – accounted for only 73. Whilst these results are, inevitably, an artefact of the sorting procedure used, as some early childhood education papers might be grouped under other categories, they do, nevertheless, give some indication of the relatively low number of studies in this area.

To take another small indicator, of the twenty-six published, small-scale, teacher research projects supported by the TTA teacher research grant scheme in 1996/7, three were in the area of early childhood education. Topics, which focused on pedagogy, included parental influence in education; using role-play to improve nursery children's language; and teaching infants mental arithmetic.

By contrast to the small-scale TTA projects, and at the other end of the scale, is the above-mentioned, DfEE-funded, five-year longitudinal study of the effectiveness of provision of preschool education of Sylva, Melhuish,

Sammons and Siraj-Blatchford (1996), at an initial cost of £1.48 million. The results of this study are intended to have relevance for educational policy, planning and practice, in comparison with the TTA teacher research projects, which will provide contextualised accounts of particular settings that may resonate with the experience of other practitioners working in similar contexts.

Other sponsors, such as the SCAA (now QCA), as noted by Gipps (1997), hold regular meetings with researchers engaged in assessment as well as supporting research in this area, notably in the area of baseline assessment. In fact the authority has its own early years focus group which has provided feedback – for instance, on the introduction of baseline assessment – as well as reviews of the desirable outcomes and the impact these procedures may have on the early years curriculum.

It is probably fair to say that, in terms of quality, the best available single indicator of research quality in early childhood education, beyond the attraction of the much sought-after external funding, is publication in a high-quality, peer-refereed journals. Even the educational panel for the recent RAE admitted, however, that concepts of national and international excellence were problematic in definition, bearing in mind that so much research was directed at national policy and, hence, 'not readily transportable'.

Taking account of the relatively small contribution of early childhood education to the overall educational research picture, such projects, typically externally-funded by the ESRC, have been well-represented in such a journal as *Research Papers in Education* which aims specifically to publish high-quality, longer research papers. Here, at least one or two papers each year have been devoted to work with an early childhood education focus. The *British Educational Research Journal* also regularly includes one or two papers in this area, about half of which have been externally funded. Two journals which specialise in the field in question, as well as drawing on an international authorship – *European Early Childhood Education Research* and *International Journal of Early Years Education* – have, again, carried one or two papers per volume featuring UK researchers. The former is more likely to carry empirical studies of early childhood education whilst the latter is more catholic, including reflective accounts and conceptual analyses of early years educational research issues, research reviews as well as polemic.

Early childhood education research methods

Large-scale and quantitative studies

Scrutiny of the published early childhood education research of the late 1980s, and 1990s suggests a much richer and more varied picture than was the case for the late 1970s and 1980s which was dominated by a few key figures: for instance, Bruner (1980), Clark (1989), Hutt *et al.* (1989) and Tizard (1974b), as described in the previous chapter.

Externally-funded projects in early years studies, in particular ESRC-funded projects, and the publication of these in high-quality journals have been strongly represented by established and experienced researchers working as pairs or in small groups. Some large-scale, quantitative studies marked by statistical rigour have utilised methodology developed from school effectiveness research at both primary and secondary level in the mid-1980s and were stimulated, in part, by the introduction of reporting and publication of schools' standard assessment task (SAT) results and the idea that 'value added' can be determined by reference to children's 'entry' skills. As noted earlier, interest in policy-related research predated the introduction of the National Curriculum in September, 1989 and its attendant changes to the curriculum and assessment. At the time there was already, as observed by Stierer (1990), a growing demand for educationally valid methods for recording competence at the start of school in order to establish a baseline measurement, or a starting point, so that assessment at seven years could determine 'value added' to the children. Given that national assessment has been increasingly used as a measure of school and teacher as well as pupil performance, as indicated by Sammons, West and Hind (1997), there has been a growing interest in exploring the influence of pupil background characteristics and school attended on attainment at the end of KS1 or seven years.

The largest of such studies is the *Effective Provision of Preschool Education* project of Sylva, Melhuish, Sammon and Siraj-Blatchford (1996), mentioned already, which is using multi-level modelling to enable the identification and separation of the distinct effects of preschool setting and primary school attended on performance at the end of KS1. It will investigate four different kinds of preschool education – playgroups, nursery classes, private day nurseries and local authority voluntary centres – as well as early entry into reception classes and 'home' children who have not attended preschool. At the start of reception and at the end of KS1 children's academic and behavioural competence will be related to family, community, preschool centre, agency and local authority characteristics. Those factors known to have a powerful impact on attainment – sex, age within the group, socioeconomic disadvantage, parental occupation and educational level, fluency in English and ethnic group – will, thus, be separated from effects related to schooling. Process quality characteristics, including day-to-day staff–child and child–child interactions and structuring of children's activities, will be collected since such variables have been associated with children's later development. The project will be the first of its kind to bring together the study of effects of preschool education with the study of infant school effectiveness, adopting a multi-level model design.

In fact, since the introduction of standardized assessment of pupil performance at the end of KS1, the issue of appropriate and valid ways of measuring and reporting schools' performance in the light of pupils' attainments or other indicators, such as attitude or attendance, has attracted wide interest in the field of infant school effectiveness over the period and, with this, the recognition that 'fair' indicators of schooling will need to measure the progress made by pupils at school rather than provide 'raw' results, as well as other factors related to intake. Strand (1997) tracked pupils in Wandworth schools who completed baseline assessment at the start of reception class in 1992/3 through the National Curriculum (NC) to the end of KS1 assessment in 1995 employing multi-level techniques to assess educational performance of pupils and 'value added' by schools. Girls were found to make more progress than boys, whilst pupils on free school meals (FSM) started with lower attainment and fell further behind during KS1. By contrast, pupils with English as a second language (ESL) caught up with English-speaking peers. Furthermore, in terms of school compositional effects, pupils made more progress on average in schools with a high proportion of girls and less progress in schools with a high proportion of pupils entitled to FSM, a high proportion of ESL or where the school average on baseline was high. Differences between schools in KS1 results were reduced considerably when account was taken of pupil-intake characteristics but significant differences remained, suggesting some schools were more effective than others in stimulating progress through KS1.

Sammons, West and Hind (1997) also used multi-level analysis to take account of the impact of pupil background characteristics on attainment at the end of KS1 in a sample of inner-city schools, though, as baseline data were not available to control for prior attainment, this analysis provided a more limited contextualisation of schools' KS1 results. Whilst a value-added approach would have been preferable their analysis provided strong evidence for links between specific pupil characteristics and performance in English at KS1, in particular. They also found that socioeconomic disadvantage (measured by eligibility for FSM), sex, lack of fluency in English attainment and, in addition, term of birth (especially for summer-born children) were all influential. One compositional factor – pupils from single-parent families – had a significant impact on English performance. For mathematics and science, however, only fluency in English, socioeconomic disadvantage and the term of birth had a significant impact. Like the previous study, these research findings point to the danger of using raw national assessment results to measure school performance. Moreover, this study used head teacher questionnaires to obtain qualitative information about teaching and school processes although classroom process data were not collected. This indicated that not only parent interest but also specific policies and practices related to reading, flexible grouping strategies and topics chosen for science teaching were influential. The same award provided the opportunity to carry out additional case studies of teaching and learning processes in Year 2 classes (for seven-year-olds) for children with additional learning needs (special education or language) in six, inner-city infant schools as well as an investigation of the attitude of 316 Year 2 children towards specific curricular areas.

Qualitative studies

As shown in the previous section, not all large-scale, policy-related research in the area of early childhood education has focused on statistically measurable effects of preschool education. Blenkin, Rose and Yue (1996), for instance, reported evidence from their major national survey of early years practitioners which provided descriptive data on the qualifications held by practitioners working with children under eight years (the age range for which qualified teachers in such settings were originally trained), the proportion of qualified teachers who had engaged in further study related to early childhood education, as well as factors influencing the implementation of developmentally appropriate curricula and professional development of practitioners.

Furthermore, not all research attention directed towards assessment has focused on standardised assessment and quantitative methodology. By contrast, Tunstall and Gipps (1996) derived a typology of teachers' feedback to young children's formative assessment using qualitative methods. Eight teachers in six schools with forty-nine children selected for more detailed study – two high attainers, two low attainers and two average, in each class – took part in the study. Classroom observation and recording in each class over the year focused on feedback to the class and to individuals across the timetable which, taken together with interviews with teachers and children, provided data which were analysed with the computer NUDIST 3.0 programme. This small illuminative study generated a grounded typology of styles of feedback, both positive and negative, in relation to performance-goal orientation, as well as identifying a particular feedback-type which specified attainment and improvement and, hence, mastery goal orientation. This type included many strategies described in contructivist approaches to learning, as well as self-regulating strategies.

The introduction of the National Curriculum has also focused attention on achievements brought into school, notably in literacy and numeracy, changes in curricular coverage as well as assessment at KS1 and its effect on parents, teachers and classroom practice – to identify just a few areas relevant to early childhood education research. It has also generated qualitative enquiry approaches to research on teaching. As we have outlined elsewhere (Aubrey 1997) such work can be characterised as a new emphasis on the complex thinking processes and decision-making involved in teaching, using methods which focus increasingly on data collection in naturally-occurring teaching situations; thick descriptions of classroom processes – in particular, interactive discourse; information concerning teachers' knowledge and beliefs; and individual children's understanding accessed through in-depth, interviews, the collection of work samples and observations of performance.

Work exemplifying such features can be found in early childhood education research. The study of Bennett, Wood and Rogers (1997) focused on nine reception class teachers' personal theories of play and the way these related to their actual practice. These theories were accessed through interviews based on key themes derived from their own narrative accounts. Stimulated 'reflection-in-action' through video-tapes of teacher-selected episodes of play revealed how many episodes of play did not match teachers' theories and intentions. Confronting teachers with the many dilemmas and challenges both to their theories and to their practice, encouraged reflection and change in practice.

Munn (1994; 1995) investigated the knowledge and beliefs about reading and numbers of a sample of children followed through the last year of nursery school. The data collected through informal interview and assessment showed that children of this age have beliefs and goals concerning reading and numbers which are very different from those of adults. She argued that preschool has an important role to play in making children aware of adults' meanings for reading and numbers without imposing those in overtly-directed activities.

Cuckle (1996) examined parental involvement in preschool reading by exploring parents' knowledge of and beliefs about the reading process, their reasons for helping, their perception of their role and the relationship between home and school. Parents filled in a checklist of reading and writing activities, took part in a detailed interview about their attitudes to helping, and engaged in a recorded reading-aloud session during which they were questioned about the help they offered. Their enthusiasm to help depended upon a set of beliefs about their capacity to help and about the respective roles of home and school in learning.

Some of our own work (Aubrey 1997), in the same tradition, sought to consider possible relationhips between reception teachers' orientations towards and beliefs concerning teaching the subject of mathematics and their classroom practice. This provided thick descriptions of classroom processes, in particular, interactive discourse as well as criterion-referenced measures of individual children's understanding of mathematics, accessed through in-depth interviewing. The observed diversity in practice among different teachers and their apparent lack of awareness of the rich informal knowledge brought into school – of counting, recognition of numerals, representation of quantity, addition, subtraction and social sharing, appropriate language of measurement and selection of criteria to sort objects – raised some questions with respect to the adequacy of teachers' subject knowledge. The interaction between the processes of assessment of children's prior knowledge and instruction, however, was demonstrated by the way teachers presented tasks and were able to assess the extent to which children could answer questions about content and apply knowledge strategically.

In-depth study of individual children's development in a number of subject domains has also been characteristic of research activity of this period. Many accounts have been provided of the development of children's drawing of the human figure, but such accounts have often been based on a presumed progression in children's drawing towards an adult paradigm with such exceptions as Buckham's (1993) sensitive account of continuity and change in children's drawing across the primary phase. Children's figure drawing strategies, between two and four years, in Singaporean nurseries and kindergartens in a variety of conditions – from imagination, from three-dimensional objects and from a human form – have also been reported by Matthews (1997). This enabled him to uncover their systematic investigation of visual structure and development of a cluster of representational strategies involving pigment and linear configurations. Far from being a period attributed to 'scribbling', these observed strategies formed complex visual descriptions.

Similarly, Thompson (1995) interviewed fifty-nine children of six to seven years and forty-four children of seven to eight years old whilst attempting mental arithmetic tasks. Their tape-recorded solutions and explanations suggested to him that young children continue to use counting as an important part of their problem-solving repertoire, combining this with other learned skills and acquired knowledge.

Small interventions to promote early literacy development have also been popular in this period. Hannon, Weinberger and Nutbrown (1996) devised home-based (provision of materials and home visits) and school-based (group meetings) ways of working with parents in the Sheffield Early Literacy Development Project. Both were found to have an impact though the former was more important in promoting book-sharing between parents and children. Wade and Moore (1996) were also interested in the effects of a National Book-start study which had introduced book-sharing through an information pack to a cohort of inner-city families. Two years later families were still giving priority to looking at books and buying books as presents, and book-sharing was a frequent home activity.

Whilst the majority of the research projects described in this section have been externally-funded projects which represent the work of small groups of researchers, Cuckle's (1996) study, for instance, was taken from a larger study comparing the literary experience of individual children at home and school which formed her own PhD project. Other 'lone' researchers, often lecturers in HE, carrying out research as part of a degree-bearing award, have produced work worthy of wider dissemination. Thompson's papers (1993; 1994; 1996) on her ethnographic study into the language and social behaviour of a small group of children during the period of their enculturation into nursery education also constitute publications based on her own PhD study. Broadhead's (1997) observation study of reciprocal sequences of play behaviours and discourse employed by interacting children, similarly, was based on a previously-awarded master's degree project.

Conclusions

The restructuring of higher education, the competitive nature of research funding, the cyclical RAE, as well as the massive legislative reforms of education and initial teacher training, have all created enormous pressures on academics as major educational researchers, as well as opportunities to take advantage of the huge natural experiment in changing policy and practices of the last decade. In this context there has been robust debate about the quality and practical relevance of educational research from both inside and outside HE.

Over the last ten years early childhood education research has attracted many talented and experienced UK researchers. A continuing preoccupation with school and teaching effectiveness has led, in fact, to the application of some of the most advanced and sophisticated, multi-level statistical models in educational and social science, particularly in the area of pre- and infant schooling. As Hammersley (1997) pointed out, however, there are still unresolved arguments in relation to the application of positivist methods to social science research, the human social world being quite different from the physical studied by natural science. One problem relates to the difficulty of measuring what is thought to be educationally significant. Another concerns the peculiar complexities involved in determining social causation, including interaction effects. The problem in the establishment of causal patterns as well as controlling competing factors in such a way as to assess the relative contribution of each one in what is usually regarded as a complex web of relationships should not, he stressed, be underestimated. In fact, can we ever assume causation involving fixed, universal relationships?

This period has also attracted qualitative applications of newer forms of enquiry in teaching which have turned to interpretive methods to capture naturally-occurring situations and complex, social practices. This has led to rich descriptions of domain-specific development of knowledge and understanding in young children – for instance, in the areas of English, mathematics and drawing – which have much potential to influence practice. Furthermore, some of this work has attempted to access children's own beliefs and perspectives and shown how different from adults' views these can be. The relative contribution of home and school to future achievement has led to small-scale interventions which have attempted to enhance parents' understanding of and contributions to the early stages of literacy, in particular. New conceptions of learning and teaching have informed much of the work carried out in this area, which is still a relatively small-scale activity. Again, caution is advised when drawing conclusions from qualitative enquiry where patterns may be local and context-sensitive and where interpretation and decision on the part of teacher and children play an important role (Hammersley, 1997). Goals in such settings are likely to be multiple, open to multiple meanings and, hence, to debate and different interpretation. Perhaps, most significantly, the phenomena under examination – young children's learning and development – lend themselves to being studied in real time, rarely a possibility in funding terms.

On balance, changing circumstances in HE have served as a spur to research activity and there is little evidence in refereed publications that this has affected quality. Peer review serves in a gate-keeping capacity (forty per cent of papers submitted to the *British Educational Research Journal*, for instance, are rejected outright and only two per cent accepted without major revision). Clearly all the on-going, early childhood education research logged in the NFER registers does not lead to high-quality outcomes. Many in any case, as noted above, constitute individually supervised research degree activity in progress.

Nevertheless much has been achieved which reflects a breadth in method-ological and theoretical interest. The main danger noted at the beginning of the chapter by Stronach, Hustler and Edwards (1997) is that, in times of rapid change, our methodological and theoretical concerns become inward-looking and our ways of addressing these concerns routine. One way to counteract this is to develop an international dimension to 'look outwards in order to look inwards'.

Granted that educational policy is not readily transportable from one country to another, such thoughts do immediately raise the question of whether or not our own educational problems are objective, social facts or simply artefacts of our own educational decision-making. Such issues, however, will be explored in greater depth in a later chapter.

Notes

1 Analyses which attempt to explore the relative importance of different independent variables in producing changes in the dependent variable.
2 Other ESRC projects may have been registered under different categories and, hence, are not included here.

Part III

Early childhood education research in action

7 Multilevel modelling

A case study on mathematics performance[1]

Qualitative and quantitative approaches are not alternatives, but simply different aspects of our search for knowledge and understanding. However quantitative the research design, it must still face up to criticism from the qualitative perspective, and vice versa. Suppose researcher A collected a huge amount of numerical data, measuring children with all possible precision and doing a lot of 'correct' statistical sums with the best available software. The conclusions would be of little value if they showed no awareness of the meaning of their data and refused to listen to criticisms about the influence on their results of the social context in which children operated. On the other hand, suppose researcher B became deeply involved in an observational case study, collected enormous amounts of notes and meticulously analysed them before constructing theories based on them. The conclusions would be hopelessly wrong, if they showed no awareness of the quantitative perspective and the fact that one case study provides no evidence of anything other than what happens in that one case.

Research is a search for truth. Truth can be seen from two points of view. Some philosophers emphasise a correspondence theory of truth. A statement is true if it corresponds with the way the world actually is. The sentence 'This child is five years old' is true if the speaker is talking about a child who is five years old. Other philosophers emphasise coherence theories of truth. 'This child is five years old' is true because it fits in with all the other things we might want to say in this situation. It is true because it fits in with 'This is a young child', 'This child is not yet six' and 'This child is of school age'.

It is obvious to everyone other than philosophers that it is silly to argue about which of these two approaches is best. 'This child is five years old' is true both because it corresponds with the fact that the speaker is talking about a five-year-old child and also because it fits in with the way these six words are used in English.

It is equally silly to argue about whether qualitative or quantitative research is better. No amount of collecting facts is going to lead to the truth if the data are described in misleading or meaningless terms. No amount of developing a deep understanding of situations will lead to the truth if it is an understanding not of the way the world actually is, but of some fantasy world in the researcher's mind.

We have to seek the truth through data, which are complex and subtle. We need a quantitative perspective to keep a grip on complexity and a qualitative perspective to keep a grip on the subtleties.

Uses of statistical analysis

People often think of statistics as a few routine mechanical procedures such as those taught in A-level courses or introductory university courses. Trying to do research armed only with these few techniques is rather like trying to design an aircraft without using maths for anything except adding up the cost of the materials. This would involve leaving the size and shape of the wings and tail to guesswork and making no calculations about the weight of the components of the plane. People could build planes in this way; but very few of them would fly. Statistics involves a very broad range of approaches to handling the complexity of data. The aid that statistics offers is not just a matter of a few standard significance tests but a rich variety of approaches to handling the twists and turns of questions that arise when a large amount of data is being considered. People who do research on statistics itself are very concerned that the quantitative techniques they do develop to follow these twists and turns should be capable of standing up to qualitative criticism.

Suppose a researcher had measured and analysed children's performances in a number of different social situations. Someone might object that it is misleading to look at how a child behaves in one setting without taking into account how the same child behaves in the other settings. The statistician would agree and would set about devising approaches which could look at all settings simultaneously. (This would be called a multivariate approach.)

Many statistical techniques are based on the assumption that the data are roughly normally distributed. Many people are reluctant to believe that many things in this world really do fit the convenient pattern of the standard bell-curve. However, if someone objects to the use of these techniques because it makes no sense to think of some particular data as being normally distributed, the statistician would already have set about devising approaches with assumptions that make more sense in the light of the data. (Non-parametric methods are an example of this.)

The possibilities for statistical analysis have been vastly increased by the availability of increasingly cheap and powerful computers. Theoretical ideas can now be followed through in the confidence that it is going to be possible to design a computer program that will put the theory into practice. Confining quantitative research to applying 'A-level' techniques that were invented before this computing power was available, is rather like confining the collection of qualitative data to techniques available before the invention of tape-recorders or cameras.

One of the great qualitative debates among statisticians was related to the research and analysis behind *Teaching Styles and Pupil Progress* (Bennett 1976). This research classified teachers into twelve types according to characteristics that were 'progressive' or 'traditional'. It went on to compare the progress of children in classes taught by 'formal', 'informal' and 'mixed' teachers. The book assumed a great political significance, since it claimed to show that progressive methods were less effective than traditional methods. This was very relevant to the so-called Great Debate on education, which occurred at about that time. There was a lot of qualitative debate about the meaning of the labels 'formal' and 'informal' and whether they meant anything at all. Educational research has since moved on and few people would now be seriously interested in discussing that.

Statisticians found other problems to discuss in Bennett's analysis and the results of that discussion are still very much with us. One question was (in quantitative terms), was the sample used large enough to show anything at all, or (in qualitative terms) should we try to understand the evidence in terms of the teachers' behaviour or in terms of the children's experience? Since there were only thirty-seven teachers, but 950 children, this made a big difference to the statistical analysis. The question is not an easy one to answer in a purely abstract way. Bennett wanted to look at the impact of different ways of teaching; so it made sense to think of the sample as made up of thirty-seven teachers and their pupils. On the other hand Bennett was trying to look at the way pupils responded to different ways of teaching; so it made sense to think of the sample as 950 children and their teachers.

In quantitative terms this looks like a very simple choice. In qualitative terms it looks like a very subtle distinction calling for a very subtle judgement. In 1981 Aitkin published two articles (Aitkin, Bennett and Hesketh 1981 and Aitkin, Anderson and Hinde 1981) that in terms of statistics seemed to have the last word to say on the subject. Bennett himself was co-author of one of these. The conclusion reached by the statisticians was in the best traditions of qualitative research: to reach an understanding of such a subtle situation, it was necessary look at the data simultaneously from the perspective of the thirty-seven teachers and from perspective of the 950 pupils. It was necessary to develop forms of analysis that could work at more than one level at a time. Out of this and similar problematic situations arose multilevel modelling.

The rise of multilevel modelling

Multilevel modelling is technically difficult and would have been impossible before the arrival of powerful cheap computers. Since the mid 1980s a number of pieces of software have been developed to carry out this form of analysis, notably MLWin (Multilevel analysis for Windows) in England and HLM (Hierarchical Linear Modelling) in America. The English software was developed by a group working at the London Institute of Education with Harvey Goldstein, who was involved in the original debate about Bennett's book. Goldstein (1987, 1995) gives a very technical account of the theory behind multilevel modelling (not recommended for non-statisticians) and a fuller account of the history.

As is the way with statisticians, they have gone on to find ways to use multilevel modelling for all sorts of purposes beyond those for which it was originally designed. It is even used in situations where far simpler techniques would be appropriate but happen to be difficult to apply.

By the late 1990s the use of multilevel modelling in educational research has become more or less standard. It is not surprising that many academic articles have been published using analysis of this type in a wide range of areas. A brief session with an index produced by the American Psychological Association drew attention to articles on the regional origin of migrants and the stability of their families (Tolnay and Crowder 1999), accidents to preschool children (Reading *et al.* 1999), smoking and social deprivation (Duncan *et al.* 1999), managing care of the elderly (Degenholtz *et al.* 1999), retirement decisions by car workers (Hardy and Hazelrigg 1999), changes in anti-psychotic drug use (McKenzie *et al.* 1999), preschool children's psycho-social adjustment (van den Oord and Rispens 1999), teaching reading skills (Fukkink and de Glopper 1999) and the effects of hostility on mood and blood pressure (Raeikkoenen *et al.* 1999). A recent *Journal of the Royal Statistical Society* was devoted to applications of multilevel modelling to such topics as area variations in teenage pregnancy rates (Diamond *et al.* 1999), the use of such things as grade levels for comparisons of pupil progress and attainment (Fielding 1999) and consumers' use of products (Romaniuck *et al.* 1999).

A more impressive indication of how far multilevel modelling has infiltrated educational research is that SCAA, noted for keeping the statistics in its reports as simple as possible, published a report which makes extensive use of multilevel modelling to investigate the usefulness of baseline assessment in giving schools value-added scores (Tymms *et al.* 1996). Admittedly this was a report to SCAA rather than from SCAA and its author has in other places analysed the same and similar data using sophisticated techniques (Tymms 1997, Tymms 1999, Tymms *et al.* 1997a). The report also rather sadly points out the danger of sophisticated techniques being seen as 'mumbo jumbo' if there are no obvious advantages to having used them (p.30).

A case study

A relatively simple application of multilevel modelling occurred when two of the authors were involved in an international study of early mathematical development organised by the University of Utrecht.

Researchers at the University of Utrecht devised a Test of Early Mathematical Competence to measure the progression of young children in content areas drawn partly from Piagetian ideas and partly from other views about the development of children's counting and arithmetic (Van de Rijt *et al.*, 1999). The Freudenthal Institute, another Dutch organisation has for many years been developing Realistic Mathematics. This is partly a theoretical perspective that informs research and partly a curriculum development project. The starting point for all this was the work of Hans Freudenthal, who held that people need to reconstruct mathematical knowledge from their rich understanding of the real world. Piaget's ideas are better known. The University of Utrecht team were looking independently at these ideas and at Piagetian developmental theory.

The Utrecht Early Mathematical Competence Test exists in three forms, each consisting of forty questions. Five questions address each of eight topics.

- Comparison – both of numbers and of measures
- Classification – grouping or matching objects on the basis of one or more characteristics
- Correspondence – recognising sets with the same number of elements, or making a set to match a given set
- Seriation – recognising sets which are arranged in order of size or some other attribute
- Using Counting Words – counting with numbers up to 20, backwards and forwards
- Structured Counting – counting objects in a number of arrangements
- Resultative Counting – counting without the need to point or touch
- General Number Knowledge – applying number knowledge to realistic situations.

The test was piloted on 823 Dutch children aged between four-and-a-half years and seven-and-a-half years. Age norms for success rates on each question were calculated (Van de Rijt *et al* 1999).

For the international study help was enlisted from researchers in Belgium, Germany, Greece, Slovenia, England and Finland. Each country was asked to assign about a hundred children to each of the three forms of the test and to test them three times during the course of a year. The intention was to capture the beginning of formal schooling.

Obviously there were limits to the detailed controls that the Dutch were able to impose on other countries. Each group of researchers found their own funding and selected a sample of children, which fitted their own resources and their own education system. In each country different practical difficulties were faced. For example, in England it turned out to be impossible to complete the third round of testing within twelve months of the first round. Some countries used this opportunity to pursue their own research questions. All things considered it was difficult to make simple comparisons between nations either qualitatively or quantitatively (see table 7.1.)

One simple approach to international comparison would be to look at the mean scores for children in each country. At the time of the 1998 European Conference for Educational Research (ECER) conference, when some counties had only completed a single round of testing, the mean scores for the first round in each country were disclosed (Van de Rijt and Van Luit 1998).

With this sort of information it would be possible to do some fairly simple significance testing and, whatever test was chosen, the result would almost

Table 7.1   Mean scores for children from each country in the first round of UEMCT testing

Country	Mean Score
The Netherlands	26.2
Belgium	21.5
Germany	23.5
Greece	20.0
England	15.9
Slovenia	20.4
Finland	31.9

definitely be that there were significant differences between countries and that the performance of children in the England was significantly below that in all other countries. This sort of depressing conclusion can lead to all sorts of alarmist articles in the press.

However, even the least qualitative of researchers can see that such a comparison would be meaningless. Much richer information is needed about the children in each sample before we can start to understand what, if anything, these differences in scores mean. Were the children from different socio-economic groups? Were they receiving the same sort of schooling? Were class sizes and adult–child ratios similar? Were children of similar ages in all countries?

For many questions of this type analysis has to remain in the qualitative style. However, since the sex of each child and their age at each time of testing had been recorded with almost complete regularity, it was possible use quant-itative approaches to investigate whether the differences between the countries could be attributed to the age and sex of the children sampled.

At the time of the 1999 European Conference for Research on Learning and Instruction more data were made available and it was possible to compare mean scores and mean ages for each national group in each round of testing. The graph of these data in Figure 7.1 presents a far less depressing picture of English children. Fairly obviously, the main reason why the English children were so much less successful than those of other nationalities was that the English children were much younger.

The conclusion to be drawn here feels rather qualitative. Since the differences in ages of children are so complicated, it is better to avoid looking at age groups and instead use a technique that treats each possible age separately but tries to fit them into an overall pattern. The usual way of doing this is to perform linear regression. This effectively puts a line through the graph which comes as close as possible to all the data points on the graph. 'As close as possible' has a technical mathematical definition which does not concern us at the moment. The mathematical description of this line, in the form of what is called a regression equation, gives us a quantitative description of the data. The accuracy of the description is a matter of how close 'as close as possible' turns out to be. It is possible to do significance tests on the closeness of fit.

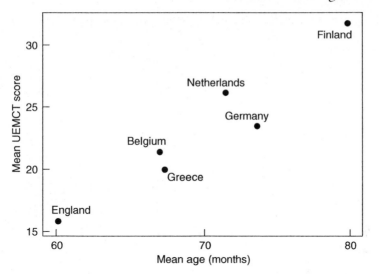

Figure 7.1 National mean scores against mean ages in the first round of UEMCT

A simple linear regression of the data shown in Figure 7.1 produces the line shown in Figure 7.2 for which the equation is

$$\text{Mean Score} = 0.78 \times \text{Mean Age} - 31.2$$

This suggests that at four-and-a-half years children are expected to have a score of about 10.9 and this expected score increases by 0.78 every month. However, this is misleading, because the data here give information only about countries and not about individual children. It is unlikely that all English children have a score of 15.9 regardless of age, but the data shown here give us no reason to think otherwise.

An alternative approach would be to go to the original data on individual children in all countries and skip the part of the analysis that finds national mean scores and mean ages. This gives the graph in Figure 7.3, which has the equation

$$\text{Score} = 0.51 \times \text{Age} - 13.6$$

This suggests that at four-and-a-half years children are expected to have a score of about 14.1 and this expected score increases by 0.51 every month. Figure 7.3 shows how this line matches the data on all individual pupils. Figure 7.4 shows the line in relation to the national averages and is more easily compared with Figure 7.2. The two equations are very different.

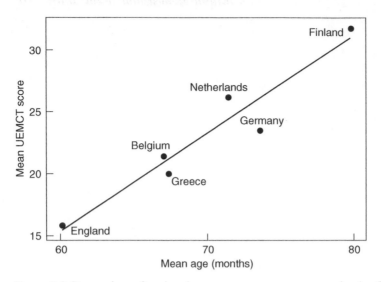

Figure 7.2 Regression of national mean scores on mean ages in the first round of UEMCT testing

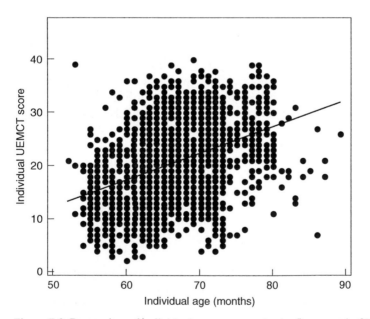

Figure 7.3 Regression of individual scores on age in the first round of UEMCT testing

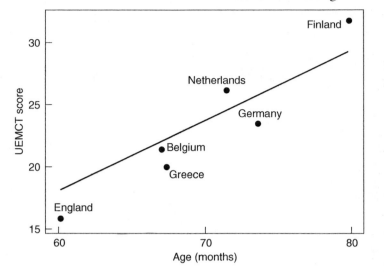

Figure 7.4 The individual regression line compared with national averages

We have not even begun to consider what happens when children are tested for the second and third time and already we are torn between, on the one hand, a model which treats all children as individuals and regards nationality as irrelevant and, on the other hand, a model which treats children as if they are uninteresting as individuals and the only thing that matters about them is their national averages. One of these approaches shows England doing much worse than should be expected and Finland doing much better. The other shows England and Finland doing about as well as expected.

One way out of this difficulty would be to do the regression using individual scores but to do it for each country separately. This would be equivalent to assuming no similarity between the development of children in one country and the development of children in another. The resulting picture in Figure 7.5 is pretty chaotic. Although it looks as if Dutch children are performing better than all others, it is very difficult to make comparisons between the other countries.

A multilevel regression model treats children as individuals and at the same time assumes that children in a single country may have similarities in their development. The result is a sort of compromise between the national differences you find by ignoring the similarities between children of different nationalists and the individual similarities that you find by ignoring possible differences between countries.

The resulting graph is shown in Figure 7.6. Dutch children still seem to be doing best overall, but there is more of a pattern to the performance of children in the other countries. Those countries with younger children seem to have a greater dependence of score on age. That is, their younger children have lower scores but the scores increase more rapidly with age.

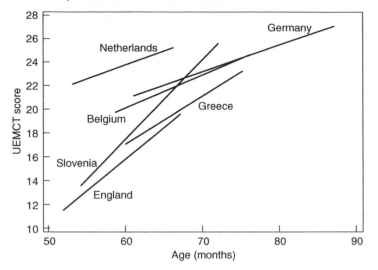

Figure 7.5 Separate national regression lines for individual scores on age

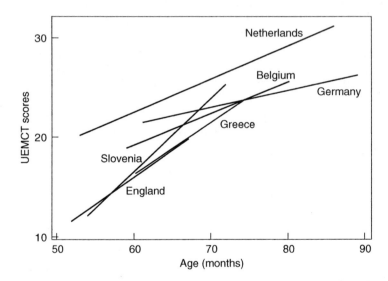

Figure 7.6 National regression lines derived from the multilevel model

It was also possible to set up a more complex multilevel model which took account of the fact that children in all countries can be expected to perform somewhat similarly and of the fact that there may well be some differences between countries, but also took into account the fact that even within countries there are quite possibly differences between the way that children in different schools perform. In the most effective of these models the underlying regression line was taken to be

$$\text{Score} = .431 \times \text{age} - 8.6$$

This line is shown against the national averages in Figure 7.7. Finnish and Dutch averages still seem to be very good and English and Greek slightly below expectation. However the interesting thing is how the model shows schools and countries differing. In principle each child can differ from its school expectation, each school can differ from its national expectation and each country can differ from the overall expectation shown in the regression line. Children were found to differ from their school expectation by an amount that had a mean of 0 and a standard deviation of 6.62. School averages were found to differ from national expectations by amounts that had a mean of 0 and a standard deviation of 2.99. The schools' rates of improvement with age differed from national expectations by very small amounts with a mean of 0 and a standard deviation of 0.14. Most importantly, no advantage was found in including any national differences at all. All national expectations in this model were the same as the overall regression line shown in Figure 7.7.

At a later time, with more data available from all countries, the analysis developed further. The results of this have yet to be published.

Once the regression model is established it is possible to go on and look at other factors that might influence children's scores and to see if the description of the data becomes more accurate once these are taken into account. For example, it is possible to investigate whether girls perform better than boys overall, or just in some countries or some schools. In fact no significant effect of sex was found in any variation on the model.

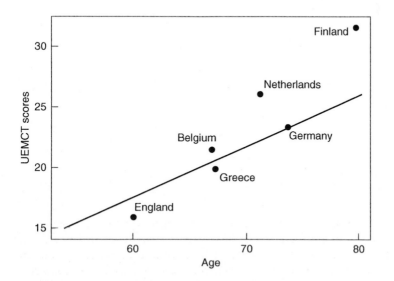

Figure 7.7 National mean scores and ages together with the international regression line for individual scores on age, taken from the multilevel model allowing for differences between schools

Another possibility, yet to be explored, is that forms of assessment that are peculiar to specific countries can be related to this model, which has some international validity. For example, relationships can be examined between the Utrecht Early Mathematical Competence Test and Baseline Assessments or KS1 Assessments in England.

The important thing to remember is that statisticians have a lot more to offer than t-tests and analysis of variance. With the advance of computing power it has become a realistic possibility for all types of researcher to make use of whichever sophisticated form of statistics is appropriate. All that is needed is advice on the most appropriate forms of analysis and probably some assistance with operating specialised software and interpreting potentially confusing computer output. It helps a lot if the advice is taken before the research is carried out and the research is then planned to make the analysis run smoothly.

Acknowledgement

1   This chapter was produced jointly with B.A.M. Van de Rijt and J.E.H Van Luit.

8 Ethnography for early childhood settings

The aim of this chapter is to offer a contrast to the previous chapter and show how research paradigms established within different fields of research – for example, linguistics and anthropology – can provide teachers and other professionals with useful insights into young children's experiences of learning and being. We have chosen ethnography as an approach that provides for contrast and comparison with the multilevel modelling approach outlined in the previous chapter. This choice is not intended to challenge; rather, the intention is to demonstrate how a different approach to research can provide the means to look at the world in a different, socially orientated way, with a view to seeing different things, or to seeing things differently; in short, to seeing the same things but in different ways.

What is ethnography?

We begin by asking the question, *what is ethnography?* The stated aim of ethnographic research is to understand people, and why people do the things they do. The answers to this question are arrived at through very detailed recorded observations of individuals and the context(s) in which they interact. The aim of ethnography is to make a person's implicit behaviours *explicit,* in the belief that these insights will lead to a greater understanding of why people do the things they do. Ethnography also aims to help us understand others and ourselves a little better. Ethnographers are interested in patterns of behaviour, and the impact and consequences of human actions. Central to ethnography is the belief that human behaviour is rule bound and rule governed. Ethnographers believe that through systematic observation they may come to identify recurring patterns of human behaviour and social activity. This is important and useful information that can provide insights into the unstated social rules that influence individuals, the ways they act and speak, and the manner in which they interact with others. Ethnographers do not believe that human behaviour can be predicted. That is not their central concern. They are interested in generic patterns of behaviour because these represent the outward manifestation of internalised rules or codes of appropriate behaviours that comprise an individual's implicit knowledge how to behave appropriately as a member of a particular group or community. For teachers wanting to know more about the children they teach, to assess what the children may already know (i.e. what they have already learned), ethnography offers an exciting opportunity to gain insights that may otherwise remain elusive. These insights may carry implications that are important for understanding the processes of teaching and learning.

Ethnography as a methodology has unique characteristic features. It has its own register (or specialist language). This is more important than it may at first appear because the terminology conveys the ways in which ethnographic research differs from other investigative approaches. For example, the people being studied or observed are referred to as the *participants*. This choice of term is not optional. It positions those being observed as equal partners in the investigation. Hence, the research becomes a joint venture, the researcher(s) and participants each learning, giving and gaining from the experience. Both parties actively engage and participate in all stages of the research. Participants provide the data and importantly, they *participate* in the analysis and interpretation of these data. This high level of participation carries obligations for the particpants. It requires a high degree of commitment from the participants who both provide the data and help the researcher(s) to make sense of them. Ethnography aims to help the researchers (*the outsiders*) and others who are not members of the observed community, to understand the group's values, culture and social activities better but also and importantly, ethnography also aims to help the group (*the insiders*) understand themselves and their way of life better. In this way ethnography can be empowering for the participant members of the observed community. Ethnographic research therefore carries dual responsibilities. Firstly, the responsibility to inform outsiders about the observed community in an informed and rigorous way. Secondly, to inform the insiders, the observed community, about themselves. However, this is a complex task. Ethnography is not merely a matter of describing the participants' behaviour. The skill of ethnographer lies, in part, in being able to report observations in different ways to different audiences. On the one hand, ethnographers will want to report their observations to other researchers, some of whom may not be other ethnographers. On the other hand, ethnographers will also want to tell the participants about themselves, in a way that is perceived as useful, worthwhile but not authoritarian, prescriptive or patronising. Communicating findings to these different audiences require different ways and approaches. Reporting ethnographic data is a demanding and complex task because ethnographic research focuses on the interrelated aspects of human behaviour – the social, the cultural and the linguistic. Ethnography does not merely describe people's behaviour; it describes people's ways of living. Hence ethnographers' reports have to reflect people's *ways of being*.

The term ethnography is sometimes used as a catch-all phrase to describe all qualitative research. This is misleading. Ethnography is highly principled approach to research, with uniquely defining characteristics. Ethnography is surrounded by misunderstandings. One example is the belief that ethnographic data are solely qualitative. It is true that from ethnographic fieldwork, there are frequently complex data sets that need to be compared, correlated and combined. However, the ethnographer is not restricted to using only qualitative analysis in this task. Ethnographic data can be analysed in the same wide range of ways that are available for all data sets, hence it can utilise both qualitative and quantitative methods. There are other factors related to ethnography. It is time-consuming, not only because of the complexity of the foci but also for very practical reasons. It takes time to collect the data from different sources and perspectives. It also requires different types of data. Since the focus is the study of *text(s) in context(s)*, the range and types of data collected demands time-intensive analyses. Ethnographic researchers spend time, sometimes several years, living and working with the people they are observing.

Perhaps one of the best known ethnographic studies is Shirley Brice-Heath's (1983) study of comparative literacy in two communities. The following description is taken from the beginning of her book, *Ways with Words*. The style is characteristic of ethnographers' ways of reporting studies.

> In the years between 1969 and 1978, I worked, and played with the children and their families and friends in Roadsville and Trackton. My entry to that community came through a naturally-occurring chain of events. In each case I knew an old-time resident in the community, and my relationship with that individual opened the community for me.
>
> (Brice-Heath 1983, p.5)

This friend-of-a-friend approach can be found in other studies (c.f. Milroy 1980). Brice-Heath's

> ethnographies of communication attempt to let the reader follow the children of Roadsville and Trackton from their homes and community experiences, into their classrooms and schools. The reader comes to know these children and their teachers and to see how both groups retained some of their language and cultural habits and to alter others.
>
> (Brice-Heath 1983, p.7)

The study focuses on each of the communities in which the children are socialised as talkers, readers and writers. The description focuses on a number of features, including:

- The boundaries of the physical and social community in which communication to or by the children was possible
- The limits and features of the situation in which such communities occur
- The what, how and why of patterns of choice the children could exercise in their uses of language, in talking, reading and writing and

- The values or significance these choices of language have for the children's physical and social activities.

In many ways her study is timeless, since many of the contextual circumstances she described are of current concern. The public, professional and political debates over standards and approaches to literacy demonstrate these common concerns. Also, given the many policy changes in education world-wide since 1988, it is interesting to note her comment that 'the influence of ... mutual adjustments on an individual level often exceeded that of the major educational policy shifts and reorganising of teachers and students which marked these times' (Brice-Heath 1983, p. 7) This comment was made in 1983 and seems equally applicable now, in the year 2000.

Brice-Heath's study spanned a decade, but not all researchers have this luxury of time available to them. However, the following comment on research and the research process indicates that she was not oblivious to the very real pressures that researchers face:

> No deadlines, plans or demands from an outside funding agency set limits on the time or direction of the cooperative arrangements between teachers and anthropologist, the timing and location. The particular inter-play of people and historic and social conditions make this, like every ethnography a unique piece of social history.
>
> (Brice-Heath 1983, p.7)

From this unique history common threads of concern emerge. Brice-Heath (1983, p.8) states that:

> the approaches to research in education have been quantitative, global, sociodemographic and dependent on large-scale comparisons of many different schools. Terms from business predominate: input, output, accountability, management strategies etc. Input factors (independent variables) are said to influence, predict or even determine output factors (dependent variables). Pieces of data about social groups, such as number of siblings, or the time of mother–child interactions in preschool daily experiences, are correlated with the output of students, expressed in terms of test scores, subsequent income and continued schooling. The effects of formal instruction have been evaluated by correlating these input factors with educational output ... From an ethnographic perspective, the irony of such research is that it ignores the social and cultural context which created the input factors for the individual and groups. Detailed descriptions of what actually happens to children as they learn to use language and to form values about its structures and functions tell us what children do to become and to remain acceptable members of their own communities.

These are precisely the educational issues that ethnographic studies can address.

With its unique focus ethnography advocates a very distinctive approach to data collection and analysis. These parameters set exacting standards. They also pose particular challenges when the participants are very young children. However, it is precisely the qualities that make ethnography a challenge, that render it a particularly appropriate research method for studying children's language and learning. This is because it includes, in its focus, socio-cultural knowledge which is understood as playing a crucial role in the ways people learn the appropriate social behaviour that is necessary for socialisation and enculturation into their own community. Ethnography also assumes that the participants themselves do not exist as *tabula rasa*, but bring knowledge and understandings with them to the contexts and events in which they are participating and where they are being observed. This is in keeping with current thinking about young children, their capabilities and development. Instead of regarding young learners as devoid of previous learning and experience, ethnography assumes them to have amassed a wealth of previous learning and experiences – in short, a huge amount of knowledge. Ethnography can be of particular interest to teachers because it aims to make explicit that which the children themselves already know implicitly but which they are unable to explain to others or to offer as display knowledge. For this reason, an ethnographic approach is particularly appropriate for studying young children's language use and development. Most language use, for both children and adults, remains a part of intuitive knowledge. It is important to note that intuitive is not to be confused with innate capacity. Intuitive knowledge can be defined as knowing something so well that the learner has first, forgotten that it has been learned, second, has forgotten *how* it was learned, and third, is able to recall, use and apply the knowledge effortlessly and unconsciously. It would be immensely useful for educators to be able to draw upon learners' intuitive knowledge and to understand it better.

The essential defining characteristics of ethnographic fieldwork procedures are that they are designed to overcome the researcher's bias and that they are grounded in the investigation of communication and other phenomena that occur in the social contexts of everyday life. Saville-Troike (1982, p.119) offers a criterion for *descriptive adequacy,* of ethnography. She suggests that sufficient data should be collected to provide a description which would enable someone from outside the observed community, who was not present during the periods of data collection, to fully understand the events that take place, the participants and their behaviour(s). It is also considered important that an ethnographic account be accepted as *bona fide* by members of the observed community, particularly the participants themselves, where this is possible. However, her prescription poses unique challenges when the participants are young children.

Context is an important dimension in ethnography. It is of central importance that the participants are observed in contexts that form part of their normal everyday experiences, going about their daily lives, doing the things that they would ordinarily do, with a minimum of intrusion from the observer(s). Since the context of the social activity is so central to ethnographic studies, the researcher should not only aim to collect information about what the participants do, but also about the social milieu in which they do it. These contextual data are what Geertz (1975) calls *thick* data. They are the extraneous detailed information that the researcher(s) gather to help them to understand more than that which they have observed. These *field notes* can be used at various stages during the research, including the early periods of observation when refining the methods of gathering data and then later when analysing and interpreting the data. In order to interpret observed human acts the ethnographer keeps records that become the *inscription* or the *thick* description. One method for obtaining thick, contextual data is through participant observation.

The ethnographer as participant observer

Participant observation is an approach to research that is established within the ethnographic tradition. It enables the researcher to observe patterned culture-specific behaviours, whilst immersed in the contexts in which these are occurring. This is achieved by becoming a member of the group or observed community, and sometimes by actually becoming one of the participants. In some ways the term is a paradox. It requires the ethnographer to be simultaneously both passive observer and active participant. Passive as a member of the group so as not to disturb the data but active as the observer, recording all possible details of context, the participants and ongoing events. Milroy (1980) suggests that successful participant observation requires 'passing oneself off' as a member of the observed community. In order to do this the researcher needs to leave behind previous cultural experiences and to learn the norms and values of the observed community. However desirable this may seem, it is not always so easy for researchers to achieve. Cultural values are not always consciously held. Individuals are rarely aware of their permeating existence and insidious influence. Cultural values are part of intuitive knowledge and people are not always conscious of their own cultural biases. The unconscious nature of cultural experiences and their inherent values makes it very difficult for a person to 'leave them behind' as Milroy suggests. There are, however, other views that contrast with Milroy's. Becker (1963) suggests that there are advantages to the researcher *not* actually being a member of the observed community. He suggests that it is easier for an outsider to act naively and ask questions, or for clarifications, that an insider would be expected to know. He suggests that as an outsider it is possible for the ethnographer to elicit more knowledge from the participants, asking for genuine information and clarification, in a more naturalistic manner. While Becker's caveat offers hope to the ethnographer studying young children, it too presents its own difficulties. Children may not feel inclined to make disclosures to unknown adults. Indeed, parents' and social caution actively discourages children from talking to strangers, with some justification.

The practicalities of ethnography

Despite advocacy of the ethnographic approach there remains an acknowledged dilemma faced by ethnographers. For example, it is almost impossible for adult researchers to pass themselves off successfully as members of a child group. There may even be difficulties infiltrating an adult community. The ethnographer is always likely to remain *an outsider* to some contexts, particularly when attempting to gain access to a community of which they have limited or even no prior knowledge. Saville-Troike (1982, pp.121–2) reminds ethnographers of their academic and professional responsibilities associated with fieldwork and cautions: 'the ethnographer should not be "taking" data without returning something of immediate usefulness to the community'. So the challenge for ethnographers researching early childhood is: what can we give that will be perceived as useful? We may be able to give things of importance and significance to the school or classroom but these may not be perceived by the children, and their parents, as being of immediate use or benefit. The researcher's legitimate contribution will vary according to the context, the participating community and researcher's own skills and expertise. In the preschool, nursery or other educational setting, the challenge is more obvious. The researchers, invariably adults, can contribute to the ongoing life of the setting as 'an extra pair of hands', classroom helper or similar. Occasionally, the researcher may be qualified to offer something more direct as a professional, teacher, nurse or similar colleague. The general point to be made is that ethnographers should contribute to their participants' community in a way that is perceived as useful and not merely treat people and their life events and experiences as data. Of course, this professional etiquette is not the sole preserve of ethnographers. It is not only ethnographers who attempt to go beyond the 'take the data and run' tactics. The approach taken by the Performance Indicators in Primary Schools (PIPS) project (Tymms 1997) also shares this philosophy. Although this research is very different in approach and concept from ethnography, central to PIPS is the commitment to provide feedback and information to schools that is wanted and useful to the teachers and pupils who have provided the data. There are doubtless other projects that make similar positive contributions. In short, educational research carries responsibilities beyond the usual ethical practices.

Among the potential problems for participant observers, the questions lurk: how to introduce oneself to the host community, what information to reveal about oneself and one's purposes and what role to assume within the community during the period of observation? When doing ethnography in the classroom, it is possible for the researcher to adopt the role of teacher or classroom helper. However, in order to do this the researcher may need professional qualifications. It is even less easy for the adult researcher to assume a *bona fide* role in the social lives of young children outside of the school setting. Adults are precluded from child activities for a variety of reasons. They are older, they look different and they are not able to infiltrate child groups in a surreptitious way. While the strategy of passing oneself off as a friend of a friend is just not possible, other roles can be assumed: bystander, babysitter, responsible adult etc. There is always the additional complication that the adult, present in a child's social world, will influence behaviour and hence distort the observations as data.

Further difficulties can be encountered when researching communities where the observer does not speak the language or belongs to a different ethnic group. Le Page and Tabouret-Keller (1985, p.209) suggest that physical markers of ethnic identity (skin colour, modes of dress etc.) may also prevent successful assimilation into the observed group. Saville-Troike (1982, p.122) raises a further issue for the ethnographic researcher to consider: 'ethnographers must first of all understand their own culture, and the effects it has on their own behaviour, if they are to succeed in participant-observation in another's culture. The idea central to participant observation is that the ethnographer should be able to enter into various events relatively unobtrusively as a participant with whom other participants can feel comfortable. Saville-Troike (1982, p.122) recommends a high level of linguistic and cultural competence as a *sine qua non* and that there should be a shared linguistic and cultural competence between the ethnographer and the observed community. This raises another obstacle for the researcher wanting to use ethnography as an approach to researching young children. There will be many times when the researcher does not share the language, culture and values of the participant group. So does this preclude ethnography as an approach to young children and classrooms? We should like to suggest that a *professional competence* may comply as genuine grounds for the researcher being present in such contexts. For example, a researcher who is professionally competent and qualified could be said to share a common concern with the other professionals in the setting. The researcher may be able to offer professional assistance and act in a professional capacity in the research setting as a co-worker. This does not of course compensate for any lack of linguistic or culture competence with the participants but it can *justify a presence*.

Whiting and Whiting (1975, p.312) advise ethnographers 'not to embark on systematic observation which is laborious and time-consuming, unless they are convinced that informants cannot report their own behaviour or the behaviour of others reliably'. This comment is pertinent to researchers of young children because the participants will generally be considered too young to undertake a meaningful investigation. However, older members of the participants' families, including their siblings, can be consulted and involved in the data analysis and interpretation stages of the research. While acknowledging that ethnographers need to consider these demands, if we are keen to understand children, their behaviour and how they learn, ethnographic studies – based as they are on detailed observations – can lead to insights that differ from the large-scale surveys. Hence the perceived advantages of participant observation as a research method should be considered, the major advantage being the high quality of naturally-occurring data that it yields which provides insights into the everyday lives of a group or community.

The observer's paradox or the ethnographer's dilemma

However strong the advantages associated with ethnography, they have to be considered alongside critical comment. Claims that the data are unreliable and the analyses invalid have stemmed, in part, from the view that researchers exert undue (and hence distorting) influence on the participants who provide the data, on the data that are gathered, and on the subsequent analyses. The impact of the researcher's presence on the participants is a wider concern within the social sciences and it is referred to as the *observer's paradox*. It was Labov (1972, p.113) who formulated this concept with special reference to sociolinguistic research. Labov's (1972) claim is that the most consistent and natural language data for analysis are those of the vernacular, or casual speech. This is not easily elicited in interview situations or laboratories where its use would be inappropriate and hence unnatural. Since Labov's claim, many socio-linguists have put great emphasis on obtaining samples of the vernacular. However, in order to achieve this the researcher needs to inhabit the social world of the participants. To obtain these data, researchers have to observe how people speak when they are not being observed. This seeming contra-diction has become established as the *observer's paradox*. Although the laboratory is not the usual research milieu of ethnographers, there are ways in which interview situations, laboratories and indeed classrooms are indeed similar. In all of these contexts it would be inappropriate for the young child to behave in a completely natural manner. Classrooms are public places. Hence, data gathered there may not be totally unguarded and hence may not be truly representative of private acts.

The observer's paradox is of paramount concern to researchers eliciting data from very young informants. There are other facets to this paradox which we shall term the *ethnographer's dilemma*. The teacher in the classroom is invested with a particular role, with responsibilities for the group, and this influences the way they behave towards others in the classroom, particularly towards the children in their care. The asymmetrical power relations that can ordinarily exist between children and adults, are compounded when the adult also enjoys the status of teacher. The power imbalance may be further accent-uated when the teacher and pupil belong to different social or ethnic groups. The presence of a white adult (researcher or teacher) in the black child culture of the classroom is a further dimension to the observer's paradox. While it is an undeniable factor, it reflects the reality of life in a number of classrooms. Researchers, however, should remain sensitive to the effects which their presence may impose on the participants and their behaviour, and hence the data and subsequent interpretation. Individuals will construct differently even those experiences which they share. Teachers and pupils are no exception.

Researchers will always face personal and professional ethical dilemmas. In ethnography (in common with other areas of social science), there is also the general issue of reconciling an academic interest with an ethical commitment to oneself and the participants. This is particularly pertinent when the researcher is not a member of the observed community. Smith (1985) presents an account of some of the broad ethical issues raised by white academic researchers studying poor non-white minority communities in Britain. These issues are all compounded when the informants are very young children.

The ethics of candid recordings

Trying to capture an individual's behaviour when they do not feel that they are being observed is central to ethnography. Capturing what people say presents a particular challenge. Spoken language is fast, fleeting and utterances are spoken only once as authentic. Hence, there is absolutely no possibility of repetition. So in order to capture linguistic data, the ethnographer is entirely dependent upon the available electronic equipment to make audio-quality recordings that can be played and replayed repeatedly. How these recordings are secured is more problematic. The current state-of-the-art technology provides a wealth of choice in unobtrusive surveillance equipment that is capable of making candid recordings. However, they also support an approach that remains highly controversial.

Audio-taped recording is central to linguistic enquiry, yet linguists are divided in their use and the acceptance of it. Labov (1981, p.32) has rejected the practice on ethical grounds, while others rely on candid recordings and surreptitious observations with some qualification and an accompanying discussion on ethics. For example, Milroy (1980, p.173) endorses the method as necessary for theoretical advancement of sociolinguistic description. She states that

> the study of the vernacular speech of the individual in its everyday social context is an important task for sociolinguistics. Since most current models of communicative competence and language structure rest on a rather narrow base derived from relatively formal styles or relatively educated varieties, it is particularly important to obtain more information about the facts of specifically non-standard speech in a range of everyday contexts. Not to have such information is undesirable for practical as well as for theoretical reasons.
>
> (Milroy 1980, p.172)

While using audio-tapes for recording people is becoming established practice, the use of video recordings, which can provide a much richer account of human behaviour, is less widely used in ethnography. There are a number of reasons for this. On a practical note, video recording is not easy to conceal and hence can render the ethnographer obtrusive in the task of data gathering. Also, while there are some theoretical models of multi-semiotics (c.f. O'Toole 1994), they are still emergent, and leave unresolved issues about how to analyse video-taped data. On a practical level, video recordings cannot offer the participants the limited confidentiality of audio-tapes. Hence currently audio recordings remain the most widely used way of collecting linguistic data. On an ethical note, Labov's (1981, p.33) general principle is pragmatic. He advises the researcher to 'avoid any act that would be difficult to explain if it became a public issue'. Collecting data in the classroom, a public domain, generally helps the researcher to respect this proviso. Individuals are being observed in a public setting, which to some extent normally prohibits, or at least restricts, displays of very private behaviour. It is usually more prosaic concerns that dominate ethnographers' lives, like which recorder to use and how to overcome the difficulties inherent in collecting high-quality recordings in noisy public places, like classrooms and playgrounds.

The role of the ethnographer

The primary task facing the ethnographer is to gather information – that is to capture the data. Ethnographers are primarily concerned with naturally-occurring human behaviour. This occurs in real time and there are often aspects of human behaviour that happen so quickly, they can go unnoticed. It is behaviour of which the participants themselves frequently remain unaware. Yet if insights are to be gained, the data must be captured and be available for scrutiny and retrospective analysis. Human behaviour occurs in *real time*. The primary role of the ethnographer is to devise ways by which human behaviour can be captured and recorded for retrospective reflection. This of course poses difficulties and challenges.

There is a point when actual human behaviour, occurring in real time, is recorded and made available to others who were not present at the events which have been recorded. This is the point of transformation from naturalistic human behaviour to research data. It is the ethnographer who stages and manages this transformation. As the manager, the ethnographer holds responsibility to two audiences. On the one hand, the ethnographer must be held ultimately responsible for maintaining the authenticity of human behaviour that has been observed so that it remains recognisable to the original participants. On the other hand, there is also a responsibility to provide rigorous data sets in a format which makes them both accessible and acceptable to a wider audience. The ethnographer has ethical loyalties to these two separate groups: the individuals observed – the participants – and the wider research community. Since ethnographers are engaged in describing acts of human behaviour it is quite likely that their investigations will also appeal to a much wider group, the general public.

The role of the ethnographer can therefore be described as comprising the following components or series of acts:

- capturing on record naturalistic human behaviour
- transforming these behaviours into data sets
- analysing the data in terms of the perceptions and cultural values of the participants
- presenting insights that are acceptable and comprehensible from both inside and outside the participant community

In order to achieve this, it is inevitable that the observed human behaviour will undergo some changes and transformations. This has been a recurring criticism of ethnography. In order to address this concern we should like to outline a series of stages in a procedural process that will make the approach more transparent. The potential for influence on the data will be explored at each stage in the procedural process. Thus it is hoped that greater accountability can be achieved through this transparency of approach to the data collection, analysis and subsequent interpretations.

A procedural approach to ethnography

This section will outline a systematic practical procedural approach to ethnographic investigation. It is based on strategies devised during the Box Hill Nursery Project, an ethnographic study of young bilingual children's enculturation into formal education. The approach has been revised and refined in subsequent classroom-based research. The project was designed in four phases. Phases 1 and 2 each took between six and eight months each to complete, and phase 3 took one school year from (September to July the following year). Phase 4, the final phase, took six months but contact with families, participants and the school have endured over several years. One could add that just as ethnography becomes a way of observing life as it is experienced by the participants, the project itself becomes a way of life for the ethnographer who becomes drawn into the observed community in a way that endures. Ethnography is, however, more than a mere lifestyle shift. The research tasks that have to appear so spontaneous and natural in situ can only arise from forward planning and meticulous psychological and practical preparation on the part of the ethnographer.

A four-step approach to ethnographic research design

Figure 8.1 presents a four-step approach to planning ethnographic research projects.

Step 1: Preparation

The aims of this first step are:

- To identify a number of potential settings where it would be realistic and feasible to carry out an ethnographic study. It is inevitable that this preliminary step will be dominated by practical considerations like time, geography, finance and specific interests. It is therefore important to identify at least two, and preferably more, potential settings.
- To negotiate access to these settings with the observed community who are to be the focus of the research. However, in the case of child informants

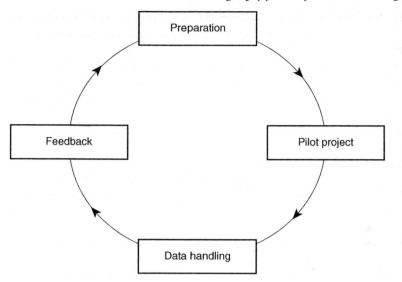

Figure 8.1 A four-step approach to planning research projects

this will also mean wider negotiation with relevant authorities: for example, if the setting is a school, then the school governing body, the local education authority (or in some countries the Ministry of Education) the headteacher, teachers and other school staff will all need to be involved in the negotiation. It will also probably be necessary to secure the necessary written permission from all relevant parties.

- To make a decision about the research location, or in the case of a comparative study, the settings where the observations can be conducted
- To negotiate a bona fide role for the ethnographer within the setting, for example, as a helper, teacher etc.
- To identify the participants, that is, the specific children who will be observed.

This phase can take several months to complete and so it is best to allow at least one school term for this phase of preparation.

Step 2: The pilot project phase

This is an important preparatory phase when the researcher will:

- Decide on the project name and decide on preliminary methods for making the observations and collecting thick contextual data. The name of the project assumes increasing significance during negotiations with relevant parties. It is important to have some written information about the project prepared for distribution. If possible this should be written in non-technical style that can be readily understood by a general readership. This information should go some way to explaining the relevance and usefulness of the planned study.

- Prepare the observation schedules to be used during the project, or if existing schedules are not to be used, a decision needs to be made about how observations are to recorded. There are a number of possible approaches that can be adopted. For example, Sylva *et al.* (1980) used structured, pre-coded schedules; Tough (1976) used more open, semi-structured schedules. Whichever form is the preferred format, in the tradition of ethnography, these observation schedules should be designed and refined in consultation with members of the participant community and/or their representatives. When the participants are young children, collaboration should be between responsible adults, family members or older children.

- Decide on ways of collecting the thick contextual data or inscription material that will be used for interpreting and illuminating the observations. This will necessitate establishing systems for recording and storing inform-ation. It is important that these data are easily retrievable by those not involved in the *in situ* observations but who may be involved in the coding and subsequent analysis of the data. These events will invariably take place long after the observations have been concluded – sometimes, many years later – so systematic data storage will be very important if the later stages of the project are to be successful.

- Plan systematic ways of storing and retrieving the data. Since the project could last over several years it is important to establish ways of keeping meticulous records that are relatively easy to access some time after they have been collected.

- Maintain cordial social and working relations with all of the participants involved in the project as well as with other corroborators including the teachers, parents and children other than those participating. This aspect is unquantifiable in a number of ways. It means being around, being a friend, being prepared to become involved in the lives of the people you are observing. These field friendships (as we call them) frequently endure beyond the research project and become established as life events in the ethnographer's own life. For some, they are one of the greatest rewards of being an ethnographer.

- Begin data collection as a pilot project with the purpose of refining the methods and approaches outlined in the points above. However well planned and prepared the observers are, there are inevitably changes to be made. These generally come about as the result of undertaking the obser-vations and the changes are best made on a day-by-day basis, as need directs. Time will need to be allowed within the project for this preliminary stage when alterations to the data-collection approaches are being refined and modified. It may not be possible to use these early data in subsequent analyses. It is also important to allow time during this process for the necessary consultation with member from within the participant community.

As with step 1, this pilot project phase is also likely to take *at least* one school term to complete. It may even be necessary to extend over two school terms to allow sufficient consultation, feedback and adjustment to plans and preparations.

Step 3: Dealing with the data

Ethnography is less like other approaches to research when it comes to collecting and analysing data. Hence, designing a framework for ethnographic descriptive analysis is inextricably linked to the collection of the data. This step of dealing with the data therefore needs to be forward looking and to take into account the ways in which the data collected will eventually be analysed. The next sections outline a number of stages that will allow the ethnographer to collect, collate, analyse and interpret a variety of data sets, in a complementary, systemic and transparent way.

Collecting raw data

The first stage in the transformation process is the collection of materials that are to form the *raw data*. This term is used for the naturally-occurring human behaviour that is observed in naturalistic, everyday settings. In other words, what people actually do and say as they go about their daily routines. These data are recorded as candidly and as unobtrusively as possible, given the ethical constraints discussed previously. Raw data come in a variety of forms, including: audio- and video-taped recordings; *thick* inscription or contextual data; observations of individual participants, obtained through the use of observation schedules or other means; the researcher's field notes, diaries and other thick inscription or contextual data; as well as documentary evidence from the research setting and wider context. Once this task has begun and some raw data have been assembled, the research can progress to the next stage. Not all of the raw data sets have to be completed before this stage begins. In ethnographic study, it is almost inevitable that the researcher(s) will be engaged in a number of different stages in the research process simultaneously.

Preparing verbatim transcripts

The second stage in the transformation process is the production of verbatim transcripts from the audio- or video-taped recordings. There are a number of established ways available for doing this but, in the interests of transparency and accountability to the participants, the use of the standard orthographic alphabet is perhaps the most straightforward. An alternative would be a phonetic (ipa) transcript. This can be useful and indeed necessary for selected extracts from the transcripts but its exclusive use will limit dissemination to a technical, expert audience. Specific aspects of the data, including the names of the participants, need to be included as part of the transcription process. Depending on the purpose and focus of the investigation, it may also be useful to include more specific, detailed information on the form, structure and functions of utterances, including features such as pauses, phonology, turn-taking etc. The approach adopted will depend in part on the focus of the investigation and the features that are needed to exemplify and illustrate that.

Coding verbatim transcripts

Codes will then need to be added to the verbatim transcripts. These codes should identify salient features that will contribute towards identifying significant patterns of recurring behaviour. At this stage, features essential to the analysis and interpretation of the data are added to the verbatim transcripts. These features may include the names or identities of the individual speakers; the language(s) or varieties of the interactions; particular linguistic features – for example, discourse topic, self-correcting or a multitude of other features. Once this coding is complete, thick contextual data, field notes and other relevant comments and observations can be added to the transcripts to form *composite data* sets of complementary data sets. These become the bases for subsequent stages of the ethnographic analysis. These stages outlined in phase 3 can take several years, depending on the amount of data to be processed and the number of researchers available to carry out the transcription, codings and analysis. It is useful to have a number of ethnographers working on the data to avoid over-subjectivity of interpretation and to provide the opportunity for discussion between informed colleagues on matters of procedure and inter-pretation. A collegial approach assumes greater significance in ethnographic studies where the researcher intuitions and interpretations are central to data analysis. The essential task here is for the ethnographers to begin to make sense of the diverse data sets collected. There are numerous and diverse ways of approaching this. With very large data sets it may be better to establish a computer corpus of the data. This is optional and, of course, increases the time taken in the process of data handling. However, it saves time later by making it easier and more efficient to handle the analyses of large, complex data sets. Systematic analyses of these data are important and there are now an increasing number of appropriate software packages available for both qual-itative and quantitative approaches to analyses. The aim is to identify recurring patterns of relevant behaviour that allow the ethnographer to abstract the generic structure of the participants' social behaviour in the context(s) observed. The ethnographer's task is to analyse the data with the aim of revealing patterns of behaviour. Once the data have been analysed, and interpreted, the emerging observed behaviour should reveal a generic structure of behaviour, within the observed contexts, that are both familiar and expected. When this is achieved, the research can move onto the fourth, defining element of ethnographic study, reporting and feeding back to the observed community.

Reporting back to the participants

This phase entails presenting the outcomes of the previous stages – the analysed data and emerging generic structures – to the participants and their advisors, representatives and other informed parties. The purpose is to continue the collaborative spirit of the ethnographic approach and to involve the participants and their wider community in discussions of the data. The focus of the collaboration will be the ethnographer's analyses, to date. The aim of this stage is for the ethnographers to seek insights and views from the participants and the wider observed community. The ethnographer is here engaged in gaining feedback, agreement and, hence, validation for the analysis of the observed behaviours. The ultimate goal of ethnography is to describe what happens in social contexts, in order to provide greater understandings of why these things happen, in the particular ways that they do, and hence to arrive at an understanding of what this means for the participants and the observed community. In short, the aim is to understand how people communicate with each other and create shared meanings within their community.

The next section will elaborate this procedural approach by describing an ethnographic study of a preschool setting.

The Box Hill Nursery Project: An ethnolinguistic study

In keeping with the traditions of ethnography, the title of the project is a pseudonym, derived from the name of the nursery school setting where the observations were carried out. It was been named retrospectively, and at various times during the investigation was known by different names, including the Cleveland Project, after the geographical region in the north-east of England where the nursery school was located but which no longer exists. The aim of the project was to describe the linguistic and social behaviour of a group of children during their process of enculturation into the nursery school, their first experience of the formal education system, through a range of macro to micro level descriptions of the children's social behaviour and use of language.

Identifying the research site

Following Milroy's (1987, p.28) advice, the first step was 'to select a community where speakers of the appropriate types might be found'. In this case, the first task was to identify a nursery school that had within its catchment area a significant number of bilingual children who were eligible for nursery education, and who were representative of one of the major community language groups in the UK. Other considerations were also considered important. A research site was sought which met the following criteria:

- There should be a small (between six and ten in number) group of children representing one of the main settled ethnic-minority communities in the UK
- There should be both girls and boys in the group
- The group should be a minority within the nursery
- There should be both bilingual and monolingual adults working in the nursery on a routine basis
- Community-school liaison links should be firmly established

Through consultation with Local Education Authority (LEA) officers a number of potential establishments were identified and contact was made with a number of schools that met the criteria stated above. Preliminary visits were made to each school and discussions were held with school staff, covering issues including practical aspects of their participation in the project and the feasibility of this. Since ethnographic studies require the active involvement of the participants, it was important that the staff in the nursery were sufficiently interested in the investigation to devote time to the project. In retrospect we all underestimated just how much time this was going to take. It was acknowledged that participation in the project would also make demands on other material resources. It is important that staff are given time to consider the implications of participation and hence it is suggested that at least a week or two should be given for them to reach their decision. This precaution prevents staff from feeling pressurised into participating, however unintentional this may be on the part of the researcher(s).

The research setting eventually selected for the project was Box Hill Nursery School, a thirty-nine-place, purpose-built nursery school, attached to a (then) Group 4 primary school, catering for children aged between three and eleven years. There were a number of nursery schools that were all considered to be equally suitable. However, Box Hill was chosen because in addition to meeting all of the stated criteria, the nursery staff were regular attenders at in-service training courses and as a result were informed and keen to be involved for their own professional development. The nursery, the children and staff were all previously unknown to the researcher. Milroy (1987, p.35) stresses the importance of identifying a pre-existing social group with which the researcher has no pre-existing personal ties. All of these factors combined to make Box Hill Nursery a suitable site.

Negotiating with the professionals

Staffing allocation to the nursery was one full-time main professional grade (MPG) teacher who was the head of the nursery; one full-time National Nursery Examination Board (NNEB) qualified person; a nursery assistant, and the equivalent to one full-time bilingual classroom assistant. In practice this meant that two assistants worked on a weekly rota, dividing their time between the adjoining primary school and the nursery unit. Throughout the project one of the writers was working in the nursery on a regular basis as a teacher. Maintaining professional credibility with nursery colleagues with whom she would be working was regarded as important. She was a qualified infant teacher with several years' professional experience. It was agreed that she would work in the nursery, unpaid, for one term before the data collection began. This enabled her to become established as a member of the community in a number of ways including:

- becoming enculturated into the nursery routines
- becoming established as a professional, establishing working relations with the regular nursery staff
- becoming known to the families and within the local community
- being able to trial and refine data collection techniques in the ethnographic tradition

Home visits and family interviews

It was the established practice in Box Hill Nursery to make home visits to potential pupils and their families before the child entered school. This familiarisation procedure provided the ideal opportunity for the next stage of the project. During these visits the aims and procedures of the project were explained to families with the help of the bilingual classroom assistant who acted as an interpreter. For those who expressed an interest, a follow-up visit was arranged. During the second visit, written permission for their child's participation in the project was sought. All information was presented orally in English and the families' own mother tongue by a native speaker of the language, who was known as a member of the local community. Written details of the project and permission forms were given to the families in both the home language and English. Families were asked to return these written permissions to the researcher by post or via the school, as preferred. It was hoped that this would reduce (perceived) pressure to participate in the project. At these informal meetings it was quite usual for a number of female members of the family to be present, including the grandmother(s), sisters, sister(s)-in-law and interested friends and neighbours. A follow-up visit was made to gather additional information on the child who was to start in the nursery school who would be participating in the project. The data collected included:

- the family's perception of their child's linguistic repertoire (families were asked to comment on their child's relative competence in their home language and in English)
- the number of siblings in the family and their ages
- the language(s) spoken in the home between siblings and family members
- the family network of children attending the same school
- the composition of the family (aunts, siblings, grandparents etc.)

These data collected in semi-formal home interviews were the beginnings of the fieldnote diaries that were kept for the duration of the project. Comments, notes and explanations from the nursery staff, as well as the researchers' own, were added to the diaries throughout the project. These observations provided, in part, some of the *thick* inscription data that were integrated into the subsequent analysis of the data. Their function was to supplement the observers' fieldnotes, to help with the retrospective illumination of the data collected.

The setting

As indicated already, the research site, Box Hill Nursery School, drew its pupil intake from a multilingual community. Children attended either a morning or an afternoon session, for five days per week, Monday to Friday. The intake included a homogeneous group of Urdu-Punjabi speakers, one of the major UK community languages. The observed group comprised both boys and girls. This group constituted a significant, but not dominant, group of the nursery intake (twelve of the thirty-nine pupils). Since context is considered integral to ethnographic description, the organisation and structure of the nursery setting is considered to be significant.

The large open-plan room was divided into twenty-eight learning domains, each containing structured learning activities and materials which had been designed to address specific aspects of social, cognitive, physical, moral or aesthetic development of the child. Each learning domain was delineated by the positioning of furniture and 1.2-metre-high screens, thus allowing supervising adults an overview of the room while simultaneously providing maximum seclusion to the children inside the individual domains. This carefully planned learning environment remained unchanged throughout the observation period, with one exception. During the last four weeks of the autumn term two of the domains were merged to accommodate the Christmas tree which became the focal point for a great deal of activity towards the end of the term. The educational rationale underpinning the layout and design of the nursery was to encourage maximum learner autonomy. It was a good, but not showcase, example of the LEA policy. Children were expected to select their learning activity and to be responsible for the collection and storage of all learning materials required for the chosen activities. Materials were available with each domain, stored in labelled units.

Identifying the sample and the participants

The first question for the researcher in relation to sampling is: does size matter? There was no clear-cut answer to this question. The size of the sample is linked to the type of planned study. One seminal study involving relatively small samples includes Labov's New York City project which was based on a sample of eighty-eight speakers. By contrast, Halliday's (1975) description *Learning How To Mean* was based on a study of only one child, his son Nigel.

Piaget's learning theories were based on data from three children, as was Roger Brown's (1973) study of A *First Language*. So small samples can lead to big ideas! However, it is always important to consider the potential difficulties associated with handling the data. Huge amounts of data can be derived from all methodological approaches. Large-scale survey projects can yield vast amounts of data, as can smaller-scale projects that aim to carry out multilevel analyses on the data collected. So it is not necessarily the approach that determines the amount of data. It is important to consider, at the planning stage, what is *manageable* and realistic. For the lone investigator working on a personal project (for example, an academic exercise for a higher degree) there will be resource and time constraints that will set the parameters of what is possible and achievable. This does not necessarily reduce the impact of the findings. Sankoff (1980, p.2) suggests that large samples bring increased data-handling problems with diminishing analytical returns. She suggests that the *selection* of the sample may be more crucial than the quantity collected. It is inevitably the case that only a fraction of the data collected can be selected for analysis. The most important task for the researcher is to make these kinds of choices: to select the data that are to be analysed and those which will not. At each stage in the research process, decisions will need to be made about what is to be discarded and left out and what is to be included and used for detailed analysis. The challenge for the ethnographer is to make judicious choices.

Collecting discourse data

Wearing protective clothing is an established practice in many UK nursery schools. Since ethnographers should aim to disturb the natural interactions as little as possible these garments were used for the data collection. Naturally-occurring discourse data were collected in this case with the use of lightweight Sanyo 6000 Micro-Talk Book micro-cassette recorders. The physical stature of the participants, in part, determined the type of recording apparatus used. These machines weighed 145 grammes when loaded with batteries and tape. A lapel microphone with its lead and wirings was sewn into the lining of the protective clothing worn by the children. The microphone with its range of five metres (fifteen feet), allowed for data to be collected from the child wearing the jacket, their fellow discourse participants, together with some of the linguistic environment of the classroom, as experienced by the child. Continuous audio-taped recordings of one hour were made. These were chosen in preference to the radio-microphones used by Tizard and Hughes (1984) and the time-sampling methods of Wells (1985). This approach was considered more appropriate for ethnographic study for the following reasons:

- they provided an instantaneous record of the linguistic events
- the method allowed for unlimited playback of the recordings, thus ensuring maximum access to the original data for transcription, analysis and discussion

- it was a less obtrusive method of data collection, allowing the unfettered movement of the children both indoors and outside

Collecting thick contextual data using observation schedules

In keeping with the tradition of ethnography the linguistic data were complemented by thick contextual observations. It is the expectation that ways of gathering data for ethnographic studies will be generated in the field and designed specifically to match the participants under investigation. However, it is sometimes useful to consider those used by other researchers as a starting point. These can then be trialled and refined to meet the need of the new investigation. In this case, observation schedules used in previous research were considered and two were trialled before the final version was achieved. The observation schedule used by Sylva *et al.* (1980) was considered inappropriate because this schedule comprised a relatively large number of closed categories of behaviour. It was therefore considered to be too inflexible to record the actual behaviour of the children in this study.

A more open-ended Observation Schedule Version 1 was based on the one devised by Tough (1976) for individual child observations. In light of the need to amalgamate thick data with discourse data, amendments were made and Observation Schedule Version 2 was eventually trialled. This too was refined (Thompson, 1999, pp.81–2). This final version incorporated a number of features specific for the researchers. To help with the amalgamation of data collected it was decided to include space where data from the contextual observations and the fieldwork diaries could be brought together. Hence the Box Hill Nursery Observation Schedule included space for details such as the time of the observation; the activity in which the observed child was engaged; the other participants present at the activity, including adults and teachers; and any other points considered to be of note or interest. The fieldwork diary notes were made at the end of each nursery session, in collaboration with the nursery teachers, workers and helpers and any other adults present, including parents or visitors to the nursery. These acted as an aide-mémoire during the later analyses, some of which took place some years after the observations. The Box Hill Nursery Observation Schedule was also used during the data analysis phase of the project when further information, from other sources was added. This included information to facilitate with the retrieval of data for further scrutiny, like the number reading on the tape recorder and transcriber, as well as details of the language used by individuals for specific interactions.

Ethnographic observations have to be prolonged and repeated. As noted, each period of observation lasted one hour and a total of twelve observations were carried out for each child during the first year in the nursery school. Each child was observed on the first day in the nursery school and then on eleven subsequent occasions. These observations and recordings yielded a total of twelve hours of naturally-occurring, audio-taped discourse data for each child, together with twelve contextual observations, as well as an amount of documentary data from the school and home contexts. The primary function of the researcher is to make sound judgements and this involves making choices. The best available option is to ensure that these choices are as fully informed as current thinking allows. There is of course always scope for development. Having got thus far with an ethnographic approach is only the beginning! The analyses of the data take much longer to complete!

Approaches to ethnographic data analysis

It should be emphasised that the final reports, research papers and books reporting on ethnographic studies that are eventually published appear as tidy accounts that belie the unwieldy data sets which they report. This should not be construed as misrepresenting the data or of being selective with the evidence. Instead it should be seen as part of the ethnographer's task to *select* that which is noteworthy and representative, and to discard judiciously that which is not. Ethnographers are not alone among researchers in the quest to present their evidence and research findings in more accessible forms. However, they do have a particular responsibility to their participants to do this. Hence ethnographers should consider ways of reporting their findings that are both rigorous and simultaneously accessible to a wider audience than the conventional audience of peer group researchers. This is partly because the reporting back to participants is central to ethnography but also because the ways in which data are presented go beyond the merely representational. They also reflect the researcher's view of the world they have observed and their construction of it. The Box Hill Nursery Project exemplified ways of reporting data which adhere to the principle of feeding back, in accessible forms, to those who have contributed the data.

Research focus: Asking an obvious question

The first level of the data analysis for the Box Hill Nursery Project aimed to answer a common question, frequently asked by parents of their children, 'what did you do at school today?'. Standing in an emptying classroom at the end of an infant school day one hears this question asked as many times as there are children in the class. The replies vary, but only slightly. If asked, the teacher's response to that question might be to cite any of the carefully planned and structured activities that had been prepared for the children throughout the day, and then add play time, lunch time, music, art, craft, PE or games as well. However, the usual response from the children is a shrug, grimace or the mundane, 'Nothing much!' How can our experiences be so at variance? One way to resolve the difference is to observe and find out exactly how each child did spend time in the classroom. There are a number of observational studies which have aimed at providing a descriptive analysis of young children's learning experiences (for example, Bennett 1976; Sylva *et al.* 1980; Tizard and

Hughes 1984 and Tizard *et al.* 1988). Although they differ in their aims and foci these studies all share the view that the amount of time an individual child spends on a learning activity is a significant factor in the learning processes that are taking place. This phenomenon has come to be known as *time-on-task* (Bennett 1976). The findings of time-on-task analyses have conventionally been reported as graphs with the time plotted along one and the tasks or activities along the other. Thompson (1999, chapter 5) is just one example of this approach.

Using graphs to report findings

The time-on-task analysis is a useful quantitative structure from which to form impressions of children's experience of school. However, there are aspects of detail that it is not possible to include in this level of data analysis. These details can be important because they may provide a greater understanding of the observed behaviours. The cognitive complexity of specific learning tasks has been suggested by Bennett (1976) and Sylva *et al.* (1980) as one reason for the sustained periods of time spent on a task by individual learners. If cognitive complexity were the crucial factor, one would expect to find a pattern to emerge in the range of tasks selected. However, this is not always the case. Further, the Box Hill Nursery project found diverse patterns of tasks for the individual learners. Some of the twenty-six learning activities in the nursery remained unvisited and occasionally a child would return to a particular task (Thompson 1999). These details are not so easy to report in graphs and yet they are precisely the kind of details that may interest parents and teachers. Also time-on-task analyses leave one very important detail unexplored. Why is it that children differ in the duration of time spent on the same task(s)? What are the factors that influence the time individuals spend on selected learning activities? It is precisely these questions that educational researchers need to explore if we are to come closer to understanding the motivations of young learners and the experiences from which they can derive immediate (social and cognitive) gains – and even pleasure! This kind of information cannot be included in a graph. Hence reporting findings as graphs have limitations. To some extent this could be overcome with the use of colour graphics or shadings.

Also, though reporting data in this way is informative, the graphs do not capture the essence of the classroom, the spirit of the young participants or the ways in which these tasks on which they spent their time were linked. Nor do they show the order in which the child engaged in the chosen activities. In the Box Hill Nursery project this information was reported by tracking each child's movements (Thompson 1999, chapter 6).

Using maps for tracking movement

Contextual data are the very essence of ethnographic investigation. Presenting the data as maps combines what Geertz (1975) refers to as the *thick*, contextual data. These include aspects of detail like the nursery setting and the organisation of the people and furniture within that setting with the movements of the observed participant, Ishtiaq, around the nursery. Presenting contextual data as maps demonstrates the interdependence of language, what is said, with an individual's behaviour, what they do, within the nursery context. By combining what is said with what is done, the activity, in this way we are able to provide a more detailed description of the children's behaviour. A map also captures more authentically the frenzy of movement and the buzz of activity that characterises life in nursery classrooms. Maps are also more reader-friendly. Graphic representation is increasingly used in all kinds of texts for reporting information, from academic scientific papers to information that we receive with the household bills. When shown the maps of their child's activity, parents get not just a picture of their child's nursery day but also a flavour of the variety, diversity and complexity of that experience. The maps enhance the time-on-task data presented as graphs because they contain further information about each of the informants, including:

- the order in which each learning activity or domain was visited
- the period of time to the nearest minute spent in each domain
- a summary of the activities in which the informant was engaged
- a categorisation of each activity.

The maps also aim to capture something of the essence of the child's movements around the nursery in a more naturalistic way than can be achieved through the static representation of graphs. Contrast, for example, the methods used here with the formal and quantitative analyses used for structured observation in Chapter 7.

Different research paradigms suggest different philosophies and also offer different ways of reporting findings. When deciding on their research focus, researchers are also making other decisions. This is not merely the simple dichotomy between qualitative and quantitative approaches. It is a more complex balancing act whereby the researcher struggles to combine a variety of conflicting priorities. It is important that the chosen paradigm complements the research focus and is compatible with the researcher's own values and beliefs. There should run, almost invisibly, through the research, an inter-connecting silver thread that joins the aims of the investigation to the method-ology, which in turn links with the ways and means of data collection and analyses and which is still just perceptively evident in the interpretation and synthesis of the data. This interconnection should provide coherence, connecting all stages in the research project both philosophically and logically. This silver thread of connectivity is *de rigueur*. Inherent within research paradigms are established conventions for collecting and reporting the data and the findings. These need to be made explicit for those new and unfamiliar with the established conventions, so that the researcher's views are more transparent. In the next section we shall discuss other approaches to analyses that are particularly appropriate for ethnographic studies.

Social network analysis

The second level of analysis from the Box Hill Nursery Project combined complementary data sets of inscription data with the audio-taped recordings to provide a social network analysis. This is an established paradigm within sociolinguistics and anthropology. It was originally introduced by Barnes (1954) to describe an order of social relationship that he considered to be important for understanding the behaviour of the inhabitants of the Norwegian village of Bremnes. It has been defined by Milroy (1980, p.174) as 'quite simply ... the informal social relationships contracted by an individual'. Social network analysis is appropriate for both qualitative and quantitative analyses. Milroy (1980, p.48) outlines a six-point scale indexed from 0 to 5 for recording contacts quantitatively. By comparison Gal (1979) uses a much more straight-forward measure based on the actual number of contacts a speaker makes within a given observation period. These analyses can be reported as diagrams (c.f. Thompson 1999) or as tabulations (c.f. Li Wei 1994).

Ethnographers sometimes need to move beyond the established ways of doing things and devise new approaches that are more appropriate for their current investigation. The Box Hill Nursery Project complemented time-on-task analyses with social network analyses. However, the types of social ties observed in the nursery were different from those observed by Barnes, Milroy, Gal and others when observing adults in less confined communities. Hence it was necessary to devise a different way of reporting the social networks observed. Thompson (1999) reports two particular types of social networks that were identified from the observations of the children in the nursery. The first are the *dense friendship networks,* characterised by children choosing to interact, and the second are the *loose pupil networks,* where the children came together as pupils for the purpose of instruction or other classroom activity. The contacts within each network remained relatively stable while the contact between the two remained separate. The task was, therefore, to find a means of portraying the two types of contacts observed and to include in the diagrammatic representation the unique identifying features. When observation reveals characteristics previously unreported, the researcher has to respond by finding new ways of reporting.

Diagrammatical ways of reporting findings can make the information more accessible to a wider group of non-specialist readers. This is an important consideration for ethnographers who are devising ways of reporting back to audiences beyond the conventional research community. But the significance of the research method is more than a mere professional preference. In their analysis of ethnicity and friendship patterns observed among schoolchildren aged between 7 and 11, Denscombe et al. (1993, p.142) note the contrast in findings yielded from two different methodological approaches: sociometric tests using the Cresswell Index and ethnographic observations. They note: 'while there is no inherent contradiction between ethnographic research and the quantification of data, there are complexities vital to our understanding of inter-ethnic friendship patterns which exclusive reliance on quantitative research methods cannot hope to unravel'.

Perhaps the greatest challenge for researchers undertaking ethnographic observations of young children is: *what should we tell the children*? How can ethnographers involve very young informants in the interpretation of the data that they have collected from them, and how do they give feedback on their findings to the informants in ways which are accessible and meaningful? The Box Hill Nursery Project found photographs and the children's tape recordings a useful and even entertaining way of providing feedback to the children, parents and teachers.

In summary, it is important to emphasise that ethnography is only an approach to researching early childhood and it is easy to understand why there are fewer studies in this tradition than in other approaches. Generally, ethnographers approach their tasks in ways that differ from researchers using other methodologies, as this introduction from Brice-Heath (1983, p.19) illustrates. Her book begins:

> A quiet early morning fog shrouds rolling hills blanketed by pine-green strands of timber, patched with fields of red clay. As the sun rises and burns off the fog, the blue sky is feathered with smoke let go from chimney stacks of textile mills: this is the Piedmont of the Carolinas.

It is inevitable that future researchers will seek out a model of practice for their studies. The following section outlines what we can term a principled approach to ethnographic study.

Ethnography: A procedural process for a principled approach

At this point, we should like to propose the following framework as a principled approach for ethnographic studies.

- Ethnographic observation focuses on human behaviour.
- The people (participants) are observed as they go about their everyday lives, doing the things that they ordinarily do.
- During the process of observation the ethnographer should aim to be as unobtrusive as is humanly possible.
- Ethnographic observations are contextualised within wider social, cultural, political and economic settings.
- Ethnographic observations should be prolonged and repeated.
- The instruments for eliciting data are generated during the field work in the research setting.
- Hypotheses and research questions emerge and become refined as the study progresses.

- The ethnographer needs to capture human activity as data. Any form of legal technical device which facilitates this – for example, audio-tapes and video-tapes – that are acceptable to the participants and which permit the cultural knowledge of the participants to unfold naturally, should be used.
- The insiders' view of their world is brought out from the data by inferences that describe their observed behaviour(s).
- A major task for the ethnographer is to understand what sociocultural knowledge participants bring to, and generate within, the social settings that they create together.
- Ethnographers should involve the participants in all stages of the research, especially the interpretation of the data.
- Ethnographers should report their observations, analyses and insights to the participants.
- Ethnographic observation should inform the participants about their ways of being and help them to understand themselves better. Ethnography thus makes explicit to a community, that which they already know implicitly. It is through this process of moving from implicit to explicit knowledge that the observed communities come to understand themselves and their collective behaviour in more depth and detail.

Summary

There are two broad approaches to educational research: macro surveys that identify general patterns and trends and micro projects that address details. If you want to know *what?* the macro studies may be appropriate. If you want to know *why?* or *how?* then a micro study is. These approaches are frequently being presented as alternatives or competitors. It makes more sense to view them as *complementary*. Macro studies identify trends and can monitor changes. However, they are not able to pinpoint the causes or reasons for these changes. These matters of detail are best obtained through micro studies of specific groups. The (re)current debates in early years' studies are linked in part to those taking place within the educational research community more generally – namely, researchers' tendency to be compartmentalised. Findings from macro and micro studies are rarely put together in a complementary way. Yet they should be. Macro studies can identify the big issues that are of interest to public policy-makers and educators. Micro studies can address aspects of details. Both are necessary and both are different. In an earlier chapter the writers posed the question: is it possible to mix paradigms? In this chapter the writers hope that they have demonstrated some of the ways in which methods can be combined in a beneficial way, to provide complementary insights. Combined research methods have the advantage of providing triangulation through their differing perspectives.

The last decade has seen a burgeoning of research in early years and education generally. Despite this, as the previous chapter has shown, no specific education paradigm is emerging. Each new piece of research remains self-contained and generally unlinked to previous work. The result is that while each individual piece of research may be sound in its own right, it is not directly contributing to a general theory of education or to learning in early childhood. Perhaps the challenge for research in the next decade is to address the fundamental questions, including: How do young children learn? What role do adults, particularly teachers, play in that learning? Early years researchers should perhaps do more than merely locate their research within educational settings. Perhaps it is time to consider the wider aspects of how children learn in both educational and other settings. Ironically, this will require educational researchers going beyond schools, classrooms and places of formal education to informal settings. The need for researching education has never been stronger. The need for coherent theories of learning (and teaching) founded in well-formulated research is now essential. The question is: where is this initiative to come from? University departments and schools of education are fettered through their engagement in teacher training by OFSTED and the TTA. More of the national research budget for higher education is to be distributed by TTA and although this is an ideal opportunity to engage more classroom practitioners in research, it seems likely that the projects funded will need to be achieved and results reported be set within a very narrow time span and with a very specific focus. Where they do flourish it is likely that these projects will have to be carried out on a part-time basis by teachers who are facing an increasing workload with the introduction of baseline assessments in reception classes and the implementation of the DfEE new foundation curriculum blueprint. It is therefore not surprising that the current funding arrangements will tend to favour particular paradigms. Ethnographic studies lasting several years, like Shirley Brice-Heath's (1983) and the Box Hill Nursery Project reported here, would not be possible to complete within six months. The next decade will be a difficult time for early years researchers, the majority of whom are women. It has been established practice for many of us to gain our research training while registered as students reading for higher degrees that have a strong core of taught courses. University departments of education have traditionally remained fairly autonomous in the content, design and scope of the higher degrees that they offer. This may be about to change. In 1998, the TTA secured from the HEFCE responsibility for those taught courses which relate to the in-service training of teachers. This is subjecting universities who offer such courses to external audit by the TTA, in the same way that initial teacher training courses are. If the same skills/competence approach to the education and profession preparation of teachers is applied to post-experience awards, including higher degrees, advanced diplomas and certificates etc. it seems unlikely that the research training and focus provided by these current courses will survive. If this does happen, then the funding and autonomy necessary for practising teachers to engage in meaningful research may be in jeopardy and university departments of education may fail to influence future policy and practice.

Part IV

Current policy, perspectives and practice in the field

9 Roles, responsibilities and relationships

When Ann Phoenix (Phoenix *et al.* 1991) was investigating the lives of teenage mothers, she realised that, despite all her efforts to work sensitively with these very young women, there were times when their participation in the research was lost through difficulties she had not been in a position to predict. In one case, interviewing a young mother living in her parent's council flat, where the walls were so thin it was possible for the parents to hear their discussion, Ann Phoenix was aware that she could have caused pain to the whole family because she asked if the interviewee would really like to have her own home.

In another example, this time from a research student project, Elaine Herbert (unpublished – personal communication) interviewed fathers of children born with recognisable learning difficulties. She had already carried out a study involving mothers of children with Down's Syndrome and this had made her aware of the fathers' shadowy presence, their absenting themselves from interviews, despite there having been no indication she wished to interview mothers only and despite her arranging to visit homes during the evening. From the point of view of roles, responsibilities and relationships, Elaine's experiences interviewing fathers made all of us question the boundary between therapy and research, asking: where does a researcher's responsibility to participants end? For many of the fathers said to Elaine that they were telling her about aspects of their lives and their feelings which they had not shared with anyone before – including their wives. Thus, despite knowing that her research demanded even greater than usual sensitivity, Elaine, like Ann Phoenix, recognised that researchers need to be clear about their roles and the responsibilities towards the *people* involved – including *themselves* – and to the *research process*.

The majority of research reports, whether articles in journals, books or reports to funding bodies, leave readers to glean whatever they can about the process of the research in terms of the roles, responsibilities and relationships the researcher (or researchers) have had during the life of a project. In this chapter we will unravel aspects of those roles, responsibilities and relationships, highlighting issues of which anyone undertaking research needs to be both aware and sensitive.

As we have pointed out in Chapter 2, research on children under five used to be the domain of developmental psychologists and many of the teams for the large-scale projects of the 1970s and early 1980s were headed by psychologists (see, for example, Tizard 1974a; Hutt *et al.* 1989). Naturally, research on infants and young children is still a key area for developmental psychologists but many more researchers in this field in the UK are now current or former early-childhood educators. Further, with the new government initiatives requiring local authorities to set up multi-agency, multi-professional Early Years Development and Childcare Partnerships to foster higher levels of, as well as improvements in, provision for under fives, there has also been an increase in statistical research by local authority officials. In addition, some extremely useful research is currently carried out, or commissioned by, organisations such as teachers' unions (e.g. Barrett 1986; Campbell and Neill 1992; Moyles and Suschitzky 1997; Stainton and Evans 1999).

What this means is that there is a multiplicity of research being carried out for a multiplicity of purposes and by people with varied experience of young children and early education and care. In some cases, there have been examples of research being deliberately commissioned of agencies without experience in the field because they were thought to come to the issues 'without any baggage'. Unfortunately, it is unlikely anyone has no baggage at all in relation to early childhood and the expectations, assumptions and prejudices which can influence the research process. If researchers have no knowledge about a field they can end up taking so long to understand it in more than a superficial way that they are unable to 'hit the ground running'. On the other hand, teams which include colleagues without 'insider knowledge' can be especially incisive because an 'outsider' will not accept the 'taken-for-granted' aspects of the research field.

This chapter approaches the discussion of roles, responsibilities and relationships in connection with three main areas – people, process and self. Each of these three areas is explored firstly in relation to all researchers, whether working alone or in a team, and secondly in relation to the added implications for team research.

Roles, responsibilities and relationships: People

Participants and others

In taking on the role of a researcher one is usually expected to be knowledgeable about the research area and the approaches being used. This can be quite disconcerting for novice researchers, such as research students, for they are learning by doing, by being involved in the process of research. However, all researchers are actually steeped in a continual learning process and no two projects in education settings will be identical, even those which set out as replications of previous research, because of changes in time and contexts.

Nevertheless, a researcher needs a clear idea of what is going to happen when they visit a research site, what they are hoping to see or hear about. In his account of the earliest phase in his doctoral research, Stephen Ball (1984) recounts his initial visits to his research site and how he came to realise he would need to make decisions about a systematic way of collecting data. Prior to this he had spent time in open-minded observations. In most cases, researchers in early childhood settings have quite considerable knowledge of the settings where their research will be carried out. It is quite difficult to open their minds enough to clear them of existing knowledge and assumptions, which they need to do in order to be able to acknowledge that they are indeed making assumptions, while on the other hand being able to ask appropriate research questions and choose appropriate methods. Like Stephen Ball, early years researchers are likely to be asked by people at the site what their research is about and why and how they are conducting that particular project – all questions to which those who will be involved are entitled to answers.

Even research which does not involve participants but which gathers its data from documents means that the researcher must access those documents and thus it will be through other people's cooperation that they will be granted that access, in libraries, book shops and archives. Here the researcher has the responsibility to offer as much information as possible to help in the search for appropriate documents and on accessing them, to use them respectfully and according to any rules which govern their use, for example not copying from or plagiarising a thesis borrowed through the inter-library loan system. The aspect of relationships in this case includes trying to develop positive working relationships with the librarian, book seller, or archivist.

Research which includes fieldwork demanding interactions with other people as one or more of the modes of enquiry is naturally much more complex, because each human being involved will not only have their own history and expectations of researchers but also their own perceptions of the particular researcher and of the project focus and approaches.

Charmian Davie (Davie *et al.* 1984) used to tell a story about an event which occurred during one of her two-hour-long observations of four-year-olds, when a parent and child she was observing went shopping. Charmian wandered into a supermarket in pursuit of her 'target child' still armed with clipboard and stop-watch. The staff of the supermarket decided she was a time-and-motion officer and downed tools, thus closing the shop. It took some time to convince them that she was not observing them but the small child, such behaviour being seen as rather strange. We learn from examples like this that even when we think we have explained fully to those from whom we wish to gather information, other people's misunderstandings can impact upon the work.

The major responsibilities researchers have in relation to participants are that they will do no harm, that they will treat those who agree to participate with respect, that they will be trustworthy and that they will maintain confidentiality and anonymity if this has been agreed (some research may need to use real names because of a person's position and this must be made absolutely clear at the outset, before their engagement with the project). In particular, in research involving children, researchers need to gain permission of parents, from educators too if the research is to occur within their settings and, as far as is possible, from the children themselves. As Pauline Evans and Mary Fuller (1996: p.17) point out,

> it is unethical to subject participants to experiences which might be stressful or promote anxiety. Such situations might easily arise whilst interviewing young children, due to the unequal balance of power between the adult interviewer and the child.

Their solution to this, and to the problem of children's suggestibility in order to please adults, involved role play and the use of play telephones wired up to a four-track tape recorder so that both child and interviewer could be made audible on playback. The children were made fully aware of the tape recorder and were able to choose – or not – to participate. In this situation a child might choose to speak on the phone but could hang up at any point and so curtail the interview – the power was placed in the children's hands.

In a similar way, research with babies in day nurseries, carried out by Peter Elfer and Dorothy Selleck (2000), explored the ways in which both researchers and staff could use the babies' behavioural signals as indications that they were uncomfortable with what was happening.

Sometimes parents or staff may refuse, or later remove, permission for a child to be involved in a research project and sometimes older children, when asked, will not consent to aspects of the research, for example being tape-recorded during an interview. Margaret O'Brien *et al.* (1996) experienced both children refusing to be recorded and head teachers withdrawing pupils aged between seven and ten from a project about children's constructions of family, because the children concerned were at the time experiencing family difficulties. Although this would mean that the research would fail to capture important and difficult phases which occur in many children's lives, the teachers rightly felt that they must protect those children from both intrusion and the pain the research could have caused.

Increasingly, researchers are aware that not only do they need to provide participants with a written outline of the research and forms on which to indicate their consent to participate – or allow their child to participate – they also provide the participants with opportunities to review data collected and correct any errors. For example, they are given transcripts of interviews or notes on observations which have been followed by discussions based on those observations (or on video recordings). Some researchers feel that they must be completely open about the aims of the research, while others argue that there are times when research on particularly sensitive issues can be described in less explicit terms so as not to warn certain respondents of the nature of the project. For example, if a researcher were exploring racism among the echelons of power in a schooling system, some argue that to fully explain the focus to those elite being interviewed would destroy the research and so not provide evidence of a need to change the situation. Individual researchers must decide for themselves which of these two positions they believe they should take up.

Clearly there are particular areas of research where the power of the researcher needs to be at the very least recognised and strategies for dealing with imbalances sought. In Chapter 10 we discuss the issues involved in research involving children and other groups that should also be acknowledged as potentially vulnerable – for example, some parents, particularly those from ethnic and linguistic minorities, or from educationally disadvantaged groups, may feel threatened by the researcher or the research process.

Gatekeepers

In the example above where the head teacher withdrew certain children from a project, the head was behaving as a *gatekeeper*. In most projects there will be gatekeepers through whom the researcher must gain access to research information, access to documents and access to people. In the past, most educational researchers required not only the permission of the head teacher of a school or nursery, but prior to this, if the nursery was administered by a local authority, also the permission of the director of education or social services for the area. Nowadays, it is the heads and members of governing bodies or management committees whose permission is vital, but most researchers send letters informing local authority officials of their involvement as a matter of courtesy.

There are occasions when gatekeepers in the form of ethics committees hold up a piece of research because they wish to be assured that all ethical aspects have been taken into account by the researcher and that committee members are happy with the researcher's competence in this area. For this reason it is important to include a sound exploration of ethical issues related to the project's work at the proposal stage, together with an exposition of how they will be surmounted.

Funding bodies

Obviously all agencies which fund research, whether the project is large or small scale, wish to be assured of the trustworthiness of the person in whom they have invested. They expect the person in whom they have invested to be competent, conscientious and careful in carrying out the project they have agreed to fund. In return, they will normally expect that the agency will be acknowledged in any publications and that they will receive reports as agreed by their terms at the outset.

In some cases there may be departures from this more open relationship between funding bodies and researchers. In particular, some government agencies expect a complete embargo on any dissemination of the results of the research until permission for such a process of informing the public has been granted. In work for central government departments and agencies this rule is generally clear from the beginning but in some cases where work is commissioned by local government bodies, it is the researcher's responsibility to discuss and clarify their position regarding the ownership of data and rights to publication. Some local authorities will be aware of exposing their workers to potential criticism if a research project finds aspects of practice – or policy – which need improvement. Yet without research or evaluation studies, such potential improvements may not be identified. Thus providers of services who have put themselves up, or been put up, for external scrutiny are bravely attempting to find ways to improve what they do. Where such work is made public, the people involved deserve praise, not ridicule or criticism, at least if they pursue the improvements recommended by the researchers or evaluators.

One example of an authority which allowed its work to be exposed in this way was Leeds, when Robin Alexander's (1992) evaluation of the PNP (Primary Needs Programme) provided rich material for both the teachers and advisers in Leeds, as well as for the rest of the field, for many could identify with the principles and practices reported.

Clearly, most research is funded either because a proposal is considered of sufficient merit to warrant investment – this would be the case where research students receive bursaries from colleges, universities and bodies such as the ESRC or because an organisation has identified an area of need for information, perhaps in order to maximise future funding for such services. An example of this type of research would be Department of Health or DfEE funding research into the efficacy or practices of nurseries and preschools (e.g. Brophy *et al.* 1992).

Where an experienced researcher seeks funding from a charity or an agency such as the Nuffield or Leverhulme Foundation, again, as with the student projects, funding would only be granted when peer review has judged the proposal and the lead researcher to merit such investment.

One of the issues which exercises researchers in relation to funding from external agencies is that of control. We have already pointed out that some agencies forbid the dissemination of findings to the field or to the press without their permission. As a result some researchers are wary that they will be unable to act independently, that some of their data may fail to see the light of day, and that they may find themselves simply being used to produce findings which will endorse particular beliefs or policies.

This discussion was taken up by David Halpin and Barry Troyna (1994) in their book, *Researching Education Policy*. They came to the conclusion that much of the research being commissioned by central government at that time was merely of the type in which the researchers were being required to find ways to 'tweak' or 'tinker with' the system as prescribed. They lamented the fact that funding was targeted away from people whose work would address the system itself in a more radical way and possibly provide alternatives to the system itself as outcomes of their findings. However, within the same volume, Bob Burgess argues that it is possible to accept funding for the project required by the agency concerned and to conduct other more visionary projects at the same time. This is a way of working which is reminiscent of how the great artists must have had to operate in order to produce works demanded by their employers, since the employment gave them their living and allowed them the freedom to paint or compose those works they themselves felt inspired to produce – a kind of 'Mozart/Titian effect' (David 1998).

Research students and supervisors

One relationship in particular which involves working together in ways that can often be mutually beneficial and mean both parties learn from each other is that of research student and supervisor. Here the role is at first one in which the supervisor is likely to be the more knowledgeable but by the end of the period of study the student will be an expert on their own specialism and the supervisor will have learnt much during the period they have shared the project.

Both have a responsibility towards each other. The supervisor should act as an adviser and as a person who challenges the student's thinking and choice of approaches – but in ways which enable rather than disable the student! Few research students sail through their period of study unscathed by doubt and misgivings about their work. One of the supervisor's roles therefore is to be a support at such times, an encourager, while also being a critical friend.

The student's responsibility, on the other hand, involves working rigorously and assiduously towards completion, arranging convenient times for tutorials and rarely demanding to see the supervisor without a prior appointment – in other words, there is a responsibility to respect the supervisor's own time and other work commitments. Being clear with each other about expectations and work to be completed, setting reasonable deadlines and trying hard to stick to them (both for writing and reading parts of the thesis), where appropriate co-presenting papers at conferences or in co-authoring articles for publication, are all examples of positive supervisor-supervisee relationships. Delamont *et al.* (1997) found that what many supervisors have difficulty with is getting the balance right between heavy-handed dominance and 'hands-off' neglect. Each student has individual needs, both professionally and personally. It takes time to know a student well enough to be in a position to tell when they are struggling and when they need challenging, for by this stage in their academic lives few will be as open as small children in expressing their feelings of frustration or even pride and elation.

This core relationship also involves additional relationships for both supervisee and supervisor – with other supervisors or chairs of supervisory panels, with examiners, and sometimes with academics in the same or other institutions who may be researching similar areas to that of the student and who may be asked to give advice or discuss issues. Supervisors will sometimes feel it is their responsibility to warn their students to be somewhat reticent about aspects of their research and especially their findings until after they have completed their thesis and possibly until after publication in book and article forms, for fear of the odd 'academic vulture'. Of course it has been known for the 'odd academic vulture' to be the student's own supervisor, while outsiders have freely offered help!

Another area in which supervisors may feel they must protect their students is during their presentations at research conferences. Fortunately most of the sessions at early years conferences, whether regional, national or international, are very supportive even when challenging – the most useful type of critical friends. However, at some conferences there may be a more macho ethos and supervisors therefore have the responsibility to either prepare or 'be there' for their student.

Family and friends

One's responsibility to one's colleagues (other students and researchers), in a personal sense, is debatable – that is, how much one feels obliged to offer support, guidance or other kinds of help to one's colleagues will depend on one's values and viewpoint. However, a collegial way of working in research, where support is actually reciprocal, could be argued to be more beneficial than one in which competition and aggressive rivalry prevents collaboration, mentoring and the true education of the next generation of researchers.

Similarly, since family and friends are often sources of emotional support, they too require researchers to be sensitive to their needs. Research can be extremely demanding work and it can occupy the mind to such an extent that personal relationships can be neglected. Maintaining a balance, ensuring – for one's own health as well as that of others and our relationships with them – that we switch off sometimes and are really 'present' in the time we spend with family and friends, is essential.

One of us recalls telling a daughter home from university for a vacation that we would go out shortly, after a piece of work was finished, with: 'I'll be back (*from my study*) in five minutes.' The reply was salutary: 'That will be on your tombstone, Mum: I'll be back in five minutes.'

Team research

In addition to the aspects mentioned above which apply equally to individual as to team research, there are additional roles, responsibilities and relationships involved when a project team is being, or has been, set up.

It is likely that team research is being funded by an external agency – thus the whole team will need to bear in mind the implications of the requirements laid on them by that agency. Also, there will be deadlines which apply to the research funders' need for information, issues relating to dissemination and recognition for the funding through acknowledgements on all publications.

The project director will usually have written the original proposal. Although in reality the original proposal may not be a focus of an early team meeting, because of time constraints, discussion of the proposal can be a useful learning device for the whole team. Firstly, it can help everyone understand the project better, but also it is an important part of induction into research design and strategy, since the team is likely to include younger colleagues who may be the directors of the future.

The director will, in most cases, select the team members, either from among the colleagues in their institution, or through advertising and interviewing candidates. Throughout, it is therefore their responsibility, in conjunction with others in their institutions (such as personnel officers), to ensure that equal opportunities policies and legislation are properly followed.

In addition to other researchers, the team will probably include a project secretary – again, it is a responsibility to ensure that equal opportunities policies and laws are enacted and that the secretary is kept informed of the project's stages and his or her own responsibilities. Remembering that the secretary works only part of the time on a project is another point for teams to recognise, and to be explicit and sensitive about the workload they ask their secretary to undertake.

Most projects these days will also involve the support of technicians and computer or statistical advisers. Again, remembering the extent and varied nature of their continuing jobs and recognising that they may work only briefly with the project team means that organisation of time and duties needs to be both tight and respectful.

How a team gels together, how they work out any disagreements, may depend to some extent on the director, who sets the tone and provides guidance on different responsibilities for the work to be done. Where disputes occur between team members, whether overt or covert, they can affect the work of the project, so at times a director may need to intervene, or to work out a way of separating the duties of those involved for a time. The frequency of team meetings, together with the tone and purpose of them, and the extent to which the team director's other duties allow them time to succour the team, can also influence how well the work is conducted.

There is, of course, the possibility that a team member disagrees with the project director about some aspect of the research process, since it is most important that the ways in which one conducts research are in accordance with one's own values and philosophy. For example, although failing to articulate the problem at the time, one of us, some twenty-odd years ago, was frustrated by working for a project director who believed in positivistic approaches and who selected research methods which did not take account of any 'inner life' or cultural meanings of those children being observed. In a case like this, members of a research team may believe one can operate within only one paradigm at a time – either positivist, interpretive, critical or postmodern. Furthermore, some years ago using both quantitative and qualitative approaches would have been seen as a betrayal by one 'camp' or another. Resolving difficulties of this nature between members of a team is probably impossible, so providing sufficient information for an applicant to judge their suitability for work on a project is essential. At the same time, it would be naïve to assume that colleagues working as contract researchers have much choice, so it is probable that they will either not reveal their own views, or they will reveal them later and possibly provoke useful discussion (depending on how their ideas are handled and how much time there is for this). The question of whether having a team member who is not wholeheartedly convinced about the project's approaches will have a negative impact on participants and findings is a moot point.

Roles, responsibilities and relationships: The research process

Perhaps the most significant aspect concerning responsibility to the research process is the integrity of the researcher. One project which results in research or researchers having a bad name in their field can influence the willingness of practitioners, policy-makers and parents to be involved. For this reason, the ethical considerations mentioned earlier (and in Chapter 10) are of paramount importance.

In addition to paying attention to ethical guidelines and behaving sensitively towards participants, respect for 'the truth' in the sense of giving an unbiased account of one's findings, carrying out the research to the best of one's ability and in 'good faith' means checking the authenticity – that is, the relevance – of one's findings. It also means that subsequently one needs to write up the research in appropriate ways, according to audience. Most importantly, researchers are expected to tell the truth as they have witnessed it and not to fabricate results.

One aspect of research planning and reporting which signifies work of a higher quality is the inclusion of theorising. The ability to use existing theories, to create conceptual frameworks which synthesise theories or which develop new theory based on findings, is a mark of greater intellectual functioning than is work which is purely pragmatic. Thus one of the key roles of a researcher is that of theorist. What often passes unrecognised, however, is the fact that as human beings we devote much of our time to theorising, because we speculate about people and events in order to try to make sense of our lives.

In the nurseries of Reggio Emilia, the staff, when asked whose theories underpin their work, respond by saying it is their own theories which provide their conceptual frameworks for action – although these often develop through consideration of the 'grand theories' of psychologists like Piaget and Vygotsky (Dahlberg 1998).

In her review of the papers contributing to Ruddock and McIntyre's (1998) *Challenges for Educational Research,* Rosemary Deem points out the contributions feminist researchers have made to the field, particularly in relation to personal experience. She states: 'As consistent with research directed towards practical as well as theoretical purposes, feminists have also considered researcher reflexivity ... [and] explored how to involve those researched in the research process ...' (Deem 1998, pp.178–9).

Although not alone in recognising the importance of reflexivity – the ability to interrogate one's own influence on the research process – feminists have indeed been at the forefront of this challenge to the idea that we can allow our own histories, experiences and assumptions to go unquestioned when we explore every phase of the research process. Such self-questioning is more evidently part of the process for qualitative researchers than for quantitative. The way one handles not only data analysis and interpretation but also confronts the initial assumptions made in order to choose approaches are signals that one is assiduously seeking to eradicate bias from one's project. That said – can we ever be totally aware of our own understandings of the world and how we think it works? We are products of a particular culture or cultures at a particular time, we can only do our best to have others interrogate our position, as well as making sure we experience others' cultures even if it is impossible for us to visit their times, except vicariously and through the imagination.

Role, responsibilities and relationships: Self

As a result of its history and the association in people's minds with scientific research in laboratories, research is often thought of as an isolated and remote job. Yet in the field of education, especially early childhood education and care, research is likely to involve demanding emotional experiences. Michael Schratz and Rob Walker (1995) argue that

> involvement in social research inevitably means involvement in relationships, and often involvement of a peculiarly intense kind ... Most of us want to make the world a better place and becoming involved in research seems to be an appropriate, congenial and effective way to do this.
>
> (Schratz and Walker 1995, pp.127–8)

In other words, our emotional investment in our work makes us vulnerable, in some cases to such an extent that the act of caring can eventually be worn down if the research creates little change in the field. At the same time, there is a contradiction in the expectations: firstly, that research findings may not be interpreted in alternative ways by other readers and, secondly, that researchers should have the right to change others' lives. The emotional aspects of the process are part of what Schratz and Walker (1995) refer to as 'the politics of research'.

How work is received at any stage, but particularly when published, will involve the depletion of emotional energy. Our ability to accept criticism and dissent, to be confident enough to listen to ways in which we can improve our work, means we must be mature and open minded. Patti Lather (1991) suggests researchers should neither require the reader to be passive nor expect acceptance of the writer as 'hero'. Ways of overcoming the insider/outsider divide and issues of researcher power are taken up in the development of the model of research as 'cooperative inquiry' by John Heron (1996).

Keeping abreast of developments in research methods and attending seminars and training sessions is a responsibility we have to ourselves. Jean Ruddock (1998) provides a report on the changes and progress in educational research over the last thirty years and she quotes Huberman in arguing that we must chase after paradigm shifts, particularly when these have 'restored the balance of power between researchers and user communities' (Ruddock 1998, p.8).

We live in a society which has traditionally had little respect for academics and learning, where reading and thinking are not considered to be 'work'. Taking care of ourselves, in both the physical and the mental senses, as well as allowing time for reading, thought and reflection and for the development and maintenance of other interests, is important. In his book *Hare Brain, Tortoise Mind*, Guy Claxton (1997) explains the failure of Western/Northern cultures to encourage the more intuitive ways of knowing. An overemphasis on logical, analytical thought processes has meant that we miss out on half our brain's powers, and these are the ones which come into play when flashes of insight provide the ideas and solutions to problems which have proved intractable. These flashes usually occur when we are doing something other than our usual tasks, so we should take time to work in the garden, listen to music, or to relax and simply laze around.

Conclusion

One final note which must be included in this chapter concerns the researcher's role, responsibility and relationship with the press. There have been celebrated examples of publicity about research projects which, because of misunderstandings, have caused adverse publicity in newspapers. Providing (with the necessary approval of any funding body) press releases does not always prevent this, for sometimes journalists will use the material they are given to write their own copy and they will put their own inflection upon the 'story'. Unfortunately educational researchers can always see the complexities of their research while journalists want clear-cut, unequivocal opinions. Radio and television journalists may end up editing an interview or video footage in such a way that the messages you wanted portrayed are either lost or misrepresented. Having said this, they do not generally do this out of malice; it behoves the researcher to ask as many questions as they expect to be asked in their turn, to check the aims and objects of the programme, and to try to attend training sessions about working with the media. Above all, the researchers' responsibility is to present their work in language which is meaningful to the public.

The most essential areas for researchers to dwell upon in recognising issues cerning their roles, responsibilities and relationships are the ethics and cs of their conduct and focus. Understanding the meaning of academic freedom and continually questioning any compromises they may appear to be asked to make – either by funding bodies, employers, participants, or through their own pragmatism – invokes the integrity of educational researchers. Recognising the dangers of self-absorption in reflexivity, of failing to take account of context and the need for authenticity (one's research focus, approaches and outcomes 'making sense' in particular contexts), requires considerable sophistication on the part of researchers. If the researcher either 'goes native' or is impervious to the effects of the internal lives of human beings and the cultures they have co-constructed, their research is worthless. One example of reported research which actually invites the reader to consider the applicability of the findings to their own experiences and situation – in other words, inviting interaction with the text – is Paul Connolly's fascinating and illuminating ethnographic study of the 'complex range of racialised social processes that can exist and potentially influence and shape young children's gender identities' (Connolly 1998, p.7). Another example of a study which seeks to be 'authentic' is that by Vi McLean (McLean 1991), in which she uses a phenomenological perspective to explore the ways in which her early years teacher participants reflexively construct and respond to the meanings they hold about the life within their settings, for she sets out to treat her participants as 'knowing beings'. As a result the 'story' her research tells can actually be identified with by early years practitioners in many different contexts. Recent studies of educational research and its influence on the field (e.g. Hillage *et al.* 1998) have indicated that policy-makers and practitioners are often left ignorant of findings which could make a difference in the lives of the children for whom we are all responsible. Dissemination through a wide variety of channels, following the testing of processes and outcomes in seminars with colleagues, is perhaps one of the paramount responsibilities of educational researchers, for as Lawrence Stenhouse (1975 p.157) pointed out, research is systematic enquiry placed in the public domain.

10 Ethical issues

What are 'ethics'?

Deciding whether a piece of research is feasible involves not only the ability to frame a research question and then plan relevant methods; it also requires a researcher to consider whether the ways in which the research is to be conducted are in harmony with the moral code by which the researcher lives and wishes to be identified. The making of moral judgements about the aims and methods of a study is what we call *research ethics*.

The dictionary definition of ethics states: '1. (as singular) Science of morals, study of principles of human duty; treatise on this. 2. (as plural) Moral principles; rules of conduct.' (From Coulson *et al.* [Eds] [1981] Oxford New Illustrated English Dictionary, p.570.) Thus, from a research perspective, ethics means the moral philosophy or set of moral principles underpinning a project.

An important point made by Cassell and Jacobs (1987) concerns the fact that many of our daily life decisions and our research decisions are made imperceptibly and there are sometimes decisions we come to regret, with hindsight, because they had unforeseen consequences. It is easy to identify the big, dramatic issues which may confront us. It is the ones we fail to recognise because they are embedded in our assumptions or our particular knowledge that can rise up afterwards and haunt us. Further, as Burgess (1989) points out, ethical definitions can sometimes seem to have little bearing on the daily life which social researchers ⌐ ⌐ttempting to explore.

For te⌐⌐⌐ ⌐ ethical issues in a particular research project ⌐, each day, a teacher is making split-second, ⌐Unfortunately, the reduction of philosophy ⌐nean that we are developing a professional ⌐e not been inducted into recognising the ⌐derpinned by ethical considerations. ⌐⌐se of punishment in schools demands ⌐t of view of its efficacy but from the point ⌐, and so on. If teachers have not had ⌐rsonal philosophies and beliefs, together ⌐ongside the school's policies, they risk ⌐h conflict with a more measured, and more morally grounded, approach. Similarly, an individual planning a piece of research or those involved in team research will need to go through their planned project meticulously in order to identify potential ethical pitfalls or disagreements.

Historically, the discussion of ethics in social research has been largely confined to studies which have created an outcry. Such studies have made us aware of the danger inherent in a lack of sensitivity to secrecy, the use of deception, falsification of data, and disagreements over the publication of results. More recently, we have become more aware of other aspects of the research process which also demand attention in this respect. These include issues such as power imbalances between the researcher and the participants; the extent to which the researcher should explain the nature and purpose of the research; the age at which children should be asked to give their own consent to participate, in addition to the consent of their parents; the extent of the researcher's responsibility to participants where the project involves sensitive personal disclosures.

Planning ethically sensitive research

In an early paper on child development research, Urie Bronfenbrenner (1952) argued that if we become too overwrought with anxiety about ethical issues and reach the conclusion that we must avoid them, we can only do so by refraining from carrying out any research at all. So, at the planning stage of a project, a researcher will think through each part of the process in order to eliminate, as far as is possible, the ethical blunders and insensitivities which could occur.

The fact that most early childhood education research tends to involve personal interactions means that it is difficult to eliminate human error or misunderstanding completely, and it is important to acknowledge human irrationality and inconsistency, which can give rise to difficulties. Being able to show that one has done one's best to consider and attend to all potential sources of grievance, followed by sensitivity to the people involved as well as to the research process, acting 'in good faith' at all times, are all indications of research expertise.

Having said that, there will still be disagreements about what such ethical considerations will mean, because researchers adhering to different research paradigms will have differing views about what some of the ethical issues actually are. A researcher who subscribes to the positivist paradigm and who decides, for example, on non-participant observation of children's behaviour, according to carefully selected categories based on knowledge of early years settings and child development, will argue that their work is both rigorous and ethically sensitive. They are attempting to log what happens in such an environment without, as they see it, influencing the children and adults in the setting. To do otherwise would, from this point of view, constitute interference, thus affecting the research data. Such researchers would also be attentive to their impact in terms of causing discomfort. Staff, relevant authorities and parents would have been informed about the research and would have given their consent.

However, a researcher subscribing to a different paradigm would argue that from an ethical, as well as a 'rigour', standpoint, such research is flawed. Firstly, because it does not seek the views, explanations and meanings of the participants and therefore represents only the researcher's view of events. Further, since early childhood settings, like classrooms for older children, develop their own culture and meanings (Edwards and Mercer 1987), researchers operating under an interpretive, critical or postmodern paradigm would argue that to ignore the very special meanings for those whose lives one is studying constitutes a lack of regard for the cultural constructions particular to the setting. Moreover, some would argue that this constitutes a disregard for the humanity, the 'inner life', of the people involved, treating them as if they are observable and measurable, data-generating machines. In addition to this, if the only view presented by such positivist research is that of the researcher, the ethical issue of power then enters the debate. The ethical question being: 'Whose view or explanation of a phenomenon is it right to present to the world, especially when policy decisions may be made as a result of reporting this research?'

Whatever paradigm a researcher or team espouses, therefore, it is important for those involved to present the moral discussion and rationale for their approaches, as well as their strategic rationale. Both are implicit within their methodology, and need to be made explicit.

Looking for guidance from earlier work

There are now many more references to ethical issues in research methodology publications than there were a decade ago (e.g. Breakwell 1995; Burgess 1985 and 1989; Hammersley 1995; Hitchcock and Hughes 1989; and Robson 1993 provide useful, brief discussions of various aspects). Cohen and Manion's 1994 publication of their popular text *Research Methods in Education* is the first edition in which the authors incorporate a chapter on ethics, in response to constructive comments on the third edition of the book five years earlier. In other words, prior to the late 1980s, ethical issues had only fleetingly exercised the minds of many influential educational researchers. As Cohen and Manion (1994) relate, the eighties saw a growth in awareness of the moral dilemmas surrounding educational research to the extent that in both the USA and the UK key professional bodies, such as the American Psychological Association, the British Psychological Society and the British Educational Research Association, developed regulatory codes of practice, and a number of papers in academic journals reflected this increased sensitivity.

Similarly, it was rare, in the past, for educational researchers writing accounts of their work for publication in books, reports and papers to include a section on research ethics. Medical researchers, however, have a long history of concern for this aspect of their work, for obvious reasons perhaps, but it is possible that the ethics committees and ethical debates of medical research can help those of us in the field of social research, especially those of us in early childhood research, for there are already so many points of contact with the health field and many opportunities for inter-disciplinary cross-fertilisation. According to Alderson (1995), the rationale for early medical ethics guidelines rested in

> etiquette: relations with colleagues, and promoting public respect for the profession. Some of these standards benefitted patients, but a main concern was also to benefit the medical profession. The Hippocratic tradition saw no conflict between doctors' and patients' interests, and assumed that the patients' 'good' was defined by doctors, not patients.
>
> (Alderson 1995, p.50)

Following the horror at the evidence disclosed during trials of Nazi doctors, the Nuremburg Code was written by lawyers in 1947. This was the first time ethical guidelines for research had been laid down. Sadly, the Code has been broken on a number of occasions since that time. In 1964 doctors themselves wrote new guidelines, named the Declaration of Helsinki. Alderson connects this development with the public concern which followed the harm *in utero* to children as a result of the drug Thalidomide being administered to their pregnant mothers. This code placed the responsibility for humans involved in research as 'subjects' on the doctors, so that it is the researcher who must protect subjects, balancing the *hoped-for* benefits of the research against *anticipated* benefits.

Perhaps as a result of the increasing recognition for ethical issues and the need to make them more explicit in writing about research, one recent publication (Pollard with Filer 1996) reporting on a longitudinal study of the lives and learning of young children contains a thoughtful account of the researcher's ethical dilemmas:

> I set out the ethical code which I proposed should frame the study. The first principle was that nothing would be done if it was likely to be harmful or distressing to the children. This underpinned the whole project. Second, the code stated that all data would be held confidentially and would not be released to anyone else, parent, teacher, child or peer. However, there was provision that this principle could be broken if I, as the researcher, came to know of something which I felt to be 'seriously damaging' to the child ... The ethical agreement also recognised my need to keep records, make analytical judgements and, eventually, to publish research results.
>
> (Pollard with Filer 1996, p.292)

Why do we seem more concerned today than in the past about research ethics?

Ideas about human rights are under constant revision. During the last fifty years or so there have been some significant developments in public awareness about the meaning of rights for both adults and children. When the atrocities of World War II became known, people were incensed at what had been perpetrated, not only in the death camps, but also the medical experiments which had been performed and the inhumane physical and psychological treatment of both soldiers and civilians.

The United Nations Convention on Human Rights and the 1989 Convention on the Rights of the Child (United Nations 1989) continue to gain wider recognition throughout the world. It behoves educational researchers, therefore, to know of these and to understand the ethical questions and practices which flow from support for these international legal agreements.

One way in which the Convention on the Rights of the Child has an impact is in its recognition for the personhood of children. Childhood is defined as the period from birth to the age of eighteen. If we are to acknowledge the capacity and the right of children to make their wishes known, researchers need to reflect on the assumptions they make when planning and organising a project (see Chapter 2).

Whereas parents have traditionally been asked to give their permission for their children to be part of the group involved in a research project in a nursery or school setting, after permission has been granted by the school's management, the staff to be involved and/or the local authority, the question of whether individual children's agreement needs also to be sought is now important.

Asking children if they are willing to take part does not completely solve the problem, however. Firstly, how does one decide at what age or stage the child's consent is needed? Secondly, bearing in mind that the child may not fully understand what is to happen or the implications, they may agree to take part in order to please the adults who ask them, particularly at the ages we are concerned with here.

On the other hand, depending upon the practices the children are used to at home or in a group setting, and upon the researcher's sensitivity, young children can prove quite powerful because they will move away, where possible, if they are bored or uninterested (David 1992; Evans and Fuller 1998). Indeed, they will change the topic of conversation if a researcher's questions fail to interest them, for example.

The assumptions made in the past about children's ability to take part and to give consent are evident in comment contained in earlier research. For example, Ronald King (1984) suggested that it is not possible to interview four-year-olds. However, someone experienced in work with this age group can do so, although as in teaching such young children, the response will depend on the appropriateness of the questions and the ways in which they are presented (see Chapter 2).

Codes of ethics and ethics committees

There are three main frameworks in ethics. They pose a number of different questions for researchers. The three frameworks comprise: *duties*; *rights*; and *harm/benefit*.

Firstly, the questions relating to duties, according to Alderson (1995) are as follows:

- Are the aims and methods of the research fair and right? (Thus this is a question of justice)
- Would you wish to be treated in the way you, the researcher, are intending to treat others? (This concerns respect for autonomy.)
- Might the research prove harmful or useless? (This relates to the tenet of a researcher not doing harm.).

Three useful codes for a researcher to consider, and perhaps to use as aides memoires, when planning an educational research project involving young children are those of the British Psychological Society, the British Sociological Society and the British Educational Research Association (see Appendix 4 for further information).

Fieldwork

Clearly codes of ethics can be very useful in helping us question our own (and others') research approaches throughout the process, but especially in the field. However, it is also important to remember that ideas about young children and their capabilities have changed and we are now aware of their active attempts to make sense of the situation in which they find themselves from very early in life. This mean that as we come to understand more about children's understanding and learning and as we develop our view of children as people with rights, not as objects or possessions, so we adjust our ideas about the 'right treatment' of children generally and as subjects of or participants involved in research.

For example, presumably many people in the UK a century or so ago accepted the idea of tiny children cleaning chimneys to provide a living for themselves. Our ideas of what is acceptable behaviour towards children change with time, so it may be that certain research approaches currently accepted as 'normal' will become unacceptable in the future.

An innovatory research project by Peter Elfer and Dorothy Selleck (1996) of the National Children's Bureau has raised a number of issues about the sensitivity of both educators and researchers in settings with babies. In this innovatory project, the researchers tried to assess the positive or negative impact of an adult's behaviour on a baby in a particular nursery setting by being observant of the child's reactions, facial and bodily postures and vocalisations.

An additional point to be considered will also be: who owns the data about a participant? Does it 'belong' to the researcher or the participant? If the raw data are shown to a participant in order to have them check it, for example in the case of a transcription of a taped interview, how much should the researcher agree to alter following the participant's reading back of what was said? This is even more crucial in the case of interviews where the participants do not wish to be taped. Clearly if one promises to alter transcriptions one must keep one's agreement, so a decision as to whether this is to be offered must be made at the outset. There are also some instances where qualitative researchers have found participants telling them key, but potentially damaging (to themselves or another participant), information at a time when they thought the researcher was 'off task'. For example, if a participant thought that the researchers were gathering ethnographic data in a nursery and they then met them outside and the participant divulged information which was of central importance in understanding the nursery, but which was really confidential, 'off-limits' information, how should researchers treat that knowledge?

Using the data: Analysis and writing

One of the main issues relating to data analysis is the extent to which the researcher is able to recognise areas of potential bias. For researchers taking a positivist stance, this may mean they should examine the categories they choose – for example, in a checklist to be used for observing children's play. For qualitative, ethnographic researchers, not only might their notes contain such a bias, as they make notes on those aspects of a situation they consider important, but they may also find their 'themes and surprises' relate more to their own concerns than to those of the community being studied. Bertrand Russell's 1927 comment is used by Ely *et al.* (1997) to highlight his view of how researchers are often unaware of bias and assumptions in their work – Russell argued that reports of animal behaviour seemed to him to depend upon the nationality of the observer, with animals studied by Americans being apparently very lively and those studied by Germans being more static and 'thoughtful'.

In other words, researchers must ask themselves if they are 'projecting' their own views of and feelings about the world onto their research population. Ely *et al.* (1997) suggest that by keeping logs or diaries, or by adding Observer Comment (OC) to their fieldnotes, researchers can access their research stance and thus be aware of its influence on their decisions. They add that researchers can make an asset of personal sensitivities as long as they are balanced by 'rigorous questioning and method' (Ely *et al.* 1997, p.353) and that by scrutinising the way we align ourselves in the process of reading is a further self-regulatory mechanism.

When one writes up the research one is often into yet another series of dilemmas, as Pollard shows from his own study of the lives of five young children:

> ... ethical issues in the process of writing up, remained. The ethical code which had been agreed at the start of the study was maintained without problems. However, part of this agreement was to treat data ... confidentially and this meant that it was only at the writing-up stage that

each party formally learned of the perspectives of the others. Anonymity from each other was clearly impossible to provide. I was extremely concerned about this, fearing for the possibility of people feeling uncomfortable with their portrayal in the accounts or by awareness of the perspectives of others, and I deliberately reminded people of the problem from time to time.

(Pollard with Filer 1996, p.301)

Andrew Pollard goes on to discuss his care that information gleaned during the fieldwork and interviews would only be used if it related directly to his research argument. Data which the researchers believed to have potentially sensitive aspects for a child or an adult participant, but which it was important to include, was edited and negotiated for inclusion because omission would result in sanitised accounts of the children's experience.

Anonymised drafts of chapters were vetted by parents and teachers and Pollard admits that some participants did feel 'somewhat uncomfortable when reflecting in this way' (p.301). As a result of the time involved in this particular study (the children were studied from age four to seven years), the children were capable of reading their own draft case study, completed as they were leaving the primary school, and the decision to give them access was left to their respective parents. Where this occurred, children were said to be positive and to some extent amused about what had been written. Andrew Pollard adds that one can, of course, never be certain that the children will continue to feel this way as they move through their teens and young adulthood.

Pollard is right to wonder if the children will still feel positive in later years, if some of the children may have had qualms about being the focus of such attention, yet unable to express or understand their 'gut reaction' and going along, apparently happily, with the research. Here one is back to Bronfenbrenner's comment mentioned earlier. We can only act 'in good faith' and try to enable children to tell adults when they perceive that a project is denying them privacy or is insensitive to their feelings.

A psychologist colleague told one of us a fascinating anecdote about a young man she had once known whose mother had worked with Piaget in Geneva. Because the mother was so used to logging children's behaviour, she kept many notebooks of observations of her son as he was growing up and, on his fourteenth birthday, presented him with 'his life' (the notebooks) bound up in a ribbon. The son related that while he did not demur at the time, he was in fact very hurt and angry: this was not 'his life', he had kept some thoughts very private and he had resented his mother's note-taking. Perhaps it seemed an unwarranted intrusion by someone he thought should care for him and protect him and it seems likely that the power imbalance in the relationship meant he felt powerless to stop his mother's well-intentioned behaviour. Further, in his early years he may not have had the understanding and the complex language needed to explain his sensitivity.

Ethical aspects of dissemination

The difficulties relating to dissemination include not only the dilemmas involved in ensuring confidentiality, but also the added possibility that one's research may be seized upon and rendered overly simplistic in the press. This happened in the mid-1970s, in the case of Neville Bennett's (1976) research on teaching styles, and more recently when research on children's achievements and mothers' employment was used in a television programme (O'Brien 1997).

The problem can be more to do with the ethics of journalists who may not allow the researchers to fully explain their own ideas about their results and who, perhaps because they do not fully understand, or because they believe the public want straightforward rather than complex messages, end up distorting the evidence.

While there are many respectable journalists who would not knowingly distort a researcher's findings and one must pay homage to their ability to grasp a wide range of topics very quickly, it is often difficult for a non-specialist to make sense of education research jargon. Additionally, there are times when the restrained language used to put forward tentative research claims must appear confusing to those outside the field. Researchers themselves probably have far less confidence in the strength of their results than those with less knowledge of either science or social science. On other occasions, only part of a 'research story' may appeal to an uninformed journalist writing from a particular political angle. An example of this last point appeared in a *Sunday Times* article entitled 'Revenge of the Progressives' (Judith O'Reilly 1999, p.19) arguing that 'our children's education is in the hands of a powerful quango' of academics.

It is generally regarded as 'good practice' for researchers to provide feedback to those who have been involved and clearly here again sensitivity is needed if some participants or children's parents feel they are easily identifiable and appear in what they perceive to be 'a bad light'. Sometimes it is impossible for a researcher to know that a person will feel this. Trying to put yourself in the shoes of those reported upon can go some way to ensuring sensitivity in this respect, but having another person with different views from one's own would be an added security.

Participation or exploitation? Special concerns for research involving young children

Research involving young children or children with communication difficulties probably requires more sensitivity to the power relations than most. It may be almost impossible to inform young children fully about the research, so their consent may seem more like exploitation. Further, because most young children are very trusting and wish to please adults, it is often difficult to know if they feel comfortable both with what is being asked of them and with the person who is asking, who may be relatively unfamiliar.

Although relatively little research of this nature has been reported, some development of cooperative research (Heron 1996) in which children's parents and carers actually participate may be a solution that could provide the field with more intimate and fine-grained evidence. Such research might be conducted in a similar way to the documentation of the workers in the celebrated nurseries of Reggio Emilia in Northern Italy (Edwards *et al.* 1998; see also the Swedish project along these lines reported in Dahlberg and Åsén 1994).

Ethics and the independence of research findings

A number of other issues relating to how the research evidence might be used in policy and practice include the suppression of research data. This would be unethical if it were done in order to skew the findings or if dissemination of the evidence would result in benefits to particular groups. For example, one story from the 1970s concerns a project team whose main finding was that boys' underachievement in reading was linked to their lack of role models – the young boys who had been studied rarely or never saw a man reading. The sponsors declared that this could not possibly be the main finding, things could not be that simple, the researchers must return to their data and reexamine what they had gathered. It seem rather ironic that at least something like this is implicit in the current literacy projects involving footballers and football clubs and that later research by Cochran *et al.* (1990) has reinforced the central message of the earlier research – that male role models and males who take an interest in a boy's learning are crucial to academic achievement.

It is difficult to imagine why some sponsors, such as a government department in a democracy, would seek to gag researchers. It appears more understandable when the sponsor is a commercial company. For example, if a firm making children's computer games was told that the games were linked to increases in violence, the firm might wish to suppress the evidence at least until they had managed to reform their products to eliminate the features considered to be responsible. The researcher has, naturally, responsibilities to the sponsors but also responsibilities to participants, to other researchers, to the field and knowledge, and it is therefore important to negotiate the terms on which any findings may be made public before the sponsorship is accepted if censorship may be part of the deal.

Unfortunately some, such as Caroline Gipps (1993), Helen Simons (1995) and Halpin and Troyna (1996), argue that interference from funding bodies has increased in recent years. Simons (1995) takes Gipps's review of the evidence of misreporting and ignoring of research findings post-1998 to suggest that most government-funded research is evaluative and policy-driven; that while past research was ideological (committed to improving educational provision) it is now more or less forced to be political; and thirdly that to speak of ethics means not the ethics of an independent researcher but the ethics of a 'captive researcher' (Simons 1995 p.437). Helen Simons adds that there has been a change in research sponsorship from 'the customer pays' to 'the customer owns'. It is hardly surprising that it has been during this time that the need to establish ownership of the 'intellectual property' emanating from any project has become firmly fixed in the procedures of HE fund-seeking. Where researchers are forbidden from making their findings public, the issues of professional checks on the quality of the research and the controlling of information available to the public are serious matters.

When a government or one of its organs seeks to control the dissemination of independent research findings this can indicate a power differential between the parties involved. Simons points to the period following the 1944 Education Act, when power was more evenly distributed 'in a partnership of governance of education between central government, local government and the schools' (Simons 1995, p.437). She adds that in the early 1990s this balance no longer existed and she reiterates Gipps (1993) in placing educational researchers in the 'front line' where they are expected to research highly contentious 'reforms' after, rather than before, legislation setting them in place. What we need to ask ourselves then is, are those researching the field of early childhood education – much of which has been relatively unregulated in the past, being in the private and voluntary sectors – experiencing a similar effect? Or is the New Labour government, elected since Simons's (1995) critique was written, more open to the idea of pilot research projects, independent evaluations of policy and practice, and the 'ownership' of their data by researchers in a way that ensures both high-quality research and the employment of appropriate ethical policies and procedures?

A further issue concerns the influence of the researcher's own political standpoint on the research process. There are two divergent views of whether researchers should use their findings for 'political ends'. Some believe research should be politics-free, while others argue that it cannot be and, like the academics who were involved in the late 1960s worker-student protests in France, believe that it is the responsibility of researchers to expose inequalities and injustices in society. Martyn Hammersley (1995) suggests that the question of whether or not research is or can be political is unclear in any case, that the definition of 'political' is in question. He argues that research should not be directly concerned with any goals other than the production of knowledge. However, he adds that 'research should be value relevant without being designed to serve particular political causes' (Hammersley 1995, p.118) and he reminds readers of Becker's (1967) questioning of the extent to which one's own values should be permissible as part of the research process in his paper 'Whose side are we on?'

Meanwhile, Page Smith (1990), reviewing the emasculation of scholarship and research in US universities, argues that too much sensitivity to not taking sides simply results in academia which supports the status quo: in other words, that it is the responsibility of academics to take a particular moral stance. In early years research it is difficult to avoid the numerous political questions surrounding provision for young children, the position of women in society, differences in the availability of edu-care in different parts of the country, the variety of and differences between forms of provision, the range of teaching appoaches adopted and the different levels of training for workers, to name only the most obvious.

Ways forward in this include the strategies Simons (1995) promoted: negotiation by the British Education Research Association (BERA) for a re-formulation of restrictive legal clauses in research contracts; working collectively to reduce the effects of market ideology; the development of an ethics policy for each individual project which outlines the behaviour expected of the researcher and other responsible participants – including the sponsors – and which must be agreed; and the development of a 'pilot project' culture. In the Netherlands and in Denmark, pilot projects are often funded in order to examine the effects of a policy on a relatively small population before widening implementation (Broström and Vilien 1998; OECD forthcoming).

Research by Hillage *et al.* (1998) suggests that neither policy-makers nor practitioners in education pay a great deal of attention to research findings. In fact it has been argued that, in the UK, policy-makers of all political persuasions listen to only those researchers who tell them what they want to hear.

Although these are legal, rather than ethical considerations, we note here that researchers must pay attention to the requirements of the Data Protection Act and the Children Act 1989. For some, the Official Secrets Act is also invoked where the sponsor is a government department. In the case of the Data Protection Act and the Children Act, such laws are intended to protect the rights of the individual (here this would be children and family members, teachers and individual policy-makers, for example). However, it is difficult to imagine the purposes of invoking the Official Secrets Act in relation to educational research, other than to protect the status of a government's position with the electorate or to prevent potential demands on the economy.

Values, morals and principles

To sum up, we have suggested in this chapter, as Tschudin (1994) has pointed out, that there are different areas to be considered in relation to ethics and research: 'the personal and professional integrity of the researcher, the responsibility of researchers to their subjects, and the relationships with sponsors, employers and colleagues' (Tschudin 1994, p.50).

A researcher's values will be largely those subscribed to in the wider community and the research community of which that person is a part. Each individual's personal history, religious experiences, values and, particularly, education will have helped shape their beliefs and their ability to think through the different moral dilemmas involved in the undertaking. Honesty and sensitivity are aspects of what is required, but to avoid unethical practices – such as deceiving participants, diminishing their self-esteem, exposing them to mental or physical stress, invading their privacy, withholding benefits to some participants in comparison with other groups, or not treating them

Table 10.1 Ethics and the roles, responsibilities and relationships of an educational researcher

Phases in project	Role	Responsibility	Relationship
Planning			
Literature search			
Devising instruments			
Fieldwork			
Data analysis			
Writing			
Dissemination			

fairly and with respect – requires not only certain personal qualities on the part of the researcher, but also the ability to reflect on abstract concepts such as justice and relate them to the real world and practical situations. Such reflection requires time, even though on some occasions an ethical dilemma may arise in the research setting and demand an immediate response. For this reason, devoting time to imagining what ethical issues might arise and making provision for them beforehand, through the development of a statement of principles, ensuring every member of a team is fully informed and party to the underpinning ethical position embedded in the statement of principles, is a useful prerequisite of all research, especially that involving young children. A practical way to consider the whole research process and the ethical issues which must be confronted is to examine the roles, responsibilities and relationships involved set against that process (see Table 10.1). This matrix is merely an outline and the cells can be extended or augmented as necessary. When this has been used with new researchers they have always expressed surprise at the number of relationships engendered during an education research project and the potential flash points which must be considered before the project gets under way, highlighted by such a device.

Finally, it is not only the participants and the funders of a project to whom a researcher has a responsibility to behave according to ethical principles, but also the researcher has a responsibility to the research process itself, to other researchers and to the population at large, and their interests can be included in the ethics matrix. Sometimes the issues, the responsibilities or proposed action may not be clearcut and dilemmas have to be faced, but the matrix can form the basis for the development of an ethics policy for the project.

11 A Canterbury tale

The researcher's inside story

...Redy to wenden on my pilgrimage
To Caunterbury with ful devout corage...
At nyght was come into that hostelrye
Wel nyne and twenty in a compaignye
Of sondry folk, by aventure y-falle
In felaweshipe, and pilgrims were they alle,
That toward Caunterbury wolden ryde...
But nathelees, whil I have tyme and space,
Er that I ferther in this tale pace,
Me thinketh it acordaunt to resoun
To telle you al the condicioun
Of each of hem, so as it semed me,
And whiche they weren, and of what degree,
And eek in what array that they were inne...
(Geoffrey Chaucer,
The Prologue to the Canterbury Tales)

The chapters in this book provide accounts of quantitative and qualitative research methods and analyses, as well as offering illustrative projects and describing particular issues which confront a researcher in the field of early childhood education. Attention has already been drawn to the manner in which researchers report on their work and the implicit assumptions these may carry about their own implicit theoretical and methodological beliefs and goals. Whatever views are held concerning the role of theory and the sequence and significance of research procedures involved, the research process – as observed in Chapter 3 – is, in practice, a much less rational and far untidier business than the average research report would suggest. Accordingly this chapter will attempt to report the authentic 'lived experience' of carrying out a piece of research in which two of the writers have been engaged. The intention is to give the reader some insight into the problems and dilemmas which can be associated with carrying out real research in the real world.

The project in question investigated children's early numeracy competence in a number of European countries and an outline of the analysis has already been provided in Chapter 7. This chapter will focus upon aspects of the research process which do not usually find their way into the research report and, hence, do not reach the public domain. It will start by examining the area for study and will follow the sequence which is conventionally adopted for reporting research, as advocated in Chapter 3. At the same time, it will attempt to uncover some of the more difficult matters which can arise and which demand resolution but which are not usually discussed.

Conceptualising the topic or area for study

As already noted in Chapter 3, the area or topic of research may be generated in any number of different ways. In this case, involvement in the project arose from a chance meeting with the Dutch researchers at the European Early Childhood Education Association Lisbon Conference in 1996, in an early mathematics session in which both parties were participating. The intention of the Dutch team had been to collect data on children's developing numerical competence in a European context, over the 1997–8 period. As it happened it was impossible for one of the writers to carry out any research or to engage in much writing of any kind during the academic year 1996–7. She was engaged in designing, planning, recruiting, administering and carrying out a large portion of the teaching for a new early years degree course which she had been asked to set up. This activity, in the event, absorbed all available time for a whole academic year during which time the writer also changed academic institutions. This created further disruption and discontinuity. It was agreed with the Dutch team that the English data could be collected over the years 1998–9 although, from their point of view, this meant that the project's data collection phase would now be extended by a further twelve months. Moreover, it transpired that the Finnish children selected for the project were so much older than participating children from other parts of Europe that they reached the ceiling for the test norms on the first data collection point and were, thus, effectively disqualified from further involvement. This constituted a second set-back for the Dutch researchers, reducing the participating countries to Belgium, Germany, Greece and the Netherlands over the 1997–8 period. Their invitation to the writer to take part in a Dutch-led mathematics symposium at the European Association for Research on Learning and Instruction Athens Conference in 1997, however, led to their introduction to the writers' Slovene colleagues and to the agreement of Slovenia to take part in data collection during 1998–9.

The field of study – early numeracy – was one in which the writers had been involved since early in the 1990s, first of all in an investigation of mathematical thinking that young children bring into school. This revealed their rich informal knowledge – of counting, recognition of numerals, representation of quantity, simple addition, subtraction and social sharing, language of measurement and selection of criteria to sort objects. The project led to a subsequent ESRC grant being awarded for the investigation of teachers' subject knowledge and the processes of instruction in reception classes. A diversity of practice among different teachers was observed, as was an apparent lack of awareness of children's prior knowledge. Later, this interest in young children's numeracy was extended in a small case study of children's arithmetic, problem-solving and mental calculation strategies for ages six to twelve years in England and Slovenia, sponsored by the British Council and in collaboration with the University of Ljubljana.

Results from the British Council case study showed that six-year-old English pupils scored significantly higher than Slovene preschoolers of the same age, yet by seven years, when the Slovene children had been in school for barely a year, there were no significant differences between the two groups of pupils for a criterion-referenced arithmetic test. Thereafter the Slovene children forged ahead. On a standardised test (the British Abilities Scale), English six- and seven-year-olds scored significantly higher, yet by eight years there were no significant differences. Mental calculation also showed that by the end of the Slovene children's first year at school there was little difference in accuracy between the two groups and, in fact, the Slovene pupils were already beginning to use more efficient recall strategies. The English pupils maintained 'the edge' in problem-solving until nine years, when the English low-achievers group still scored significantly higher than the low-achieving Slovene group. Overall, however, there appeared to be little benefit to be gained from the English early school-entry and, hence, early start to formal schooling. The opportunity to look in more depth at the performance of five- to six-year-olds in the Dutch project was particularly attractive, especially the prospect of having the comparative dimension of a number of other European countries.

This section illustrates how a researcher's interests, areas for investigation and, hence, research focus, may extend and develop over time. A significant influence in this respect is the meeting and exchanging of ideas which takes place in the context of conference activity, at home and abroad, and in the networking which ensues. Identifying other on-going research activity in similar and overlapping fields provides a major source for information exchange – substantive and methodological – conducted increasingly by e-mail and e-conferencing and keeping researchers in touch with emerging work in their field. This section also indicates some of the common threats to the successful completion of research projects, as research teams grow in size and an international dimension is included. The particular life circumstances of a single team member may tip the time-scale of the project quite out of kilter. More seriously, when individual member countries do not adopt a common sampling strategy for the project concerned, the entire data-set and, hence, the involvement of the particular country concerned may be thrown into question.

Reviewing the existing literature

That the existing English and US literature in the area of children's early numerical development was already familiar to the writers was an advantage. Access to Dutch realistic mathematics education theory and practice through a visit to the Freudenthal Institute at the University of Utrecht was an added bonus. A visit to one of their experimental schools and a contact made with the Dutch publisher of primary realistic mathematics textbooks fed into another research project being conducted by the writers with the University of Ljubljana.

It was more problematic that topics in the Dutch assessment instrument to be used for the European project included tasks such as classification and seriation associated with Piagetian theory, since the relationship between such activities and the development of children's early numeracy has been increasingly questioned in this country (see, for instance, Aubrey 1997a; Thompson 1997). Moreover, in the Netherlands, van den Heuvel-Panhuizen (1996) has also raised doubts with respect to the relationship between these skills and arithmetical development. Activities such as classifying objects and sorting sets according to different criteria, matching identical objects to find equivalent or non-equivalent sets and ordering activities, influenced by Piagetian theory and presumed to constitute logical operations which underly more abstract numerical concepts, have come under increasing attack as cognitive research has delineated children's number skills development in a fine-grained manner (see Geary 1994 for a scholarly review of the area).

In fact the Dutch realistic approach to counting was first formulated as a *reaction* to the practice of developing structuralist concepts – that is, logical forms of reasoning such as correspondence, seriation and classification – at the expense of counting activities. In this respect *most* Dutch mathematics educators regard it important to identify a number of sub-skills in the counting process: verbal control over the number-word sequence, including counting forwards and backwards, which develops separately from what they term as 'resultative' counting to determine amounts, and 'abbreviated' or structured counting, on the basis of taking in small or larger amounts, with ordered and unordered sets of objects, which may be visible or only partially visible. The range of activities in the test, including both logical forms and counting activities, if anything increased its interest to the writers since it allowed consideration of the relationship among different sub-topics, at specific testing points and over time.

In fact, when the international teams eventually met as a group, it was interesting to note that the Flemish team had included additional assessment results and analysis in their arm of the project – with general arithmetic achievement test results available at mid-first grade (at the second testing point) and school results at the end of Grade 1 (at the third testing point) being utilised. They concluded from additional analysis that the predictive validity of the test was 'relatively weak', that the theoretical framework underlying it was 'not supported by the factor analysis' and that there was a 'significant difference between results for the classical Piagetian skills and the counting skills' (Guesquiere *et al.* (1999) p. 1). The Greek team, by contrast, were interested in the relationship of cognitive style to cognitive development. This, in turn, they hypothesised to be influenced by children's sociocultural environment and they accordingly attempted to distinguish between 'analytic' and 'holistic' processors in carrying out the Piagetian tasks, from so-called 'privileged' and 'deprived' neighbourhoods, as well as comparing performance in these respects at the first moment of testing with the third.

Suffice it to say, at this point, that although a number of European research teams came together in a common project, using a common research instrument and following a common research design, the theoretical assumptions of the originating Dutch team were by no means shared by the international group as a whole. This, in turn, influenced the additional procedures that were carried out by individual teams, the additional analysis which took place, the claims that were made about the cases tested and the conclusions which were drawn concerning the research focus. The theoretical framework in this project clearly became a contested area.

This section demonstrates powerfully how substantive and methodological dimensions of a project interact in a researcher's ongoing research activity and how, in the context of the project being reported, implicit theoretical assumptions of researchers in participating countries were made manifest in the adjustments and modifications made to the original research design which took place in national contexts.

Designing the procedures

Since ostensibly the design, the procedures and main instrument had been planned in advance by the Dutch team, this left the English team with a major problem – how to gain financial support for the project. The project was not regarded as suitable for seeking a grant from an external funding body who would expect a significant theoretical or methodological advance to be proposed and in fact it is likely that few research teams would be prepared to pursue such a project *without* the support of a major funding agency. This, in turn, constituted an indication, in its own right, of the relative quality and standing of the research in question, in research assessment exercise (RAE) terms. That the writer continued at all in these circumstances is an indication that researchers *may* continue to be driven by curiosity rather than by more instrumental career motivation or, indeed, by institutional pressures to conform to conventionally-assessable research, given that part of a senior academic's salary is regarded as ring-fenced for research activity.

The project *did* seem a suitable one for the support of the higher education institution of the two writers concerned; thereby it became associated with sponsorship for a European-wide project and, hence, international research. Accordingly, a research proposal was carefully prepared and costed, with the help of the finance department, for submission to and consideration of the relevant internal assessment panel. This led to a prompt interview with a very senior manager who pointed out that granting the request in its entirety would mean that almost all of the institution's research budget for a whole year would be swallowed up by one project. It was proposed, therefore, that the institution should support the first data-gathering cycle, which left the resear-chers with the challenge of seeking alternative funding sources for the second and third data-gathering cycles. In the event further funding from a related project became available and additional financial support was promised by the department of one of the writers.

Obtaining external funding can prove the most challenging aspect of a project and in a recent conversation with a senior researcher at another insti-tution it was concluded that established researchers of national and international status may expect no more than a one-in-six 'hit' rate with prestigious funding agencies, for whom competition is extremely keen. The same researcher ob-served, moreover, that rejection is not only an inevitable setback in professional terms but can also be quite personally distressing in terms of self-esteem. Such observations do *not* usually find their way into reports of researchers' activity for external assessors, where self-presentation is all-important and display of emotion inappropriate. Nevertheless they *do* reveal the extent of personal investment in time, energy and intellectual effort which is involved in engaging in research and the inevitable, ensuing disappointments and discouragements which are part and parcel of the 'jobbing' academic researcher's lot, most of whom have heavy teaching and administrative loads as well, unless they are contract researchers without a full-time academic post.

With respect to the project's design, the overall objectives had been set in advance to:

- make an international European comparison among different countries with regard to the development of early numeracy
- investigate the usability of the Early Numeracy Test in other countries;
- set norms for each country, offering the possibility of determining possible lags in early development
- follow the development of early numeracy for a sub-group of low-achievers in each country.

This left individual countries free, as noted above, to pursue additional aims, our own being to:

- assess the relative progress of pupils between five and six years, with a view to tracking them from the authority's baseline assessment through to seven years when they carried out standard assessment tasks (SATs)
- evaluate the predictive value of the test in the light of this (as the Flemish team had done)
- determine the effect of pupil factors such as age, sex, class or school upon progress during the first phase of formal schooling
- compare the progress of pupils in different parts of Europe who have had different social, cultural and educational experiences, largely outside the context of formal schooling (this was not only most important, but was

also where the project had the most potential to extend the previous work of the writer – national and international).

For the English design, as noted in Chapter 7, it was decided to use a multilevel modelling method of analysis to incorporate the hierarchical structure of the data collected, with pupils nested within classes, within schools and within different areas.

Before the design could be finalised, however, gaining access had to be addressed. In fact, one of the writers had already made an unsuccessful attempt to gain the cooperation of a large education authority which, for reasons of multiple staff changes at senior-education-officer level and an existing commitment to a nation-wide, preschool project, was reluctant to be involved. A second authority approached, in the south-east of England, was extremely cooperative, agreed to discuss the details of the project promptly, and undertook to seek the support of local inspectors involved. This led to letters being sent to more than three hundred infant and junior-mixed-infant schools, requesting their involvement. The response was overwhelming with only five schools declining the offer to participate. In the event the researchers attempted to select schools carefully to include the east, west and the centre of the region, urban and rural areas, large and small schools, with high and low concentrations of children having free meals (commonly used as a crude social index) and special educational needs, as well as a broad band of achievement levels based on previous standard assessment (results of schools selected ranged from the twentieth to the ninety-fourth per centile).

The sampling strategy adopted is critical to the quality of any piece of research since it is upon the cases examined that the claims of the research team are based, as noted in an earlier section. In the case of international research this is, arguably, even more important where claims from the cases examined form the basis for conclusions relating to the research focus, which may imply national differences. Eventually, twenty-one schools were selected to take part with groups of ten children (five boys and five girls) from each reception class included, so far as possible. Information on the ages at the first cycle of testing is shown in Table 11.1.

Approximately one hundred children took each form of the test on each testing cycle. Additional children were included to allow for 'sample attrition' or loss to the project. There was little movement of children between the first and second testing cycles although a number of children were ill, absent or had changed schools by the time of the third testing cycle. As a result of this, considerable extra trouble was taken to follow up children who were absent through illness at the time of the final testing in order to maintain a total of three hundred participating pupils. This added considerably to time required for testing and, since the research associate's time was the most expensive aspect of the project, it added significantly to the costs of the project. Moreover the research associate, as a contract researcher, was at the same time attempting

Table 11.1 Mean ages of children at first cycle of testing

	Mean Age (Months)	SD	N
Boys	60.1	3.56	163
Girls	59.8	3.57	156
Total	60.0	3.56	319

to complete the data-base in order to move on to a new full-time post in another part of the country.

Despite all efforts, the number of pupils involved dropped from three hundred and nineteen, at the first testing point, to two hundred and ninety-nine, at the second testing moment, and finally to two hundred and ninety, at the last testing point.

This section has attempted to demonstrate the intimate relationship which exists among research design, research questions or aims, sampling strategy adopted and data collection methods used. It has also shown how difficult in practice it is to examine, never mind treat, these aspects separately. It also indicates some of the problems and pitfalls in trying to manage a large international project which has separate national administration and funding, as well as independent researchers with their own distinct goals and motivation.

Collecting data

Since the original test was written in Dutch, this had first of all to be translated into English. Translation costs in themselves can be huge – even for a single sheet of A4 text – and, in this case, were borne by the Dutch team. This meant that the Slovene team, however, were faced with retranslating the English text into Slovene before their data could be collected. The wording of instructions in English, moreover, had to be adjusted to take account of different usage of, for instance, comparative terms such as 'high' and 'tall' or 'thick' and 'fat' to avoid confusion for children, and care had to be taken to ensure that instructions given were idiomatically correct. This still left unresolved the influence of the picture stimulus to the orally-administered number and word problems which inevitably, in some cases, depicted familiar Dutch contexts – for instance, the so-called Dutch 'goose' board game – with compatible, but nevertheless different, versions obtaining in the different national settings.

Judging how many children could be assessed within a day was problematic and, hence, making firm plans for visits to different schools remained a little precarious. Testing times varied according to the pace at which individual children worked and the arrangements made by individual schools for collecting children and returning them to particular classrooms, as did the location of the research associate in relation to individual classrooms.

Problems with loss of subjects have already been described above. Accessibility of schools in terms of public transport was another problem for the research associate and, indeed, certain rural schools were virtually inaccessible without private transport. This added to time spent in travel as well as the enlistment of additional researchers to work in particularly remote areas of the authority. These may appear to be trivial difficulties scarcely worth mentioning but their reporting serves to indicate that the greater the care that is taken in planning the sampling strategy, the greater is the likelihood of creating additional challenges to data collection. Although such aspects of data collecting were neither discussed nor reported by individual teams in the current project, issues of feasibility and manageability in data collection are bound to influence the strategy adopted and, therefore, the quality of data obtained.

Analysis of data

It has already been reported above that individual countries carried out their own additional assessment and analysis. The basic requirement for each country was to provide a factor analysis for the various components of the test, based on the first testing point; to provide mean results and standard deviation on the first, second and third testing moment, for the total group as well as for boys and girls separately; and to carry out a reliability analysis on the first testing moment, for the three forms of the test.

The Dutch team alone had access to the full data-set and carried out a reliability analysis for each country on each form of the test; a factor analysis of the eight components of the test for each country; and an analysis of variance, with the country representing the 'between-groups factor' and the moment of measurement the 'within-groups factor'.

The international teams finally met face-to-face at the poster symposium for the project, held at the European Association for Research on Learning and Instruction (EARLI) Gothenburg Conference in 1999. Considerable interest was taken in and careful scrutiny made of the presentations of individual countries by other participants. There was a general feeling that the analysis carried out was inadequate to capture the complexity of the data-set and it was agreed at the post-symposium discussion that the full international data-set should be analysed using the multilevel modelling method of the English team. Furthermore it was agreed that these data should be sent to England in advance and that the Dutch team would make a follow-up visit so that the procedure and results of analysis could be explained in more depth by one of the writers, as statistical expert and adviser to the project.

Before releasing these – and without reference to other participating countries – copyright restrictions were placed upon the full international data-set in order to protect their use. This action placed in some doubt the spirit of trust and cooperation in which the project had begun. Moreover it was a reminder of the concern expressed by three of the participating countries that the Dutch team had *not* enlisted the services of an independent discussant for the EARLI 1999 poster symposium, who might have acted as independent assessor and critical friend.

Writing the research report

At the time of writing, the precise manner in which the joint report will be written remains to be negotiated, though mini-collaborations with sub-groups of countries have been encouraged, and a joint paper, to appear in the journal *Learning and Instruction* has been proposed. Meanwhile the Dutch team have already reported results relating to the project at conferences in 1998 and 1999 *without* making adjustments for the ages of the pupils. At the 1998 European Conference for Educational Research in Ljubljana, results for the first testing moment were reported without providing information on mean ages of the children concerned, and without prior consultation with the countries involved. By the time the writers of this chapter returned from the Ljubljana conference last year, a journalist from the *Times Educational Supplement* had left a phone message and was ready to run a research article based on the first testing cycle of this project. This was to be based on the Dutch conference paper, with results unadjusted for age, and reporting: 'The first results on the first moment of measurement show that the UK has a score below the scores of the other countries' (van de Rijt and van Luit 1998, p.8)

It was explained to the journalist that it was not appropriate to report the results for the project before the data were fully collected and analysed, and without the participating schools being informed. Moreover the findings, as presented, were not entirely consistent with the results of our own previous British Council project. The reply was: 'Oh, you researchers, if you never agree with one another what *are* reporters to make of your research findings?'

In this case the England and Slovene team had met the Dutch researchers prior to the 1998 conference presentation to express concern that findings were being reported with no prior consultation or agreement with the participating countries. In fact, their first intimation of the Dutch intentions had been through reading the conference abstract in the conference proceedings, when the conference was in progress.

More recently, at the 1999 EARLI Conference the Dutch team reported the mean scores and deviations for total samples, as well as for boys and girls separately, for each country, and for each testing cycle, again without providing mean ages. Their paper concluded that: 'There are differences in the development of early numeracy between the different countries over the three moments of measurement. Especially the United Kingdom, Slovenia and Greece fall behind compared with the other countries' (van de Rijt and van Luit, 1999 p.10).

Bearing in mind preliminary analysis, the use of multilevel modelling now suggests that there may be little variation among countries at the start of the project, once age has been taken into account, and it is a matter of some relief that these data were *not* reported in the English press at the time. It appears, moreover, that this position may be substantially *unchanged* by the end of the project. Taking account of the fact that the English pupils have been in formal schooling throughout the testing cycles, the Slovene children not at all, and the rest of the participating countries from between the second and third testing moments, the end-results have a particular interest whatever their nature. As pointed out in Chapter 3, numerical data require statistical procedures which are technically appropriate and reveal the likely patterns in the data – with expert statistical expertise available throughout the research process. Moreover, as noted by John (1993):

> Can we learn … from cross-cultural comparison? It hardly needs pointing out that any social phenomena, whether it be practices in relation to the provision of education for women … or curriculum development in the teaching of mathematics, or whatever, is necessarily multivariate, yet frequently the comparative studies that are undertaken are univariate studies which fail to take account of the other variables.
>
> (John 1993, p.4)

The stage of reporting the results to a wider conference audience is certainly *not* the time to be seeking appropriate statistical expertise.

The research project described in this chapter does raise some genuine issues of ownership, design and technical expertise as well as ethics of research which, in this case, go beyond the treatment of the subjects to the conduct of the researchers themselves. It is clear, with hindsight, that a formal contract should have been prepared, specifying roles, responsibilities and duties, at the start of the project instead of trust being assumed.

It is at the stage of reporting that the quality of the research comes under closest scrutiny and when it will be judged by the wider research community. Moreover it is probably true to say that there is a *less* widely-available statistical expertise to judge the quality of data production and analysis than any other aspect of the research process to be considered. Obviously different audiences will have different background knowledge, different motivations and different interests. At this stage peer reviewers will serve as the major gate-keepers in the process; however, the integrity of researchers must be taken on trust at all times. The particular issues associated with research involving international comparison will be addressed in a future chapter. In this case study the appropriate analysis *will* take place and in due course a reliable research report produced which takes full account of the subtleties of the data. As John (1993) concludes:

> A final feature of the research itself which has been regarded as conducive or otherwise to having an influence on policy is whether or not it is of a high quality, whether it is clear and readily comprehensive, whether it has clear messages or is inconclusive and woolly.
>
> (John 1993, pp.15–16)

Conclusions

One intention of this chapter has been to emphasise to the reader that without a high level of technical expertise it is difficult to judge the quality of studies reported at research conferences, in research reports and journal articles. Furthermore the conventions of research reporting tend to indicate a smoothness, a progression and an orderliness which provides a highly sanitised version of the process and which belies the real-life experiences of the researchers concerned. Added to this, it is usually the case that any senior academic, at any one time, will not only have several research students to supervise and be working on diverse projects, but the exigencies of his or her life are such that there will be a number of other ongoing activities, at different stages of completion, requiring a different set of skills and making fairly unpredictable demands. All of these will require ongoing rigour and vigilance throughout the process to their conclusion. One of us, for instance, is currently awaiting the galley-proofs for one book to be received from the publishers as *this* book reaches the final stages of completion. At the same time book proposals for a further two await preparation. A numeracy project evaluation is in the earliest stages of data collection whilst another realistic mathematics intervention is at a tender stage of development. Meanwhile a magazine series on mathematics and learning difficulties is being juggled whilst two chapters, a journal article and three book reviews are also awaiting attention. In the circumstances it is just as well that there are clear checks and balances as it would be easy for an unscrupulous academic to 'cut corners'. And, perhaps, it is a healthy sign that researchers *don't* just agree with one another although this places even more responsibility upon knowledgeable policy-makers, scrupulous media reporters and any other consumers of research reports, who may have to find their way around a bewildering array of outputs. In this respect, the government's latest new proposed system for commissioning, reviewing and disseminating research is timely – but that is the tale for Chapter 13.

More fundamentally, this chapter raises issues of reflexivity which are not especially novel and which relate to the claims that the research activity of the knower always influences what is known and that nothing can be known except through these activities. The problem then becomes one of recognising that knowledge claims are always dependent upon the activity of the researcher. This raises questions about the kind of reality which is being constructed by the research questions asked and the methods used. It has already been noted in Chapter 4 that the separation of the subject that carries out the research from the object researched is a process considered essential to the generating of 'truthful' representations and 'scientific' research. This process is embodied in the construction of a written text which makes use of certain strategies and textual devices to divorce it from any recognisable contextualisation. Such a text is intentionally de-contextualised and, hence, questions are raised about its faithfulness to any reality outside the text. As Derrida (1978) observed, the so-called 'narrative realism' conceals the 'writerliness' and, in so doing, creates an ambiguous relationship to reflexivity of the writer/researcher. The whole notion of reflexivity, as noted by Usher and Edwards (1994), raises a powerful question for researchers to consider – can we *avoid* researching our own research practices, including ourselves as researchers? As they note, the need to problematise the practice of research is rarely recognised by us!

Papers available from the Poster Symposium held at EARLI Conference, Gothenburg, 1999

Aubrey, C. and Godfrey, R. *The Development of Early Numeracy in England.* Canterbury Christ Church University College.

Guesquiere, P., Verschaffel, L. Torbeyns, J. and Vossen, E. *The Development of Early Numeracy in Flanders.* University of Leuven.

Tancig, S., Kavkler, M. and Magajna, L. *The Development of Early Numeracy in Slovenia.* University of Ljubljana.

Tzouriadou, M., Barbas, G. and Bonti, E. *The Standardization of the Utrecht Early Mathematical Competence Test in Greece.* University of Thessaloniki.

van de Rijt, B.A.M and van Luit, J.E.H. *Development of Early Numeracy in Europe.* University of Utrecht.

12 Policy and practice

The hand that rocks the cradle

Two senior government advisers – Professor Michael Barber and Judy Sebba – visited the September 1999 British Education Research Association Conference to discuss the government's new approach to commissioning, reviewing and disseminating research. At the same time they sought to reassure their audience that research was helping to inform the education policy-making process. It may sound cynical to suggest that there appears to be much evidence to support the view that research is used to *justify* polical decisions which have already been made. This chapter, however, will take a different approach by showing how research can be used to interrogate existing policy and, hence, evaluate it. The case to be examined will be government policy which, in response to concern at school children's current educational attainment levels, has been encouraging an ever-earlier introduction to the formal teaching of literacy and numeracy. Two assumptions underpinning this policy are that:

- early introduction to formal schooling will lead to the raising of standards
- higher levels of achievement are linked to economic progress and, hence, to future prosperity.

These two, related assumptions will be examined critically, firstly, by reference to relevant comparative, preschool educational research and, secondly, in relation to the recent Third International Mathematics and Science Study (TIMSS). The implications will then be considered and, finally, some conclusions drawn.

Concern about falling standards of literacy and numeracy

There has been a growing public concern about falling standards in literacy and numeracy over the 1990s, stimulated by the so-called Three Wise Men report of Alexander, Rose and Woodhead (1992). More comprehensive data have become available as National Curriculum standard assessment tasks (SATs) have been made available and the results of two international studies published.

SAT results for eleven-year-olds have shown that in 1997 sixty-two per cent of pupils reached the expected Level 4 or above in mathematics and sixty-three per cent in English (QCA 1998). At an international level, in 1996 an NFER study assessing reading standards and comparing them with those of the International Association for Evaluation of Achievement (IEA) 1992 study of reading literacy (Elley 1994) – in which Britain did not take part – found that British nine-year-olds would have come sixteenth out of twenty-eight countries. Furthermore, there was a 'long tail' of pupils scoring well below the British mean score. Reynolds (1996 p. 54) has also referred to the 'a trailing edge of low performing pupils' in relation to a review of international mathematics studies involving England. Most recently, the TIMSS report by Harris, Keys and Fernandes (1997) showed English nine-year-olds to be significantly below the mean in mathematics, although there is now 'no sign ... of the long tail' reducing the average score. Moreover, the TIMSS report highlighted the important role in achievement of whole-class teaching, as well as individualisation, with regular use of homework.

Successive reports of the HM Chief Inspector of Schools, Chris Woodhead, have called for a 'back to basics' approach to teaching exemplified by the new National Literacy and Numeracy Strategies introduced during 1998–9. Clearly there are grounds for concern about standards though we have, as yet, a far from perfect understanding of the conditions that give rise to these. The last government put in place a comprehensive programme of measures to ensure that individuals' basic literacy and numeracy skill needs were being addressed, from preschool to adulthood. These initiatives fell into three broad groups:

- policies to identify and meet all pupils' needs, with national testing at seven, eleven and fourteen years, and including baseline assessment at school entry
- policies to improve the quality of teaching, with the introduction of a national curriculum for initial teacher training and new standards for teaching English and mathematics
- policies to challenge current standards and promote school performance through the publication of school performance tables and regular school inspections which, for nursery education, specify Desirable Outcomes for learning by compulsory school age.

Getting it right first time?

The cornerstone to these policies was the goal to 'get it right first time' by giving young children a solid grounding in basic skills from the start of schooling in order to reduce the need for remedial action later on. Good early education was thus seen to provide an essential foundation for every four-year-old, through the short-lived voucher scheme introduced from April 1997. The provision of nursery education was intended to ensure that 'for the first time preschool children ... work towards common learning outcomes', including language and literacy and mathematics, at school entry (SCAA 1997).

Schools and teachers, it was thought, needed to be very clear about pupils' capabilities at school entry so that they could build upon what had already been achieved. Accordingly, baseline assessment – focusing on early literacy and numeracy – of all children on school entry was regarded as an important new development which would help teachers to:

- understand their pupils' needs
- provide valuable information to guide schools' targeting of resources
- give a baseline for measuring future improvement (DfEE 1997a, Foreword by Gillian Shepherd).

National baseline assessment was thus set up on a voluntary basis from September 1997 and as a statutory requirement from September 1998 when over 600,000 pupils were involved (SCAA 1997).

Similarly, 16 per cent or so of all pupils were being identified as having special educational needs (SEN), the majority of whom would be able to acquire basic skills and 'in many cases to progress much further'. The early identification and assessment of SEN – including specific learning difficulty such as dyslexia – was therefore essential if national standards were to be raised. Since 1988 the National Curriculum had required a broad and balanced programme of teaching but, in order to raise standards, more emphasis on literacy and numeracy was seen to be needed.

At the same time the Labour Party, still in opposition, was planning to phase out the voucher scheme with its own 'big idea' for early years, set out in their document *Early Excellence* which appeared late in 1996. It committed Labour to a programme to bring education and care into an integrated service to meet the needs of young children and their families, which Blunkett (DfEE 1996) wrote 'lies at the very heart of our agenda for early years services'. An integrated and radical approach was advocated, already adopted by a number of local authorities and the basis for the more successful early years services in the rest of Europe. This signalled a commitment towards a 'sound beginning' for all children, for partnership plans to expand integrated education and care facilities for three-year-olds and high-quality education for all four-year-olds whose parents wanted it.[1] In fact, on entering government David Blunkett, as Secretary of State for Education and Employment, stated in the White Paper *Excellence in Schools* (DfEE 1997c):

> Tony Blair and I have made clear that education is our top priority ... by publishing the first policy document of the new government ... Without excellence in all of our schools many of our children are not given a fair start in life ... We all need to be involved: schools, teachers and parents are at the heart of it ... we need ... commitment if we are to get our children off to a good start.
>
> (DfEE 1997, Foreward by David Blunkett)

This document pledged that *all* children should have a firm foundation for their education and that by 2002 there would be:

- high-quality education for all four-year-olds whose parents wished it

- joint local planning of early years childcare and education, to meet local needs
- a network of early excellence centres, to spread good practice in teaching and learning
- effective assessment of all children starting primary school
- class sizes of thirty or under for five-, six- and seven-year-olds
- at least an hour each day devoted to both literacy and numeracy in every primary school
- national guidelines and training for all primary teachers on best practice in the teaching of literacy and numeracy
- a great improvement in achievements in mathematics and English, so that at least four out of five eleven-year-olds reach the standards expected of them, compared to three out of five as at present.

It was recognised that children – especially those from disadvantaged backgrounds – benefit from early education – that is, those with early education are more likely to succeed in primary school (DfEE 1997b, Forword by Estelle Morris). Furthermore, as stated in the Green Paper *Excellence for All Children* (1997d), the government's targets for raising standards were for *all* children, including those with SEN, and early identification of difficulties and appropriate intervention, it was stated, 'will give children with SEN the best possible start to their school lives'. The unexamined assumption underlying the government's commitment to a 'sound beginning' is that high-quality teaching of literacy and numeracy from statutory school-starting age at five years will lead to the raising of standards, to be judged in terms of national and international results. Furthermore, embedded in this assumption, is the belief that achievement and economic success are closely related and that raising educational standards will therefore increase British competitiveness in relation to the advanced economies of North America, Western Europe and the Pacific Rim.

> All over the world it is taken for granted that educational achievement and economic success are closely linked – that the struggle to raise a nation's living standards is fought first and foremost in the classroom. What has established this idea so unshakeably in people's minds is a recent, and to many a rather alarming phenomenon: the new intensity of global rivalry. The idea of competition among nations is now familiar (albeit often misunderstood).
>
> (*The Economist* 1997, p.17)

The remainder of this chapter will examine research evidence from international studies to evaluate critically the assumptions that:

- an early start to formal schooling is associated with higher standards of achievement
- attainment in literacy and numeracy is important for economic performance in industrialised countries.

The implications for policy-makers will then also be considered.

An early start or slow development?

Given concern about standards of achievement in this country and our relatively early age of starting full-time, compulsory schooling – by the term following a child's fifth birthday – it might be reasonable to consider what advantages accrue from this practice, as the age of school-entry varies between countries from five to seven years, with six being the most common age. Moreover, whilst Luxembourg and the Netherlands also begin school at five years of age, in England children frequently begin school even earlier than statutory school requirements. Although practice varies among local authorities and individual schools, children typically enter reception classes in the September after their fourth birthday. Sharp (1995) found local authorities adopting a range of admission strategies, the most common being annual (forty-four per cent), along with termly (twenty-five per cent) and bi-annual (twenty-three per cent). Most schools took four-year-olds, just under a third of authorities having changed their policy recently in favour of admitting four-year-olds. Interestingly, prior to the current government's drive to provide high-quality education for all four-year-olds, figures for 1994 (DfEE 1996) showed that seventy-seven per cent of four year-olds attended school, local-authority or grant-maintained nurseries, full- or part-time, for at least some of the year before compulsory school-starting age. Of these, fifty-one per cent were in reception classes and twenty-six per cent in nursery classes A further nineteen per cent said to be placed in private or voluntary preschool education would suggest that almost all four-year-olds were already in some form of educational provision at least part of the time. Furthermore, as Tizard *et al.* (1988) and Bennett and Kell (1989) had already shown, in spite of appearances only a small proportion of reception-class activities were devoted to play-related activities (less than ten per cent), indicating that in spite of pupils' early admission age little time was spent in preparation for, or developing skills to, facilitate formal learning.

Perhaps more importantly, these figures give some indication of the wide variability of ages of children in reception classrooms, inevitable given a spec-ified calendar year for admissions and exaggerated still further by variations in local policy and practice as well as by parental preference. In fact, the relatively lower average attainments of summer-born children, who conceivably may be up to nine months younger than their autumn-born peers, have been well-documented by the NFER (see, for instance, Sharp and Benefield's annotated bibliography *Research into Season of Birth and School Achievement*, 1995). Sharp's own work (Sharp, 1995; Sharp, Hutchison and Whetton, 1994) has demon-strated the influence of season of birth on attainment at the end of Key Stage 1 and in later General Certificate of Secondary Education (GCSE) as well as statementing as having SEN in primary schools. These data confirm that children who are oldest perform best, although Tymms (1998) has challenged the quality of the data and analysis and hence their limitations as the basis for policy and practice.

Existing wide variations of age within one class, however, are likely to be accentuated still further by variations in general development or maturity. Not only do children starting school near to their fourth birthday appear to do less well than those of the same age starting school later but, as noted above, nursery schools with their more generous staff–pupil ratios and activity-based curricula may be better suited to the needs of the younger child, as noted by West and Varlaam (1992). Daniels, Redfern and Shorrocks-Taylor (1995) concluded that the provision of appropriate conditions for four-year-olds in infant classes appeared to be a low priority in many local authorities. Their failures, they felt, were a consequence of a combination of government, local-authority and school-governor decisions.

Moss (1994), moreover, highlighted the dangers inherent in constructing league tables for cross-national comparison of levels of provision for early preschool learning based on nationally-available data, such as the OECD *Education at a Glance* (1992). For children over three years the general pattern to emerge was that most countries now provided, or planned to provide, two to three years of publicly funded early childhood services before formal schooling began. In general, for countries with early school entry such as Britain, Luxembourg and the Netherlands, there may be more variation in provision for three-year-olds. Britain, he has suggested, was

> unique for its reliance on a combination of playgroups, a shift system for nursery education and early admission to primary school. One consequence is that for many children ... the period from 3 to 5 involves a series of transitions from one short phase of service attendance to another (e.g. into playgroup, then to nursery class, then to reception class in primary school within a two-year period). Elsewhere a two- to three-year nursery education phase, leading to primary school at 6, is the emerging pattern.
>
> (Moss 1994, p.16)

In conclusion, with one of the world's lowest school admission ages, Britain provides very variable provision for three- and four-year-olds in range and in appropriateness.

A question of organisation or readiness?

Prais (1997) has approached the long-known phenomenon of low achievement in summer-born children as a problem of teaching, in the same class, children who are at widely differing stages of their development. In other words, what organisational changes could be made to reduce the wide variation in children's attainments within a single class in order to improve the pace of teaching and learning for the class as a whole? He has contrasted our rigid calendar-age admission policies with the Continental practice of deferring entry for slow developers in order to achieve greater class homogeneity. Furthermore, he has compared our rigid, age-related promotion to higher classes regardless of attainment with the widely-practised system of 'class repetition' on the Continent, where the academic advantages of further consolidation must be weighed up – with parents – against the social-emotional disadvantages of separation from peers and possible lowered esteem. Deferred or postponed entry to normal schooling may, therefore, be recommended for a slowly-developing child, a child with a disability or a recent immigrant. Using Switzerland, specifically the Canton of Zurich, as an exemplar country with high achievement in terms of international educational comparison, Prais described how a recommendation to spend an additional year in kindergarten – normal or special – may be assisted by various school-readiness tests but depends more usually upon the guidance of the kindergarten teacher. In fact early identification of and remediation for special educational needs is a prime function of the Swiss kindergarten teacher. Whilst Swiss class repetition is used infrequently, with late entry being regarded as less disruptive, this procedure is available when necessary and where supplementary instruction has been unsuccessful. The result is a slightly more mixed-age class with slightly less variability in attainment within any one class, where predominantly whole-class teaching takes place and less individualisation is required. Prais has concluded that 'greater flexibility in age of school entry than currently practised in England may thus be a pre-condition for the extension of whole-class-teaching, and for more efficient teaching and learning' (Prais 1997, Abstract).

This suggests that current government policy, with increasing emphasis on earlier introduction to scholastic skills and taking no account of readiness, simply widens the variability of pupils and increases the likelihood of early failure.

Preschool education: A stage in its own right or preparation for formal schooling?

The Desirable Outcomes of learning (SCAA 1997) produced in response to the proposed expansion of nursery provision, outline the expected achievements of English children by the time they enter compulsory schooling. As noted by Whitburn (1996) of the six areas defined – personal and social, language and literacy, mathematics, knowledge and understanding of the world, physical development, and creativity – at least three demonstrate a concern with early academic learning and reflect the concern to develop formal skills in the preschool years. In contrast she described the Japanese preschool emphasis on cooperation, kindness and collaboration, which prepare children to take part in the class group and become a 'social person' when formal schooling starts at six years. She outlined the aims of Japanese preschool education (cited by Monbusho 1994), which over ninety per cent of children will attend for at least two years. These aims:

*   encourage basic living habits and attitudes for a healthy, safe and happy life, and nurture the foundations for a healthy mind and body

- encourage love and trust for people and cultivate an attitude of independence, cooperation and morality
- encourage interests towards one's surrounding nature and society, and cultivate sensitivity and a capacity for appreciating one's surroundings
- encourage interest towards language in daily life, develop a pleasant attitude in talking and listening to others, and cultivate language sense
- encourage a rich mind and enrich creativity through various experiences.

In contrast to the English emphasis on individual development, rights and freedoms, which allow individual children to 'progress at their own rate', the Japanese curriculum recognises the importance of both maintaining and imparting cultural values within the context of a highly controlled state curriculum, with common goals which set standards for each year and, more-over, require acceptance of individual responsibility for reaching these (Whitburn 1996). Education is valued by society, schools and parents in particular, who are expected to support children's learning at home by reviewing school work, dealing with learning problems and monitoring homework, as well as paying for private, evening preparation classes – or *juku* – to ensure that annual targets are met.

Like Switzerland and Japan, Hungary has also scored highly in terms of international educational achievement and, like Switzerland and Japan, Hungary provides a preschool system with the goal of preparing children for formal schooling, which like the others emphasises whole-class interactive teaching. The Hungarian Professor Jozsef Nagy (1989), who has been investigating the relationship – or 'articulation' – of kindergarten to compulsory schooling for more than twenty years, also sees the goal of preschool education as the reduction of pupil variation, whether resulting from developmental difference or delay, whether cognitive or from social disadvantage. In fact his own research from the early 1980s onwards, with Hungarian and Sri Lankan five- to six-year-olds, has indicated that children with a calendar age of six years could vary widely in developmental terms, which could not be eliminated by later schooling. Hence, the outcome of a child's scholastic career was deter-mined by social or biological difference in entry characteristics. These differences could be more than plus or minus one year biologically, plus or minus two-and-a-half years mentally and plus or minus three years in social development – leaving aside the five per cent of the most and least developed at each end of the distribution. The 'alternative entry model', introduced in Hungary in 1986, thus required that children be registered at school not according to their calendar age of six years but according to their stage of development. As a result, twenty to thirty per cent of children with a calendar age of six years do not enter first grade but spend a further year at kindergarten. At the same time those five-year-olds who are nearly six and whose level of development is above average for six years are accepted. As a result class-heterogeneity caused by extreme variation is avoided and early failure reduced.

A recent Channel 4 Television programme, *Dispatches: The Early Years* (Mills and Mills 1998) set out to investigate the early childhood educational systems of three cognate, European nations – Hungary, German-speaking Switzerland and Flemish-speaking Belgium – successful in terms of international school achievement. Again the focus was upon preparation for formal schooling by nursery or kindergarten education. Like the Japanese system described above, the common goal for these systems was described as preparation for effective formal learning:

> The implicit and sometimes explicit aim is that the preschool cycle should reduce the socioeconomic and genetic variation found in young children and pass on to schools homogeneous groups of children who can learn together and who are ready for the formal learning.
>
> (Mills and Mills 1998, p.3)

In each country children were being taught systematically in the preschool phase:

* attention, listening and memory skills in order to participate in an oral, linguistic approach to teaching
* appropriate cooperative group behaviour
* conceptual understanding of space, size, quantity and time which underlies later mathematical understanding
* phonological awareness and motor skills (regarded as essential preparation for reading and writing).

All children apparently passed systematically through this highly-structured and progressive, preschool curriculum – whether the Hungarian Kindergarten Handbook, the Swiss *Rahmenplan*, or Flemish Core Curriculum – with daily sessions of whole-class teaching and with special help provided for slower learners or those from less-advantaged backgrounds. Whilst gross and fine motor exercises are provided in preparation for later handwriting, written language – reading and writing – is excluded, with spoken language being emphasised throughout. The goal is to prepare children thoroughly for the rapid introduction to a formal curriculum which will be encountered on entry to primary schooling at six to seven years.

To illustrate the influence that formal preparation has on later achievement, one of the writers' own comparative case study in conjunction with the University of Ljubljana, Slovenia (historically, like Hungary, part of the old Austro-Hungarian empire) showed that by seven years – when Slovene pupils had been in school for nine months – there appeared to be no benefit accrued from early English schooling in terms of mathematics achievement. In other words, by seven years the effects of an additional two years of formal schooling for English pupils were negligible in comparison with a Central European system stressing preparation for formal schooling and a tradition of relying entirely on oral methods of instruction till seven years of age (Aubrey, Tancig, Magajna and Kavkler 1998).

The English emphasis on early, formal scholastic skills was noted in the introduction to this section. In fact, the latest OFSTED report (1998), drawn from evidence on the early education on four-year-olds in a range of settings leaves no doubt that the so-called Desirable Outcomes of learning are 'intended to help providers design a curriculum which is both well-suited to four-year-olds and relates effectively to the earliest stages of the National Curriculum' (OFSTED 1998, p.4).

The conclusions drawn in this report were that, whilst personal and social development was generally 'well-promoted', variations were noted between types of institution for language and literacy (94.3 per cent of independent or private schools contrasted with 54.3 per cent of playgroups promoting this area of learning) and in mathematics (where the figures were 91.3 per cent and 59.4 per cent respectively). Moreover the variation in treatment of knowledge and understanding of the world was 'still disappointingly wide and reflected confusion about what this area was intended to cover and how to plan and prepare for it' (OFSTED 1998, p.11). A 'key indicator of success' for these inspections was the progress made by four-year-olds towards the Desirable Outcomes.

These institutions, then, were being judged by inspectors on their effectiveness to introduce formal scholastic learning to four-year-olds. Moreover it was a statutory requirement from September 1998 for all children to have a baseline assessement with a focus on early literacy and numeracy on entry to formal schooling. Far from providing a 'sound beginning' – in other words a preparation for formal scholastic skills, especially for those socially disadvantaged or developmentally delayed, in order to *reduce* pupil variation – our educational system serves simply to confirm failure – if not confer failure – and, thereby, *increases* variation. On the one hand there is no generally-agreed curriculum for three-, four- and five-year-olds in England; on the other, whilst there *is* a National Curriculum for children of six years and above, there are no expected standards of attainment for each year of schooling. In fact it is expected that children will progress at different rates. There is no requirement and, indeed, no incentive for individual pupils to 'catch up' or a responsibility for parent or teacher to ensure that they do so.

Whilst ministers have asked advisers to examine whether formal schooling should be delayed until children are six years old (Ghouri 1998), and whether three to five years old should be regarded as a distinct phase for which new curriculum guidelines should be developed, *will* such research described in this section influence the hand that rocks the cradle?

Education and the wealth of nations?

The first part of this chapter identified a concern about current educational standards in relation to national and international performance and noted the call from policy-makers for a 'back-to-basics' approach to teaching from an ever earlier age. Lessons from abroad suggest that, far from eliminating pupil variation, too early a start may serve merely to accentuate existing social and developmental differences between pupils, which the educational system has no means to redress.

Robinson's (1997) analysis in *Literacy, Numeracy and Economic Performance* suggested that the new Labour government's educational policy was under-pinned by a belief in the importance of the key skills of literacy and numeracy, both in improving Britain's relative economic performance and for tackling the twin problems of unemployment and low wages. He identified the need to distinguish between the objective to raise average levels of attainment in literacy and numeracy and, on the other, to reduce the numbers of young people at the lower end of the attainment range.

The evidence from international studies examined above, however, suggests that effective educational systems can tackle these twin objectives in tandem. Robinson concluded that there was a strong case for putting more emphasis on improvements at the lower end of the attainment range and cited the findings from two English longitudinal studies[2] which revealed the dominant impact of social and economic disadvantage – again, recognised and addressed by the educational systems already described. Furthermore, one of the two studies suggested that preschool education had no impact, though the degree of parental interest and involvement – also recognised and required by the Continental systems examined above – was important. Robinson concluded that an individual's market prospects *are* harmed by low levels of literacy and numeracy. Whilst he could find no evidence from the longitudinal studies that class size, teaching method, homework policy or the use of setting or streaming has any impact on attainment, he concluded that public-policy initiatives needed to emphasise improvements at the lower end of the attainment range, that is, for the socially- and economically-disadvantaged groups. Green (1997), too, asserted that none of the traditional indicators – whether class size, educational expenditure, selection and grouping strategies, teaching styles or time spent learning particular subjects – correlate systematically with outcomes over a range of countries. Instead outcomes are likely to be associated with complex interactions among factors, some internal to the educational system in question and some related to features in the broader sociocultural contexts.

All of the evidence points to the need for policy-makers to address social and economic disadvantage in order to reduce pupil variability. Strategies, including preparation for formal schooling and adopting greater flexibility towards school grouping than our rigid calendar-age grouping permits, appear to offer a means to reduce variability. In the case of Hungary, for instance, these procedures are supported by sound research. But what *is* the relationship of policy to research?

Tizard *et al.* (1988), examining the issue of how research findings reach policy-makers and practitioners, identified the crucial gateways through which research findings must go if they are to become known specifically to the quality press, the media in general and the educational supplements in particular. Research which does not pass through these gateways, she opined, stands little chance of making an impact. Lack of attention does not appear to have been a problem for recent international research on school achievement in the current climate of global economic rivalry and the widespread belief that economic success is associated with high educational achievement.

One hazard, of course, is that once these gateways are opened up, journalists – or academics, for that matter – will have their own purposes and agendas for reporting research findings and, in the process of recontextualising, wittingly or unwittingly, may oversimplify, if not sensationalize and distort, these findings. In fact, as Halls (1990) has indicated, the influence of international comparisons of pupil performance has grown steadily since the early 1970s. Brown (1998) has also noted the growing enthusiasm – and growing criticism – for such work since the First International Mathematics Study was carried out in 1964. By the late 1980s, she noted, this was being used by both Tory and Labour governments to justify a return to 'basics' in terms of both curriculum content and whole-class teaching methods with their respective emphases on raising levels of literacy and numeracy, especially in primary schools. She emphasised that England's performance in TIMSS for mathematics was in fact quite similar to that of most European countries, with neither a particularly wide range of attainment nor a long tail of underachievement. Much, she noted, depends upon the match of test items to the national curriculum concerned, which is as likely to explain our higher achievement in science and as our relatively lower achievement in mathematics, with the *less*-publicised good performance for problem-solving and geometry. These findings in themselves, she concluded, cast doubt upon the need for major reform of teaching methods.

The editorial of the *Times Educational Supplement* for 20 March 1998 enquired: 'How is it that the United States remains the world's most successful industrial nation when its pupils are no better at mathematics than the English' and 'If high rates of literacy and numeracy result in economic progress, how is it that the Czechs, Slovaks and Bulgarians score so well, yet have weak economies?'

It would appear, in this respect, that value for money as well as overall educational expenditure must be taken into account. In any case, the assertion that there is a direct correlation between education and economic growth has been questioned since the 1970s. *Human capital* theory, according to Halls (1990), postulated that education is the catalyst for the progressive appreciation in value of human capital, demonstrating that physical capital must be used in conjunction with a trained labour force. More recently there has been a revival of interest in *cost-benefit* theory in which 'rates of return' are recognised as approximate indicators of the effectiveness of educational systems. As noted by Hall (1990), however, higher attainment in a cycle of unemployment does not necessarily lead the individual to a correspondingly higher placement in the work hierarchy.

Nothing new under the sun?

No-one needs convincing that education matters and, if policy-makers seek to find best practice from looking around the world, what they observe is a wide variation in performance and a wide variation in class size, hours of subject teaching and educational expenditure.

If there *has* been a growing consensus that education is the key to getting rich – for countries as well as for individuals, this view may have to be radically revised as we teeter on the edge of global recession. So, apart from casting doubt upon some widely-held beliefs about education, what lessons can be learned from abroad? It must of course be acknowledged straight away that, notwithstanding the disclaimers of any intention of 'running an international horse race', there has been no doubt that a number of ministries of education have been interested in and influenced by the findings of recent, large-scale and quantitative international studies of educational attainment. Such studies – the first, genuinely worldwide comparative studies – have generated enormous interest, and the impact on policy has been incontrovertible. The finding that levels of attainment among industrialised countries are broadly comparable and that levels in developing countries cannot match these standards is, in itself, unremarkable. Moreover, the discipline of comparative education is older – and richer – than the relatively recent IEA studies, which began in the late 1960s, might suggest.

Halls (1990) has suggested in fact that not since the 1960s have comparative educationalists seen the main thrust of their work as improving education in order to stimulate a better life for society and for the individual. By the first oil crises in 1973 belief that education would prove to be the universal social and economic panacea was discredited. As he noted, it was evident that educational expansion alone brought neither greater equality of opportunity nor greater economic prosperity. It demonstrably had not wrought more effective economic progress, as the situation in developing countries attested, and it does not appear to have reduced social inequalities in the developed world. As a result of this, comparative educationalists now generally view the world more cautiously and approach it with a more modest research agenda.

Bereday (1964), who saw the systematic study of foreign educational systems as stretching back as far as the days of Plato and Aristotle, identified practical applications of such study. He suggested: first, that 'education is a mirror held against the face of a people ... how they take care of their children tells unerringly who they are'; and second, that 'one studies foreign education not solely to know foreign peoples but also – and perhaps most of all – to know oneself' (Bereday 1964, pp.5–6)

To understand others and to understand ourselves, he concluded, is to have in hand the two ingredients of comparison. Being attuned to the importance of comparability permits comparative educationalists to serve two practical goals:

> first, to deduce from the achievements and the mistakes of school systems other than their own, lessons for their own schools (or warn policy-makers that such lessons cannot be lightheartedly sought where valid comparison is impossible); second, to appraise educational issues from a global rather

than an ethnocentric perspective, or in other words, to be aware always of other nations' points of view.

(Bereday 1964, p.6)

Both goals, he regarded, were important enough to render comparative education 'indispensible in the armoury of educational planners'.

Perhaps, then, at a time of comparative education retrenchment, as Bereday noted,

> the power to see schools of other countries not only as they appear in their own national context but in terms of other systems is an important goal ... (since) ... it bestows knowledge both by guiding students to the true face of a foreign people and by showing their own faces reflected in foreigners' eyes.

(Bereday 1964, p.6)

Mallinson (1980), in fact, provides us with a timely reminder – that preschool education in particular, at home and abroad, whether creche, nursery school or kindergarten, has a long and distinguished history. Furthermore, if various countries of Western Europe differ as to which is the best age to start compulsory schooling, there are, nevertheless many commonalities. He noted that there is general recognition in different countries that:

- children need to spend longer than ever in school to learn the complexities of modern living
- they have to face problems of dealing with children of immigrants, as with children of socially deprived backgrounds
- they are harassed by the ever-growing complexities of urbanisation (which can be associated with lack of adequate play facilities and lack of contact with children of the same age, outside the home)
- they are finding an increasingly familiar pattern of both parents working, not simply for economic reasons but often to enhance adult lifestyle
- there is a general agreement that the sooner individual handicaps are diagnosed and dealt with, the more confidently will children tackle the later steps of their school career
- as parents acknowledge that the modern condition of the home may not always meet all of their young children's needs beyond a certain age, so they become more involved with their children's preschool institutions and are fully encouraged to do so.

Moreover, there is already a widespread belief in the benefit of some kind of formal education well below the compulsory school-starting age. The influence of key educators in this area have been many – Froebel, Pestalozzi, Dewey, Montessori, Decroly – to name just a few. Again, the commonalities in their views are marked:

- an interest in the total child and the formative nature of the earliest years for all-round development (social, emotional and physical)
- the importance of a cognitive (intellectual) approach, particularly for the less-advantaged child
- the traditional acceptance of an informal approach to learning through play
- an emphasis, by the best approaches, placed on verbal development and simple calculation through activity-oriented programmes, carefully devised by a warm, supportive and stimulating teacher
- the encouragement of independence, self-control and self-discipline through teaching the child to function as a member of the group
- an important and sensitive role in all of this for the teacher to play in providing indirect guidance and inspiration rather than any kind of formal instruction.

Preschool education across Western Europe has common social and humanitarian roots in the nineteenth century, catering originally for children of working-class parents, and often including the 'underprivileged' and 'backward' child. Now preschool institutions draw from every social group and, as noted by Mallinson (1980), have become 'democratising institutions … (and) … only by such a pre-apprenticeship is the child fully prepared to benefit from his primary school education'.

What has become clear from this short analysis of international early education research is that the drive of successive English governments to introduce formal scholastic teaching at ever earlier ages serves merely to create the failure it seeks to avoid. Until our first phase of education – for our three-, four- and five-year-olds – has goals, curriculum content and appropriate teaching strategies which seek to *prepare* children for formal schooling and reduce variation with procedures for identifying, remediating, where possible, and making sensible placement decisions concerning our most socially and developmentally vulnerable children, our educational 'beginnings' will *not* be as 'sound' as we might hope.

Notes

1 Guidance for 1998–9 appeared in DfEE (1997b).
2 The National Child Development Study collected data on over 17,000 people born in a single week in 1958, and subsequently at ages 7, 11, 16, 23, 33 and 37 (10% sample). The 1970 British Cohort Study also began with a sample of over 17,000 born in a single week, who have been followed up in subsequent surveys at 5, 10, 16, 21 and 26 (10% sample). A series of studies has been carried out by the Basic Skills Agency, analysing the effects of poor basic skills on adult life.

13 Current theoretical perspectives

Directions for the future?

The new research and policy-making context

The previous chapter considered how research could be used to examine critically existing government policy. It showed that assumptions made by policy-makers about the mechanisms underlying achievement of a world-class education can – and should – be challenged. At the same time policy-makers, for their part, rightly expect the *quality* of research to be improved, to be evaluated more carefully, and to be publicised more widely:

> The Treasury is increasingly demanding hard evidence that the investment they are making in education is delivering outcomes ... Next year we will be going back to the Treasury for the next three-year funding cycle and we desperately need the best evidence possible.
>
> (Barber 1999 p.27)

In spite of a commitment to the development of nursery education in the early 1970s made by Margaret Thatcher as Education Minister, some twenty-five years ago, successive governments have failed to invest in preschool education. Now the DfEE has made it clear that investment is to be forth-coming, both to serve the long-term goal of creating an effective, top-quality educational system which can compete in international terms but also, in the short-term, one which can demonstrate cost-effectiveness. With respect to long-term goals, David Weikart (see Schweinhart, Weikart and Toderan 1993) of the High/Scope Research Foundation has long argued that we can hardly afford to ignore early education, bearing in mind the later saving to be made in terms of special services such as social welfare and the criminal justice system, which he believes his research of twenty years to have demonstrated. In this country it is hoped that the Sylva *et al.* (1997) Effective Provision for Pre-school Education (EPPE) project will provide corresponding evidence concerning children, families and settings which can inform decisions about this sector of education.

Accountability has become a watchword in a whole range of public services from education and health to social services. This has arisen partly from the political and ideological drive of the previous government to place public services within a framework which resembles private, profit-making business and partly from a general trend throughout Europe and North America to demand evaluation of the functioning of public services. In Chapter 2 evaluation as a form of research was discussed briefly and although, in itself, it does not constitute a distinct research strategy it *can* be distinguished from other sorts of research which this book has been examining in terms of its function – to assess the effectiveness or worth of a new policy, practice or public service. This means that whilst evaluation findings have a better chance than more traditional research results of influencing policy, a whole host of new questions is raised. These questions relate to the interests being served by the evaluation, in terms of clients and decision-makers, the nature of the change programme being investigated, as well as the values and goals of the audience for the technical report, which will influence its style, treatment of evidence and the time-frame within which it is prepared.

At last the present government is setting out a vision of excellence for all children by providing a programme of high-quality early years education and care to meet the needs of young children and their families, which should serve as a spur to evaluation as one type of applied research. This integrated and radical approach, described as the basis for the most successful early years service in the rest of Europe, is well on the way to being implemented through the Early Years Development Partnerships (DfEE 1997b) and, more recently, the Early Years Development and Child Care Partnerships 1999–2000 (DfEE 1998a) with:

- integrated administrative responsibility for day care and education services to provide a universal framework of registration and inspection
- local development of services through the Development Partnership and local authority coordination of service planning and commissioning
- improving training through integrated education and care, training opportunities and developing a climbing framework of vocational qualifications.

So far as research is concerned, there will be an unprecedented scope for investigation of early years policy and practice that only such large-scale natural experiment in change can bring. In addition to the provision of nursery education for all four-year-olds and the reduction of infant class sizes, the government announced in July 1998, following its comprehensive spending review, the launch of the £540 million *Sure Start* programme for under-fours which will be developed alongside a substantial increase in nursery education (DHO/DfEE 1998).

Sure Start will involve a number of government departments working to provide comprehensive support for preschool children in disadvantaged areas, by working with families to give children the best start from the beginning of life. In fact the number of children living in a household with no working adult grew from one in five in 1979 to almost one in three in 1997, or two and a half. One in three (more than three million) children live in households with less than half the average income, almost three times as many as in 1979. Some thirty-seven local authorities have reported a reduction and sixty-seven an increase in concentration of disadvantage in particular schools, indicating an increasing polarisation of social advantage and disadvantage in education and society (Howarth *et al.* 1998).

Meanwhile the Sure Start (DfEE 1999) initiative is planned as an addition to the National Childcare Strategy work in Early Excellence Centres and the expansion of nursery education. Its key principles relate to play, learning and childcare. It is claimed to reflect research which shows what works in helping child development and to focus on:

- parental involvement
- the importance of play
- accessibility
- good quality play-based preschool provision
- cultural appropriateness and sensitivity to particular families' needs (DOH/DfEE 1998).

What is proposed is a broad developmental pack for children 'so that parents and professionals can plan to help each child move towards the next developmental milestones which are set out as Sure Start Child Development Objectives under the following headings:

- personal care and emotional development
- social care and development
- cognitive development
- creative development
- physical development.

which should incorporate the full range of the child's development (Sure Start Unit 1998). This initiative, taken together with the new foundation curriculum being developed for three- to five-year-olds (QCA 1999), will provide a seamless programme for children from birth to five years, with the National Curriculum proper starting at six years (Year One). But since, unlike the Foundation Curriculum, Sure Start resources have been concentrated on areas and localities of extreme disadvantage, the expectation of the government is that their investment will deliver outcomes and, hence, local authorities involved will be expected to provide appropriate, independent evaluation. The outline of the programme provided here serves to indicate that evaluators need to have an understanding of the issues involved in its original development, as well as the proposals put forward for implementation by the specific authority concerned, before selecting a general research strategy and appropriate methodology. Moreover it serves to illustrate the political dimension to any such activity, however hard individual evaluators may attempt to focus on the specific programme workings concerned.

The challenge

If all of these new initiatives at last provide young children with the opportunity – as is the case in most of Europe – to prepare for formal schooling at six years, then they are to be welcomed. Furthermore, they may even provide the means for the preschool cycle to *reduce* the socioeconomic and genetic variation found in young children to allow:

- more homogeneous groups of children to enter formal schooling
- who can be taught together
- who are ready for formal learning
- who will respond to the whole-class, interactive teaching envisaged by the new Literacy and Numeracy strategies.

We already have overwhelming evidence that children of the poor and minority groups have been overrepresented in special education for moderate learning difficulties and emotional and behavioural disorder, as noted in the previous chapter. These two groups constitute sixty per cent – nearly two-thirds – of our special school population (see Audit Commission/HMI 1992). As Reynolds (1989), a leading American scholar in the field, has argued, the prevalence of mildly handicapped children is far greater than those more severely handicapped. These children show one or more of the following characteristics (Reynolds 1989, p.130):

- they are not responding positively to the instruction offered to them in basic academic skills (usually reading)
- their social behaviour in school is unacceptable
- they are falling badly behind classmates in learning in academic subjects
- they have significant physical limitations or major health problems
- English is not their primary language (often associated with important cultural differences as well)
- they are extremely limited in experiences which provide background for formal education

Reynolds has observed that underlying these characteristics are complex factors, many of them beyond the full control of teachers and school authorities. For example, some children live in poverty and lack proper housing, medical care, and even food. They lack the range of experiences and thus the richness of cognitive schemata upon which teaching is usually predicated. As infants many of such children are born at low birth weight, are otherwise fragile in health and show a high base-rate for developmental problems.

A recent in-depth investigation in this country by McCallum (1998) into the home-life of five thousand pupils from the age of four in the London Borough of Ealing has provided new evidence that social class is a crucial factor in determining whether a child is successful at school. This study showed that reception-aged children from the lowest social groups consistently achieved the worst results in baseline assessment tests for reading, writing, speaking and maths and were underrepresented (only fourteen per cent) in the highest scores for SATs at eleven years: that is, reaching level five and above.

According to Safford (1994), however, there is no overall consensus concerning the nature of children's development – typical or atypical – or the salience of factors that influence its course. Maybe this is a good argument for developing inclusive education and care services for the early years of life which will offer a sound test-bed for inclusion in the years of statutory schooling. As Wilson (1998) has observed, a major difficulty in describing the growth of a young child who is developing atypically begins with the problem of trying to define 'atypical'. By definition, children described as having special needs fail to develop in line with their typically-developing peers in one or more areas of development. Wilson goes on to distinguish between *delays*, which are marked by slow progress in reaching developmental milestones in one or more areas, such as communication, cognition, adaptive behaviours (feeding, dressing, toileting and so on), and *disorders*, which disrupt or change the manner of a child's developmental progress. A disorder differs from a delay in that a delay is characterised by slow but otherwise unremarkable development whereas a disruption to normal development may require alternative routes for achieving certain skills as a result of visual, hearing or motor impairment. In these cases, however, it is common that there will be accompanying delays in one or more other areas.

Whilst intervention cannot remove the disorder, the goal will be to minimise the negative impact on the child's development. The extent of delays, on the other hand, will be determined by comparison with chronological development measured in terms of norms of performance. Quantitative descriptions may be used to establish the percentage of delay or standard deviation from the mean, which require the use of an assessment instrument where standardised scores are obtained, such as an intelligence test. Arguably, atypical development should include not only delays in development but also significantly higher levels of performance than is the norm in one or more area, in order to nurture special talents and abilities at an early stage.

Certain conditions place children at increased risk of experiencing atypical development in the form of delays or disorders. Wilson has suggested grouping these risk conditions as *established risk* which refers to medical and/or neurological disorders, often with a known aetiology as such as Down's syndrome; *biological risk*, where there is a history of concerns in prenatal, perinatal, neonatal, or early development; and *environmental risk*, where experiences or conditions may have interfered with healthy physical, emotional or psychological development.

Since young children are believed to learn through play and through interactions with people and objects in their environment, it is clear that early education which focuses on removing or circumventing the barriers to play and interactions within the social and physical environment is essential for exceptional children. Wilson's analysis indicates the importance of building on early competence and confidence in order to minimise the negative impact of a disability on learning and development. This competency-based approach suggests that all children are able to construct their own knowledge so long as major barriers to interacting with the environment are reduced so far as possible or removed. As Wilson indicates, however, notions of 'best practice' evolve and establishing a theoretical framework for understanding and working with children – ordinary or special – is central to this. This brings us back to the view expressed in the Preface for this book that there is a need to examine critically both the informal assumptions about learning and teaching that early years policy-makers, professionals and practitioners all hold, as well as the formal, theoretical knowledge base upon which they draw. This will be the topic of the next section to this chapter.

In the meantime this brief examination of the existing knowledge base concerning the learning of young 'at risk' children is sufficient to indicate the need for large-scale studies of the economics of early years education as well as the wider benefits of learning. Furthermore, the DfEE's proposed new system for reviewing and disseminating research – that is, providing a version of the medical *Cochrane Collaboration* network – would allow the preparation, updating and distribution of research reviews which encompass the diverse range of educational and healthcare issues underpinning early childhood learning and development.

Models of development, developmental processes and outcomes

The previous section has underlined the importance of examining the developing child from an ecological perspective although, as noted by Bronfenbrenner (1992), overwhelmingly psychological conceptions of child development are context-free. The characteristics of the developing child are thus defined conceptually and empirically without reference to the environment and are presumed to have the same meaning irrespective of the culture, class or setting in which they are observed, or in which the child lives. Where such conceptions are still held by practitioners the life chances of children from minority groups are unlikely to be transformed.

Bronfenbrenner (1992) has suggested that the study of an ecology of human development involves progressive, mutual accommodation through the life course, between an active, growing human being and the changing properties of the immediate setting in which the developing person lives, as this process is affected by the relations between these settings, and by the larger contexts in which these settings are embedded. Here characteristics of both the child and of the environment are taken into account jointly to identify 'ecological niches' in regions of the environment which are favourable or unfavourable to the development of individuals with particular characteristics. As an earlier section in this chapter identified, there are groups of children at psychological risk, whose circumstances immediately raise questions about a 'good ecology'.

In this regard Bronfenbrenner cited a longitudinal study (Werner and Smith 1982) of a group of Hawaiian children who, despite having been born in chronic poverty and of parents with little education, managed to develop into autonomous and competent adults, outcomes which contrasted dramatically with a similar group of 'control' children. Whilst the environmental and personal characteristics of the vulnerable children with successful outcomes are richly described, Bronfenbrenner concluded that the processes and pathways remained unclear.

According to Safford (1994), however, the wealth of available psychological constructs leads to the use of a 'mixed bag' of theories by special educators – and, it could be equally argued – by early educators too. These include:

- *maturational* theories which carry assumptions about fixed ages and stages, and carry a notion of developmentally appropriate practice (DAP)
- *interactionalist/transactionalist* theories which stress the social context
- *learning* theories which focus on the careful arrangement of the environment
- *cognitive* theories which focus on global, undifferientiated behaviour which progresses to increasingly advanced skill and reasoning
- *brain maturation* theories which support the position that intervention begun in the earliest years can affect neurological development of children
- *psycho-biological* theories of affect which owe much to, for instance, Freud and Bowlby, who were also transactionalists who emphasised the importance of interactions between brain development as an affective system and the environment in which the infant develops a sense of well-being, feelings of autonomy and competence.

Psychodynamic theory has, perhaps, been the best-known in the past and a necessary counter to the behavioural theory prevalent at a similar time. Behavioural procedures have been reported as effective in both mainstream and special educational programmes and are based on a number of principles (Wheldall and Merrett 1984):

- concern with the observable
- behaviour is learned
- learning is a change in behaviour
- learning is governed by the antecedents and consequences of the behaviour.

Causal relationships between such techniques as 'modelling', 'shaping', 'prompting' and 'reinforcement' and key developmental milestones – cognitive, language, social, motor or self-help/adaptive skills – through direct teaching and extrinsic reinforcement of praise or more tangible rewards have been demonstrated. Dissatisfaction with such mechanistic approaches led, over time, to a shift in attention back towards mental events.

The evidence for maintained and long-term competence resulting from such behavioural regimes is far less clear-cut and based on the dubious belief that learning and development is promoted through direct instruction (Wilson 1998). In fact, as Safford (1994) has demonstrated from his comprehensive review of the literature, studies of play, cognitive and language development of normal and atypical children who are adult-directed, are not found to generalise to spontaneous behaviour (Kaiser, Yoder and Keets 1992).

Whilst, as yet, the more recently-developed 'social constructivist' approach is still to be evaluated more fully as the basis for an educational strategy, there is at least as much empirical justification for using this approach as for using behaviourism. So-called 'transactional' approaches, it could be claimed, have transformed our views about learning and development. For instance, in terms of parental interaction, those who support and encourage play, communication and other forms of constructivist behaviour are found to be more effective in enhancing development (Trevarthen 1992). Gallimore, Tharp and Rueda (1989) have argued that through collaboration with more 'expert' others, less competent children can have their performance advanced. Taking Vygotsky's view that as the child works with another in the 'zone of proximal development' the activity is gradually appropriated and the need for assistance declines, Gallimore *et al.* (1989) developed their Kamehameha Early Education Project. Using these principles they developed a reading programme which was both successful and compatible with the culture and language of native Hawaiian children. Moreover, the programme, focusing on the teaching of comprehension through an explicit questioning strategy, was sensitive to children's responses and supported the interweaving of new information with prior knowledge. Teachers did not find this process of constructing 'enabling' questions easy to acquire but overall the programme was found to be effective and minimally disruptive to existing classroom practice.

Such examples of 'socially constructive' practice, underline the need for both sensitive adult support as well as developmentally-appropriate interventions. Furthermore they highlight the very skilled nature of supporting early years learning in the home and outside.

Taking a rather different starting point, Safford (1994) has identified a number of principles which have been drawn from a range of theoretical perspectives which underlie current conceptions and beliefs concerning early development – typical and atypical – and we have added to the references provided:

- The brain is only partially mature at birth and continues to develop over the first five years of age (Nash 1997; Karmiloff-Smith 1992)
- The incompleteness of brain development makes it very open to the influence of experiences (Greenough *et al.* 1992; Plomin 1986)
- Experiences of all types are recorded in the brain (Greenough *et al.* 1992)
- Experience does not write on the brain as if it were a 'blank slate'; there are species-specific biological tendencies to develop some forms of behaviour such as language (Karmiloff-Smith 1992, 1995)

- These potentials direct the organism towards behaviour potentials that every person will develop if reared in species-typical environments (Skinner 1974)
- Culture is an organising influence, the impact of which begins early and which affects every domain (Hebb 1980; Vygotsky 1987)
- Development is a process of continuous change, an open biological system that is self-maintaining, self-restoring and self-regulating (von Bertalanffy 1968, 1978)
- Human beings are, from infancy, active organisms exploring the environment, whose innate abilities and dispositions help them to select what is relevant and adaptive (Plomin 1986)
- While behaviour reinforcement (Bijou and Baer 1961, 1965, 1978, 1989; Skinner 1974) and social learning (Bandura 1973, 1986) theorists consider behavioural laws involving external influences to be the mechanisms of all behaviour change, these are mechanisms of learning and teaching, not of development; change in the course of children's development results from reciprocal transactions of the biologically-maturing organisms with the social and physical environment (Bronfenbrenner 1992; Sameroff and Fiese 1990; Vygotsky 1987).

Whilst these principles represent widely diverging theoretical positions, take different standpoints and address different phenomena, they are not as contradictory as they may appear and, in fact, provide a consistent message. They emphasise the critical importance of the young child's early interactions in the social and physical world and the real potential for the transformation of development resulting from transactions with more experienced members of the culture concerned.

Schaffer (1996) has proposed that this plethora of theories has the potential to provide methodological tools to further understanding. Moreover, current scepticism about such meta-theories, which focuses on the limitations in the topic areas treated and dismisses them as of mere historical interest, may underestimate their value in providing an impetus to the development of more sophisticated methodological tools.

The broad implication of these theories for educational planning is that identification of developmental competence for *all* children, through active engagement in play, daily activities and routines, is central. These activities, psychological theories suggest, will be child-initiated, with the adult acting as both observer and active participant in interactions which provide a bridge – a 'shared consciousness' – through which cultural meanings pass and through which the child constructs a model world, learns social rules and develops self-awareness.

Suffice it to remind the reader at this point that there is overwhelming evidence to support the position that active and appropriate, adult intervention which begins in the earliest years can influence neurological development of both normally and atypically-developing young children.

Advances in neuroscience offer another potential means for exploring the importance of the child's early environment – even before birth. It has been established, for instance, that electrical activity in the nerve cells of the embryonic human brain can be identified from the earliest weeks after conception. Furthermore, it is recognised that this rhythmical 'firing' of neurons changes the physical structure of the brain. During the first years of life, the brain undergoes a series of changes, starting shortly after birth, when trillions more connections between neurons are produced, some of which will never be used and, according to Nash's (1997) review of early brain development, will be subject to later 'pruning' by ten or eleven years of age.

After birth, when the number of connections explodes, each neuron will be making links to thousands of others to form the 'synapses', or gap-like structures, over which the axon of one neuron beams a signal to the dendrite of another. Moreover, there is a time-scale to early brain development – 'synaptogenesis' or 'synaptic excess'. By the age of two it is believed that a child's brain contains twice as many synapses and consumes twice as much energy as the brain of a normal adult. It remains at this level until ten or eleven years when the growth spurt ends and, with the pruning of synaptic connections, it has been assumed, comes a decline in plasticity of the brain at the end of adolescence.

It is this synaptogensis which is assumed to be related specifically to critical periods for learning. Furthermore it has been associated with early visuo-motor development, language development and development of the feelings and emotions. For instance, we know from observational studies that at birth the neonate shows uncoordinated movement, by two months reaching and grabbing nearby objects is demonstrated, by four months depth perception and binocular vision is established. Between six months and four years, sitting, crawling, walking and running are all mastered. In terms of language development, at birth the infant is thought to be attuned to the melody of the mother's voice, at six months there is evidence of recognition of vowel sounds and by twelve months the first words appear. Between birth and six years, language acquisition takes place and, over a similar period, simple emotions of distress and satisfaction evolve gradually into a complex range of identifiable feelings. It is a small step to the assumption that the observed pattern of development in the first few years provides a 'critical window of opportunity' which maps onto the periods of synaptogenesis (Nash 1997).

This well-documented synaptogenetic pattern, taken together with findings by Greenough *et al.* (1992) that rats raised in complex environments show superior learning which is reflected in twenty to twenty-five per cent more synapses per neuron in the visual cortext, has been used to argue for an experience-dependent human brain plasticity. Greenough and his colleagues, however, were also able to demonstrate that these synaptic changes occurred in stimulated adult as well as young rat brains. This suggested that, in the case of rats at least, experience-dependence plasticity lasts through life. As Bruer (1999) has pointed out, the gap between animal and human synaptogenesis, and the relationship between synaptogenesis and critical periods of learning, is a 'bridge too far'. Whilst there may be subtle and gradual changes in brain plasticity, this knowledge can provide little guidance for devising specific educational programmes. We do know that early changes and development of the human visual cortex may well constitute a critical period which provides a strong argument for early identification of sensory disabilities to avoid the long-term impact of impairment. We also know that stabilisation in development of the frontal cortex – responsible for planning, integration of information and, hence, executive function – does *not* occur until the mid-teens. As Bruer (1999) argues, early neural development can provide no guidance on specific experiences, provision *or* policies in relation to young children since, the world over and regardless of environment, they develop in a similar manner. More importantly, we have no idea how these capacities relate to later school learning or culturally-transmitted knowledge and skills, whether acquired informally from the social and cultural environment, or whether learned through formal school subject teaching.

Such diverse theoretical and methodological approaches drive us back to consider Schaffer's (1996) fundamental question: why are people interested in child development in the first place? He has suggested two main reasons: an interest in children per se – at certain ages; and in terms of their developmental competence – to learn about the nature and end-product of development (adults) in terms of the process. Schaffer proposed that 'theoretical frameworks serve as formal guides in the search for knowledge about children's development' (Schaffer 1996, p.44).

Perhaps another and more fundamental reason for early years educational practitioners' interest in such research is to provide tools with which to interrogate current policy and practice. Furthermore, these theoretical and methodological frameworks provide insight into the processes of research itself, its nature, use, limitations and constraints. They provide descriptions of development and explanations for change, characterised at the broadest level by research methods which have moved increasingly away from the structured and experimental towards data-gathering in naturalistic settings which, so far as possible, takes account of the perspectives of the participants concerned. Each methodological approach makes its own distinctive contribution to knowledge in the field, in terms of the research questions asked, the design adopted, as well as the conclusions drawn.

Conclusion

Ball (cited in Ransom 1996) has argued forcefully that the isolation of educational research from the major research developments of the period can only impoverish its results. Educational studies overall have become increasingly isolated from the theoretical developments in cognate fields or disciplines. Key examples here are the advances being made in statistical practices, for instance in the area of probability theory, where the law of likelihood is providing objective representation of evidence and measurement of its strength, as well as measurement and control of the probabilities of weak and misleading evidence. In fact, development in the sophistication of the statistical tools available today for measurement and interpretation of phenomena in the social and physical world stands out as a major conceptual and methodological achievement of the period. Such advances – such as likelihood theory – however, have made little impact on the social sciences.

It is evident from this chapter's brief consideration of the theoretical bases to early childhood education and special education that it connects in the closest of ways to broader concerns and issues facing our society, for instance those of poverty, divorce and social exclusion. Moreover, early education research cannot be isolated from the social sciences and the theoretical construction of generalisable knowledge, for which Bassey (1996) has blamed the educational research community. We have already noted above that educational research in general was the target of much criticism during 1998, though most of this has been directed to compulsory phases of education (Edwards 1998). Ransom (cited in Ransom 1996) himself has noted that the capacity of researchers to address the educational issues involved in a changing society will depend upon an ability to develop theoretical connections with allied disciplinary fields. More seriously, it has been argued that the preoccupation with the statutory sector has caused neglect of preschool education as well as post-compulsory education and training. In fact, by relocating learning in school to learning in society we are more likely to achieve an inclusive view of learning and development which requires the consideration of learning in the context of home, community and schooling. This is already being addressed in early years research.

Such research highlights the need for early and high-quality enrichment programmes for the children living in impoverished circumstances as well as those showing significant delays and deviant development, whatever the particular 'risk' factors involved. Accommodation to the wide variety of children from different social, cultural and economic circumstances entering early education presents its greatest challenge and a possible blueprint for the compulsory years of schooling. As Nagy (1989) has concluded, unless more flexible forms of articulation between educational settings and home, community and workplace are found, it is unlikely that life-long education, as a comprehensive concept of learning and development over the individual lifespan, can be achieved. As this chapter has shown, theoretical advances in our understanding of early learning have been achieved from the level of the micro organisation of individual psycho-biographical and social experiences, through to the level of macro forms of social and economic organisation, in a broader historical context.

Whilst much remains to be learned about the activity of the young learner from birth to the development of competence in a range of domains, as well as the role that instruction plays in facilitating this process, early years education has a rich knowledge-base upon which to draw. If this can be systematically applied to inform policy and practice in early years education, as it comes at last to the top of the agenda, then much will have been achieved. Moreover, this process could provide a model for the development of educational studies in general and inform research which attempts to investigate learning at a time of rapid economic, social and political change.

Appendix 1
Manual of observation schedule for use in pre-school units.

From: Robson, B (1989) *Special Needs in Ordinary Schools. Pre-school Provision for Children with Special Needs*. London, Cassell, pp.148–153

A. INTERACTION CATEGORIES

	+	+	+	−	−	−	0	
INI	V	M	NV	V	M	NV		Insert'C' 'P' or 'T'
RES	1	2	3	4	5	6	7	

+*V*: *Positive verbal*. A remark from one person to another which is friendly and non-threatening.

+*NV*: *Positive non-verbal*. (a) Physical contact which is friendly and non-hostile. Includes cuddling, taking hands, patting, stroking, touching an object which another is holding. (b) Carrying out an instruction, obeying a request.

−*V*: *Negative verbal*. A remark from one person to another which is hostile, threatening, aggressive.

−*NV*: *Negative non-verbal*. (a) Physical contact which is hostile, threatening, aggressive. Includes pushing, hitting, snatching toy from another against his wishes, destroying something another is building. (b) Refusing to carry out an instruction or obey a request, e.g. shaking head, running away, turning away.

M: *Mixed verbal/non-verbal*. Physical contact plus simultaneous verbalisation.

0: No interaction has occurred.

INI: *Initiation*. Record of the person who made the first move in the interaction (see C, P and T below).

RES: *Response*. Record of the person who responded or made the second move in the interaction.

C. Child being observed.

P. Peer, any other child.

T. Teacher, nurse, any other adult.

B. CATEGORIES OF ACTIVITY

Fc	Fs	GA	GM	IP	B	SG	LW		NS
1	2	3	4	5	6	7	8		14

*1. Fc: Fine perceptual-motor (creative).*Unstructured fine perceptual-motor activity; no rigid rules; no right/wrong distinction. Includes modelling, painting, drawing, Lego, small construction, stringing beads, some sand and water play, craft activities, some cutting, gluing, carpentry.

2. Fs: Fine perceptual-motor (structured). Fine perceptual-motor activity with rigid rules and goals; clear right/wrong distinction, since there are limited number of acceptable outcomes. Includes jigsaws, table games (picture bingo, snakes and ladders, ludo, etc.), cutting shapes, putting on/taking off clothes.

3. GA: Gross physical activity. Movement over the ground without use of toys or other equipment. Includes running, jumping, hopping and walking. Location will always be solitary or parallel or group or teacher – if children are involved in GA in association, then SG is recorded (see below).

4. GM: Gross perceptual-motor. Gross movement involving equipment or toys. Includes climbing frame, swings, vehicles, chute. Location records as with GA.

5. IP: Imaginative play. Child is involved in fantasy; has adopted role of particular person and is acting the part, e.g. Superman, policeman, nurse *or* is pretending that an object represents something else, e.g. child uses cutlery to 'shoot' as if it were a gun.

6. B: Book/story activity. Child is (a) listening to a story being read, (b) 'reading' by him/herself – includes books, comics, wall-posters, (c) listening to a story on record, tape or television.

7. SG: Small group activity. Two or more children involved in association without the controlling presence of an adult. Includes rough and tumble play, peek-a-boo, hide and seek, gross physical and perceptual-motor play in association. If an adult has set up the activity and is absent for a few minutes this is not recorded as SG, since adult control is present – the group must be a spontaneous one set up by the children.

8. LW: Looking, listening, waiting. The child is inactive and is looking or listening to others, waiting for equipment to arrive, or an activity to begin. Location is recorded as solitary or group (when child is sitting in group but is not involved in what the group is doing). Parallel, association and teacher cannot be recorded.

Blank box for one of five activities to be recorded by initial:

9. M: Music/dancing. (a) Listening to music on tape, record, television, piano, (b) participating in songs, dancing, movement to music, singing games.

10. H: Helping an adult. To organise, fetch and tidy away equipment.

11.   *T: Toilet/washing activities*. Includes going to the toilet area, using toilet, sink or mirror, queuing to leave toilet area.

12.   *S: Snacks*. Includes waiting for the snack to be served, and eating and drinking.

13.   *C: Conversing*. Child is talking to adult or peer and *doing nothing else*. If he or she is involved in another activity at the same time, record the other activity only. Location for 'C' is always association or teacher.

14.   *NS: Non-specific activity*. Child is wandering aimlessly, not involved in any activity which could be included in the above categories.

C. LOCATION CATEGORIES

S	P	A	G	T
1	2	3	4	5

S: Solitary play. Child is engaged in activity alone. No child within conversation distance is engaged in the same activity.

P: Parallel play. Child is engaged in activity alongside other child/children. The other(s) must be engaged in the same activity. They work independently and without roles.

A: Associative play. Child is engaged in activity *with* other child/children. Roles are taken, the boundary of the group is clearly defined, the presence of the other(s) is necessary for the activity to continue.

G: Group activity. Child is involved in formal group activity organised and controlled by adult. The child's participation can be voluntary or compulsory.

T: Teacher/adult. Child is engaged in activity in parallel or association with an adult. No peers are present. If one or more peer is present and engaged in the same activity, 'G' is recorded.

OBSERVATION PROCEDURE

1.   *Complete information* on the front observation sheet – unit, child's name date and your initials. Leave code blank.

2.   *Locate child* and start stopwatch. Observe for one minute without recording in order to tune into the child's activity.

3.   Begin 20-minute observation session. You will complete one observation of interaction, activity and location *every 30 seconds* as follows:
     Observe for 20 seconds. Mentally note activity and location in the first second then wait for the first interaction involving target child to occur. When it occurs, observe who initiated, who responded and whether it was verbal/non-verbal and positive/negative. Immediately complete the first block on schedule:
     (a) *Interaction:* 'C', 'P' or 'T' in the appropriate box on the top line for initiation and 'C', 'P' or 'T' on the bottom line for response.

(b) *Activity:* Circle the number of the appropriate category or place the appropriate initial in the blank box.

(c) *Location:* Circle the number of the appropriate category.

If no interaction occurs during the 20 seconds' observation, record activity and location only. If an interaction is clearly initiated but there is no response, record the initiation in the usual way and put 'C', 'P' or 'T' in response box 7 in indicate who did not respond.

You have 10 seconds to record before the next observation period begins.

4.   Observe and record continuously for 20 minutes, completing 40 blocks on the observation sheets. Work down the columns of the observation sheets, *not* across the rows.

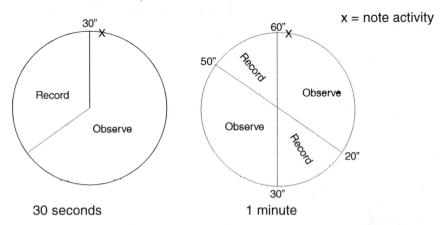

30 seconds   1 minute

Note

If an interaction is already ongoing at the beginning of a 20-second observation period, place a large cross at the side of the interaction grid. If that interaction ends and another begins before the end of the 20-second period, record the new interaction as well as the cross.

1.

	+	+	+	–	–	–	0
INI	V	M	NV	V	M	NV	
RES	1	2	3	4	5	6	7

ACTIVITY

Fc	Fs	GA	GM	IP	B	SG	LW		NS
1	2	3	4	5	6	7	8		14

LOCATION

S	P	A	G	T
1	2	3	4	5

4.

	+	+	+	–	–	–	0
INI	V	M	NV	V	M	NV	
RES	1	2	3	4	5	6	7

ACTIVITY

Fc	Fs	GA	GM	IP	B	SG	LW		NS
1	2	3	4	5	6	7	8		14

LOCATION

S	P	A	G	T
1	2	3	4	5

2.

	+	+	+	–	–	–	0
INI	V	M	NV	V	M	NV	
RES	1	2	3	4	5	6	7

ACTIVITY

Fc	Fs	GA	GM	IP	B	SG	LW		NS
1	2	3	4	5	6	7	8		14

LOCATION

S	P	A	G	T
1	2	3	4	5

5.

	+	+	+	–	–	–	0
INI	V	M	NV	V	M	NV	
RES	1	2	3	4	5	6	7

ACTIVITY

Fc	Fs	GA	GM	IP	B	SG	LW		NS
1	2	3	4	5	6	7	8		14

LOCATION

S	P	A	G	T
1	2	3	4	5

3.

	+	+	+	–	–	–	0
INI	V	M	NV	V	M	NV	
RES	1	2	3	4	5	6	7

ACTIVITY

Fc	Fs	GA	GM	IP	B	SG	LW		NS
1	2	3	4	5	6	7	8		14

LOCATION

S	P	A	G	T
1	2	3	4	5

6.

	+	+	+	–	–	–	0
INI	V	M	NV	V	M	NV	
RES	1	2	3	4	5	6	7

ACTIVITY

Fc	Fs	GA	GM	IP	B	SG	LW		NS
1	2	3	4	5	6	7	8		14

LOCATION

S	P	A	G	T
1	2	3	4	5

7.

	+	+	+	−	−	−	0
INI	V	M	NV	V	M	NV	
RES	1	2	3	4	5	6	7

ACTIVITY

Fc	Fs	GA	GM	IP	B	SG	LW		NS
1	2	3	4	5	6	7	8		14

LOCATION

S	P	A	G	T
1	2	3	4	5

10.

	+	+	+	−	−	−	0
INI	V	M	NV	V	M	NV	
RES	1	2	3	4	5	6	7

ACTIVITY

Fc	Fs	GA	GM	IP	B	SG	LW		NS
1	2	3	4	5	6	7	8		14

LOCATION

S	P	A	G	T
1	2	3	4	5

8.

	+	+	+	−	−	−	0
INI	V	M	NV	V	M	NV	
RES	1	2	3	4	5	6	7

ACTIVITY

Fc	Fs	GA	GM	IP	B	SG	LW		NS
1	2	3	4	5	6	7	8		14

LOCATION

S	P	A	G	T
1	2	3	4	5

11.

	+	+	+	−	−	−	0
INI	V	M	NV	V	M	NV	
RES	1	2	3	4	5	6	7

ACTIVITY

Fc	Fs	GA	GM	IP	B	SG	LW		NS
1	2	3	4	5	6	7	8		14

LOCATION

S	P	A	G	T
1	2	3	4	5

9.

	+	+	+	−	−	−	0
INI	V	M	NV	V	M	NV	
RES	1	2	3	4	5	6	7

ACTIVITY

Fc	Fs	GA	GM	IP	B	SG	LW		NS
1	2	3	4	5	6	7	8		14

LOCATION

S	P	A	G	T
1	2	3	4	5

12.

	+	+	+	−	−	−	0
INI	V	M	NV	V	M	NV	
RES	1	2	3	4	5	6	7

ACTIVITY

Fc	Fs	GA	GM	IP	B	SG	LW		NS
1	2	3	4	5	6	7	8		14

LOCATION

S	P	A	G	T
1	2	3	4	5

Source: M. M. Clark and W. M. Cheyne (1979) *Studies in Pre-school Education* London: Hodder and Stoughton

Appendix 2

Observation form for high-frequency events

For use when the priority problem is likely to occur four time or more in any half hour period.

Instructions: 1. Use one form per half hour period (approximately).
2. Complete section (a) before the lesson.
3. Each time you observe the priority problem being shown by the pupil, tick one of the boxes, starting with the box on the top left, and working from left to right. Put only one tick in each box.
4. After the lesson add up the number of ticks and enter this in the 'Total' box.
5. Add any relevant comments.

Section (a)

PUPIL: TEACHER: DATE:

CLASS/GROUP: SUBJECT: TIME:

LESSON DESCRIPTION:

PRIORITY PROBLEM BEHAVIOUR:

Section (b)

Tick box when behaviour occurs

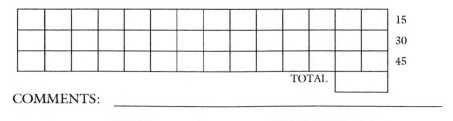

COMMENTS: _____

_____

Source: D. Tweddle *et al.* (1984) *Preventive Approaches to Disruption. A Resource of In-Service Training Materials*, University of Birmingham, p. 59.

Appendix 3

Record form for low-frequency events

For use when the priority problem is likely to occur three times or less in any half hour period.

Instructions:
1. Use one form for each occurrence of the problem behaviour
2. Complete section (a) before the lesson.
3. Fill in Section (b) as soon as possible after the behaviour has occurred.

Section (a)

PUPIL: CLASS/GROUP:

TEACHER:

SUBJECT: TIME:

LESSON DESCRIPTION:

PRIORITY PROBLEM:

Section (b)

ANTECEDANTS	BEHAVIOUR	CONSEQUENTS
(describe what happened just before the behaviour e.g. what you and/or the class were doing)	(describe the behaviour in observable terms)	(describe what happened just after the behaviour e.g. how you and/or the class reacted to the behaviour)

COMMENTS: _____

Source: D. Tweddle *et al.* (1984) *Preventive Approaches to Disruption. A Resource of In-Service Training Materials*, University of Birmingham, p. 60.

Appendix 4
Ethical guidelines

A copy of the British Educational Research Association *BERA Ethical Guidelines* can be obtained from:

> BERA Office
> Commercial House
> King Street
> Southwell
> Notts NG25 0EH
>
> *Tel:* 01636 819090

The British Psychological Society's *The Code of Conduct, Ethical Principles and Guidelines* can be obtained from:

> The British Psychological Society
> St Andrew's House
> 48 Princess Road East
> Leicester LE1 7DR
>
> *Tel:* 0116 2549568

References

Ainsworth, M.D.S., Bell, S.M. and Stayton, D.J. (1974) Infant–mother attachment and social development: Socialisation as a product of reciprocal responsiveness to signals. In M.P.M. Richards (Ed.) *The Integration of a Child into a Social World* Cambridge: Cambridge University Press.

Aitkin, M., Bennett, S. and Hesketh, J. (1981) Teaching styles and pupil progress: a reanalysis *British Journal of Educational Psychology* 51, pp.170–86.

Aitkin, M., Anderson, D. and Hinde, J. (1981) Statistical modelling of data on teaching styles *Journal of the Royal Statistical Society* A 144, pp.148–61.

Alderson, P. (1995) *Listening to children* London: Barnardos.

Alexander, R. (1992) *Policy and Practice in Primary Education* London: Routledge.

Alexander, R., Rose, J. and Woodhead, C. (1992) *Curriculum Organization and Classroom Practice in Primary Schools: A Discussion Document* London: HMSO.

Andersson, B.E. (1992) Effects of daycare on cognitive and socio-cultural competence of 13-year-old Swedish school children *Child Development* 63, pp.20–36.

Ariés, P. (1962) *Centuries of Childhood* London: Jonathan Cape.

Aubrey, C. (Ed.) (1994) *The Role of Subject Knowledge in the Early Years of Schooling* London: The Falmer Press.

Aubrey, C. (1997a) Children's early learning of number in school and out. In I. Thompson (Ed.) *Teaching and Learning Early Number* Milton Keynes: Open University Press.

Aubrey, C. (1997b) *Mathematics Teaching in the Early Years: An Investigation of Teachers' Subject Knowledge.* London: The Falmer Press.

Aubrey, C. (1999) *Changing the Subject.* First Vicky Hurst Memorial Lecture held at Goldsmith's College, 2 October 1999.

Aubrey, C., Tancig, S., Magajna, L. and Kavkler, M. (1998) Mathematics lessons from abroad *Scientia Paedagogica experimentalis* (Special Volume on Mathematics Education).

Audit Commission/HMI (1992) *Getting in on the Act* London: HMSO.

Ball, S.J. (1984) Beachside reconsidered: Reflections on a methodological apprenticeship. In R.G. Burgess (Ed.) *The Research Process in Educational Settings: Ten Case Studies* Lewes: Falmer Press.

Ball, S.J. (1990) *Foucault and Education: Disciplines and Knowledge* London: Routledge.

Ball, S.J. (1997) Policy sociology and critical social research: A personal review of recent education policy and policy research *British Educati onal Research Journal* 23, 3, pp.257–74.

Bandura, A. (1973) *Aggression: A Social Learning Analysis* Englewood Cliffs, NJ: Prentice-Hall.

Bandura, A. (1986) *Social Foundations of Thought and Action* Englewood Cliffs, NJ: Prentice-Hall.

Bandura, A (1989) Social cognitive theory. In R.Vasta (Ed.) *Six Theories of Child Development: Revised Formulations and Current Issues* London, Jessica Kingsley.

Bandura, A. and Walters, R.H. (1963) *Social Learning and Personality Development* New York: Hold, Rinehart and Winston.

Barber, M. (1999) reported in D. Budge Medicine men have the cure. *The Times Educational Supplement*. 10 September, p .26.

Barnes, J. A. (1954) Class and committees in a Norwegian island parish in *Human Relations* 7, 1,

Barnett, W.S. and Escobar, C.M. (1990) Economic costs and benefits of early intervention. In S. J. Meisels and J. P. Shonkoff (Eds) *Handbook of Early Childhood Intervention* Cambridge: Cambridge University Press.

Barrett, G. (1986) *Starting School: An Evaluation of the Experience* London: AMMA BERA Intelligence.

Basic Skills Agency with NFER (1998) *Family Numeracy Adds Up* London: The Basic Skills Agency.

Bassey, M. (1992) Creating education through research *British Educational Research Journal* 18, 1, pp.3–16.

Bassey, M. (1997) Annual expenditure on educational research in the UK *Research Intelligence* 59, pp.2–7.

Bassey, M. and Constable, H. (1997) Higher education research in education 1992–1996: Fields of enquiry reported in the HEFCEs RAE *Research Intelligence* 61, pp.6–8.

Beck, U. (1992) *The Risk Society* London: Sage Publications.

Becker, F. (1963) *Outsiders* New York: The Free Press.

Becker, H.S. (1967) Whose side are we on? *Social Problems* 14, pp.239–47.

Beilin, H (1989) *Theories of Child Development: Revised Formulations and Current Issues* London: Jessica Kingsley.

Bennett, N. (1976) *Teaching Styles and Pupil Progress* London: Open Books.

Bennett, N. (1981) Interview: High score for the new teaching with Peter Wilby. *Sunday Times*, April, 1981.

Bennett, N. and Kell, J. (1989) *A Good Start? Four Year Olds in Infant Schools* Oxford: Blackwell.

Bennett, N., Wood, L. and Rogers, S. (1997) *Teaching Through Play: Teachers' Thinking and Classroom Practice* Buckingham: Open University Press.

Bereday, G.Z.I. (1964) *The Western European Idea in Education* Oxford: Pergamon.

Bereiter, C. and Engelmann, S. (1966) *Teaching Disadvantaged Children in the Preschool* Englewood Cliffs, NJ: Prentice-Hall.

Berger, P. and Luckmann, T. (1966) *The Social Construction of Reality* New York: Doubleday

Bernstein, B. (1960) Language and social class *British Journal of Sociology* 11, pp. 271–6.

Bernstein, B. (1962) Social class, linguistic codes and grammatical elements *Language and Speech* 5, 221–40.

Bijou, S. and Baer, D.M. (1961) *Child Development: A Systematic and Empirical Theory. Vol. 1* Englewood-Cliffs, NJ: Prentice-Hall.

Bijou, S. and Baer, D.M. (1965) *Child Development: Universal Stage of Infancy. Vol. 2* Englewood-Cliffs, NJ: Prentice-Hall.

Bijou, S. and Baer, D.M. (1978) *Behavior Analysis of Child Development* Englewood-Cliffs, NJ: Prentice-Hall.

Bijou, S. and Baer, D.M. (1989) Behavior Analysis *Annals of Child Development* 6, pp.61–83.

Blank, M. and Solomon, F. (1969) How shall the disadvantaged be taught? *Child Development* 4, pp. 47–61.

Blank, M., Gessner, M. and Esposito, A. (1979) Language without communication: a case tudy *Journal of Child Language* 6, 329–52.

Blank, M., Rose, S. A. and Berlin, L. (1979) *The Language of Learning: The Preschool Years* New York: Grune and Stratton.

Blatchford, P. and Plewis, I. (1990) Preschool reading-related skills and later reading achievement: further evidence *British Educational Research Journal* 16, 4, pp. 425–8.

Blenkin, G.M., Rose, J. and Yue, N.Y.L. (1996) Government policies and early education: Perpectives from practitioners *European Early Childhood Education Research Journal* 4, 2, pp.5–20.

Blunkett, D. (1996) *Early Excellence* London: Labour Party.

Blurton Jones, N. (1967) An ethological study of some aspects of social behaviour of children in nursery school. In D. Morris (Ed.) *Primate Ethology* London: Weidenfeld and Nicolson.

Blurton Jones, N. (1972) (Ed.) *Ethological Studies of Child Behaviour* Cambridge: Cambridge University Press.

Bone, M. (1977) *Preschool Children and the Need for Daycare* London: Office of Population Censuses and Surveys.

Bowlby, J. (1953) *Child Care and the Growth of Love* Harmondsworth: Penguin.

Bradshaw, J. (1990) *Child Poverty and Deprivation in the UK* London: National Children's Bureau.

Breakwell, G. (1995) *Researching Sensitive Issues* London: Sage.

Brice-Smith, S. (1983) *Ways with Words* Cambridge: Cambridge University Press.

Brindle, D. (1994) Poverty highlighted by school meals survey. *The Guardian* 31 January.

British Educational Research Association (1998) Responses to the IES Report *BERA Research Intelligence,* 66, pp.13–15.

Broadhead, P. (1995) (Ed.) *Researching the Early Year Continuum* Clevendon: Multilingual Matters.

Broadhead, P. (1997) Promoting sociability and cooperation in nursery settings *British Journal of Educational Research* 23, 4, pp.513–32.

Bronfenbrenner, U. (1952) Principles of professional ethics: Cornell studies in social growth *American Psychologist* 7, 2, p.452–5.

Bronfenbrenner, U. (1974) Developmental research, public policy and the ecology of childhood *Child Development* 45, pp.1–5.

Bronfenbrenner, U. (1975) Reality and research in the ecology of human development *Proceedings of the American Philosophical Society* 119, pp.439–69.

Bronfenbrenner, U. (1977) Towards an experimental ecology of human development *American Psychologist* 32, pp.513–31.

Bronfenbrenner, U. (1979) *The Ecology of Human Development* Cambridge, Mass.: Harvard University Press.

Bronfenbenner, U. (1989) Ecological systems theory *Annals of Child Development* 6, pp. 87–250.

Bronfenbrenner, U. (1992) Ecological systems theory. In R. Vasta (Ed.) *Six Theories of Child Development: Revised Formulations and Current Issues* London: Jessica Kingsley.

Brophy, J., Statham, J. and Moss, P. (1992) *Playgroups in Practice: Self-Help and Public Policy* London: HMSO.

Broström, S. and Vilien, K. (1998) Early childhood education research in Denmark. In T. David (Ed.) *Researching Early Childhood Education: European Perspectives* London: Paul Chapman/ Sage.

Brown, M. (1997) Presidential Address to the British Educational Research Association Conference, University of York, 11–14 September.

Brown, M. (1998) Findings lost amid political jockeying *The Times Educational Supplement* 20 March, p.17.

Brown, R. (1973) *A First Language. The Early Stages* New York: Glencoe.

Bruer, J.T. (1999) Education and the brain: a bridge too far *Educational Researcher* 26, 8, pp.4–16.

Bruner, J. (1980) *Under Five in Britain* London: Grant McIntyre.

Bruner, J. (1990) *Acts of Meaning* Cambridge MA: Harvard University Press.

Bruner, J. and Haste, H. (1987) *Making Sense* London: Methuen.

Bryman, A. (1988) *Quality and Quantity in Social Research* London: Unwin Hyman.

Buckham, J. (1994) Teachers' understanding of children's drawing. In C. Aubrey (Ed.) *The Role of Subject Knowledge in the Early Years of Schooling* London: The Falmer Press.

Burgess, R.G. (Ed.) (1985) *Issues in Educational Research* London: Falmer Press.

Burgess, R.G. (Ed.) (1989) *The Ethics of Educational Research* London: Falmer Press.

Butler, A.J.P. (1996) Review of children and violence *Child Abuse Review* 5, 4, pp.297–98.

Bynner, J. and Parsons, S. (1997) *Does Numeracy Matter?* London: Basic Skills Agency.

Bynner, J. and Steedman, J. (1995) *Difficulties with Basic Skills* London: Basic Skills Agency.

Byrne, E. (1993) *Women and Science: The Snark Syndrome* London: Falmer.

CACE (1967) *Children and their Primary Schools: The Report of the Central Advisory Council for Education (England)* (Plowden Report) London, HMSO.

Campbell, D.T. and Stanley, J.C. (1966) *Experimental and Quasi-experimental Designs for Research* Chicago: Rand McNally.

Campbell, R.J. and Neill, S.StJ. (1992) *Teacher Time and Curriculum Manageability* London: AMMA.

Cassell, J. and Jacobs, S.E. (1987) *Handbook on Ethical Issues in Anthropology* Washington: American Anthropological Association.

Central Statistics Office (1994) *Social Trends 24* London: HMSO.

Cicarelli, V.G. (1969) *The Impact of Head Start: An Evaluation of the Effects of Head Start on Children's Cognitive and Affective Development* Washington, DC: Westinghouse Learning Corporation.

Clark, M. M. (1989) *Understanding Research in Early Education* London: Gordon and Breach Science Publishers.

Clark, M.M. and Cheyne, W.M. (1979) *Studies in Preschool Education* London: Hodder and Stoughton.

Clarke, C. (1998) Resurrecting educational research to raise standards: statement from the new minister responsible for research *BERA Research Intelligence* 66, pp 8–9.

Clarke, C. (1999) Editorial, *Research Intelligence*, 69, August, p. 1.

Claxton, G. (1997) *Hare Brain, Tortoise Mind* London: Fourth Estate.

Cleave, S. and Brown, S. (1991) *Early to School: Four Year Olds in Infant Classes* Windsor: NFER/Nelson.

Cobb, C., Halstead, T. and Rowe, J. (1995) If the economy is up, why is America down? *Atlantic Monthly* October.

Cochran, M., Larner, M., Riley, D., Gunnarsson, L. and Henderson, C.R. Jr. (1990) *Extending Families* Cambridge: Cambridge University Press.

Cohen, B. (1990) *Caring for Children: The 1990 Report* London: FPSC/SCAFA.

Cohen, L. and Manion, L. (1994) *Research Methods in Education* London: Routledge.

Connolly, P. (1998) *Racism, Gender Identities and Young Children* London: Routledge.

Cordingley, P. (1998) Educational research: a Perspective from the TTA. SCCET Seminar, London, 12 May.

Coulson, J., Carr, J., Hutchinson, L. and Eagle, D. (1981) *Oxford New Illustrated English Dictionary* Oxford: Oxford University Press.

Council of Europe (1996) *The Child as Citizen* Strasbourg: Council of Europe.

Cuckle, P. (1996) Children learning to read: exploring home and school relationship *British Educational Research Journal* 22, 1, pp.17–32.

Currer, C. (1991) Understanding the mother's point of view: the case of Pathan women in Britain. In S. Wyke and J. Hewison (Eds) *Child Health Matters* Buckingham: Open University Press .

Dahlberg, G. (1998) Everything is a beginning, everything is dangerous. UK Reggio Group Seminar, London, Thomas Coram Foundation, January.

Dahlberg, G. and Åsén, G. (1994) Evaluation and regulation: a question of empowerment in P. Moss and A. Pence (Eds) *Valuing Quality in Early Childhood Services* London: Paul Chapman.

Daniels, S., Redfern, E.D. and Shorrocks-Taylor, D. (1995) Trends in the early admission of children to school: appropriate or expedient? *Educational Research* 37, 3, pp.239–49

David, T. (1990) *Under Five – Under-Educated?* Buckingham: Open University Press.

David, T. (1992) Do we have to do this? *Children and Society* 6, 3, pp.204–11.

David, T. (1996a) Nursery education and the National Curriculum. In T. Cox (Ed.) *The National Curriculum and the Early Years* London: Falmer Press .

David, T. (1996b) Their right to play. In C. Nutbrown (Ed.) *Children's Rights and Early Education* London: Paul Chapman.

David, T. (Ed.) (1993c) *Educating our Youngest Children: European Perspectives* London: Paul Chapman Publishing.

David, T. (Ed.) (1998) *Researching Early Childhood Education: European Perspectives* London: Paul Chapman Press/Sage Publications .

Davie, C., Hutt, S.J., Vincent, E. and Mason, M. (1984) *The Young Child at Home* Windsor: NFER.

Deem, R. (1998) Educational research past, present and future: a feminist social science perspective. In J. Ruddock and D. McIntyre (Eds) *Challenges for Educational Research* London: Paul Chapman Publishing

Degenholtz, H., Kane, R., Kane R. and Finch M. (1999) Long-term care case managers' out-of-home placement decisions: an application of hierarchical logistic regression *Research on Aging* March, 21, 2, pp.240–74.

Delamont, S., Atkinson, P. and Parry, O. (1997) *Supervising the PhD* Buckingham: Open University Press.

Deloache, J.S. and Brown, A.L. (1987) The early emergence of planning skills in children. In J. Bruner and H. Haste (Eds) *Making Sense* London: Cassell.

Denscombe, M., Szulc, H., Patrick, C. and Wood, W. (1993) Ethnicity and friendship: the contrast between sociometric research and fieldwork observation in primary school classrooms. In P. Woods and M. Hammersley (Eds) *Gender and Ethnicity in Schools* London: Routledge.

Denzin N.K., and Lincoln, Y.S. (1994) *Handbook of Qualtiative Research* London: Sage.

Department of Education and Science (1972) *Education: A Framework for Expansion* London: HMSO.

Derrida, J. (1978) *Writing and Difference* London: Routledge and Kegan Paul (translated by G.C. Spivak).

DES (1944) Education Act. London: HMSO.

DES (1988) Education Reform Act. London, HMSO.

DES (1989) Children Act. London, HMSO.

DES (1990) *Starting with Quality*(The Rumbold Report). London, HMSO

DES (1992) Education Act. London, HMSO.

DfEE (1996) *The Next Steps* London: DfEE.

DfEE (1997a) *Basic Skills for Life* London: DfEE.

DfEE (1997b) *Early Years Development Partnerships and Plans* London: DfEE.

DfEE (1997c) *Excellence in Schools* (White Paper) London: DfEE.

DfEE (1997d) *Excellence for All Children: Meeting Special Educational Needs*. London: DfEE.

DfEE (1997e) *Report of the National Committee of Inquiry into Higher Education* London, DfEE (The Dearing Report).

DfEE (1998a) *Early Years Development and Child Care Partnerships: Planning Guidance 1999–2000* London: DfEE.

DfEE (1998b) *Education Action Zones* London: DfEE.

DfEE (1998c) *Meeting Special Educational Needs: A Programme of Action* London: DfEE.

DfEE (1999) *Sure Start: A Guide for Trailblazers* London: DfEE.

DHO/DfEE (1998) Sure Start. Press Release 537/98, 19 November.

Diamond, I., Clements, S., Stone, N. and Ingham, R. (1999) Spatial variations in teenage conceptions in south and west England *Journal of the Royal Statistical Society* A 162, 3, pp.273–90.

Donaldson, M. (1978) *Children's Minds* Harmondsworth, Penguin.

Duncan, C., Jones, K. and Moon, G. (1999) Smoking and deprivation: are there neighbourhood effects? *Social Science and Medicine* February, 48, 4, pp.497–505.

Dunkin, M.J. and Biddle, B.J. (1974) *The Study of Teaching* New York: Holt, Rinehart and Winston.

Dunn, J. (1988) *The Beginnings of Social Understanding* Oxford, Blackwell.

Edwards, A. (1998) A careful review but some lost opportunities *Research Intelligence* 66, pp.15–16.

Edwards, C., Gandini, L. and Forman, G. (Eds) (1998) *The Hundred Languages of Children: The Reggio Emilia Approach – Advanced Reflections* London: Ablex.

Edwards, D. and Mercer, N. (1987) *Common Knowledge* London: Methuen.

Elfer, P. and Selleck, D. (1996) Building intimacy in relationships with young children in nurseries *Early Years* 16, 2 pp. 30–34.

Elfer, P. and Selleck, D. (2000) *The Best of Both Worlds* London: National Children's Bureau.

Elley, W.B. (1994) *The IAE Study of Reading Literacy Achievement and Instruction in Thirty-Two School Systems* Oxford: Pergamon.

Elliot, J. (1977) Democratic evaluation as social criticism or putting the judgement back into evaluation. In N. Norris (Ed) *Theory and Practice* SAFARI Papers 2, Centre for Applied Studies in Education, University of East Anglia.

Ely, M., Vinz, R., Downing, M. and Anzul, M. (1997) *On Writing Qualitative Research* London: Falmer Press.

Erickson, F. (1986) Qualitative methods in research on teaching. In M.C. Wittrock (Ed.) *Handbook of Research on Teaching.* (2nd edition) New York: Macmillan.

Evans, P. and Fuller, M. (1996) Hello, who am I speaking to? Communicating with preschool children in educational settings. *Early Years* 17, 1, pp.17–20.

Evans, P. and Fuller, M. (1998) Children's perceptions of their nursery education *International Journal of Early Years Education* 6, 1, pp.59–74.

Field, T. (1991) Quality infant daycare and grade school behaviour and performance *Child Development* 62, pp.863–70.

Fielding, A. (1999) Why use arbitrary point scores? Ordered categories in models of educational progress *Journal of the Royal Statistical Society* A 162, 3, pp.303–28.

Finch, J. (1986) *Research and Policy: The Uses of Qualitative Methods in Social and Educational Research* Lewes: Falmer Press.

Fine, G. A. and Sandstrom, K.L. (1988) *Knowing Children: Participant Observation with Minors* London: Sage Publishers.

Foshay, A.W. (1962) *Educational Achievement of Thirteen-Year-Olds in Twelve Countries* Hamberg: UNESCO Institute for Education.

Foucault, M. (1977) *Discipline and Punish* London: Allen Lane.

Froebel, Friedrich (1826) *The Education of Man* Leipzig: Keilhau (English edition, New York: Appleton, 1887).

Fukkink, R. and de Glopper, K. (1998) Effects of instruction in deriving word meaning from context: a meta-analysis *Review of Educational Research* Winter, 68, 4, pp. 450–69.

Gal, S. (1979) *Language Shift: Social Determinants of Linguistic Change in Bilingual Austria* New York: Academic Press.

Gallimore, R., Tharp, R.G. and Rueda, R. (1989) *The Social Context of Cognitive Functioning in the Lives of Mildly Handicapped Persons* Lewes: The Falmer Press.

Galton, M., Simon, B. and Croll, P. (1980) *Progress and Performance in the Primary Classroom* London: Routledge and Kegan Paul.

Gardner, H. (1993) *The Unschooled Mind* London: Fontana.

Garland, C. and White, S. (1980) *Children and Day Nurseries* London: Grant McIntyre.

Gash, S. (1989) *Effective Literature Searching for Students* Aldershott: Gower.

Geary, D.C. (1994) *Children's Mathematical Development* Washington, DC: American Psychological Association.

Geetz, C. (1975) *The Interpretation of Cultures* London: Hutchinson.

Ghouri, N. Formal schooling may be put off until six *Times Educational Supplement* 27 March, p.1.

Gillan, C. (1996) Letter in *Work and Family: Ideas and Options for Childcare. A Consultation Paper* London: DfEE.

Gipps, C. (1993) The profession of educational research *British Education Research Journal* 19, 1, pp.3–16.

Gipps, C. (1997) The funding and management of research in education: two thorny issues – future and impact *Research Intelligence* 62, pp.2–6.

Goldstein, H. (1987) *Multilevel Methods in Education and Social Science Research* London: Charles Griffin and Co.

Goldstein, H. (1995) *Multilevel Statistical Models* Hove: Lawrence Erlbaum (2nd edition).

Goodwin, W.L. and Goodwin, L.D. (1996) *Understanding Quantitative and Qualitative Research in Early Childhood Education* New York: Teachers College Press.

Green, A. (1997) *Education, Globalization and the Nation State* London: Macmillan.

Greenough, W., Wallace, C., Alcanta, B., Hawrylak, A., Weiler, I. and Withers, G. (1992) Development of the brain: experience affects the structure of the neurons, gila and blood vessels. In N. Anastasiow and S. Harel (Eds) *The At-risk Infant: Vol. 3, Intervention, Families and Research* Baltimore: Paul H. Brookes.

Halliday, M.A.K. (1975) *Learning How to Mean: Explorations in the Development of Language* London: Edward Arnold.

Hallowell, A. (1955/1977) Cultural factors in spatial orientation. In J. Dolgin, D. Kemnitzer and D. Schneider (Eds) *Symbolic Anthropology: A Reader in the Study of Symbols and Meanings* New York: Columbia University Press.

Halls, W.D. (Ed.) (1990) *Comparative Education: Contemporary Issues and Trends* London: Jessica Kingsley and UNESCO.

Halpin, D. and Troyna, B. (Eds) (1994) *Researching Education Policy* London: Falmer Press.

Hamilton, D. (1976) *Curriculum Evaluation* London: Open Books.

Hamilton, D., Jenkins, D., Macdonald, B. and Parlett, M. (1977) (Eds) *Beyond the Numbers Game: A Reader in Education Evaluation* London: Macmillan.

Hammersley, M. (1995) *The Politics of Social Research* London: Sage.

Hammersley, M. (1997) Educational research and teaching: a response to David Hargreaves' TTA lecture *British Educational Research Journal* 23, 2, pp.141–62.

Handy, C. (1994) *The Empty Raincoat* London: Hutchinson.

Hannon, P., Weinberger, J. and Nutbrown, C. (1996) A study of work with parents to promote early literacy development *Research Papers in Education* 6, 2, pp. 77–97.

Hardy, M. and Hazelrigg, L. (1999) A multilevel model of early retirement decisions among autoworkers in plants with different futures *Research on Aging* March, 21, 2, pp.275–303.

Harré, R. (1983) *Personal Being: A Theory for Individual Psychology* Oxford: Blackwell.

Harré, R. (1986) The steps to social constructionism. In M. Richards and P. Light (Eds) *Children of Social Worlds* Cambridge: Polity Press.

Harris, P. (1989) *Children and Emotion* Oxford: Blackwell.

Harris, S., Keys, W. and Fernandes, C. (1997) *Third International Mathematics and Science Study: Second National Report, Parts 1 and 2* Slough: NFER.

Hazareesingh, S., Simms, K. and Anderson, P. (1989) *Educating the Whole Child – A Holistic Approach to Education in the Early Years* London: Building Blocks/Save the Children.

Hebb, D.O. (1949) *The Organisation of Behaviour* New York: Wiley.

Hebb, D.O. (1980) *Essay on Mind* Hillsdale, NJ: Erlbaum.

Hegarty, S. (1997) Sacred cows trample the garden *The Times Educational Supplement* 3 January 1997, p.9.

Herbert, E. (forthcoming) Work in progress: personal communication concerning research approaches involving sensitive issues with families.

Heron, J. (1996) *Cooperative Inquiry: Research into the Human Condition* London: Sage.

Hess, R.D. and Shipman, V. (1965) Early experience and the socialisation of cognitive modes in children *Child Development* 36, pp.869–86

Hillage, J., Pearson, R, Anderson, A. and Tamkin, P. (1998) *Excellence in Research on Schools* London: DfEE.

Hilton, M, Styles, M and Watson V .(1997) (Eds) *Opening the Nursery Door: Reading, Writing and Childhoood 1600–1900* London: Routledge.

Hitchcock, G. and Hughes, D. (1989) *Research and the Teacher* London: Routledge.

Home Office (1998) *Supporting Families: A Consultation Document* London: Home Office.

Hopkins, D. (1985) *A Teacher's Guide to Classroom Research* Milton Keynes: Open University Press.

Howarth, C., Kenway, P., Palmer, G. and Street, C. (1998) *Key Indicators of Poverty and Social Exclusion* London: New Policy Institute.

Howe, C. (1990) Can the age of entry into child care and the quality of child care predict adjustment in kindergarten? *Developmental Psychology* 26, 2, pp.292–303.

Hughes, M. (1996) (Ed) *Teaching and Learning in Changing Times* Oxford: Blackwell.

Hughes, M., Desforges, C. and Holden, C. (1994) Assessment at Key Stage One: its effect on parents, teachers and classroom practice *Research Papers in Education* 9, 2, pp.133–49.

Hutt, S.J. and Hutt, C. (1970) (Eds) *Direct Observation and Measurement of Behaviour* Springfield, Ill: C.C. Thomas.

Hutt, S.J., Tyler, S., Hutt, C. and Christopherson, H. (1989) *Play, Exploration and Learning* London: Routledge.

Ingleby, D. (1986) Development in context. In M. Richards and P. Light (Eds) *Children of Social Worlds* Cambridge: Polity Press.

Isaacs, S. (1936) *Intellectual Growth in Young Children* London: Routledge.

John, M. (1993) Educating the policy-maker? European comparative research: case studies and appraisal *Research Papers in Education* 8, 1, pp.3–17.

Kaiser, A., Yoder, P. and Keets, A. (1992) Evaluating milieu teaching. In S.F. Warren and J. Reichle (Eds) *Causes and Effects in Communication and Language Intervention* Baltimore: Paul H. Brookes.

Karmiloff-Smith, A. (1992) Nature, nurture and PDP: Preposterous Developmental Postulates? *Connection Science* 4, 3 and 4, pp.253–69.

Karmiloff-Smith, A. (1995) Developmental disorders. In Michael A. Arbib (Ed.) *The Handbook of Brain Theory and Neural Networks* Cambridge, MASS: The MIT Press.

Katz, L.J. (1993) Multiple perspectives on the quality of early childhood programmes *European Early Childhood Education Research Journal* 1, 2, pp.5–9.

Kessen, W. (1979) The American child and other cultural inventions *American Psychologist* 34(10) pp. 815–20.

Kessen, W. (Ed.) (1975) *Childhood in China* New Haven: Yale University Press.

King, R. (1984) The man in the Wendy house: Research in infants' schools. In R.G. Burgess (Ed.) *The Research Process in Educational Settings: Ten Case Studies* Lewes: Falmer Press.

Klein, M. (1932) *The Psycho-Analysis of Children* London: Hogan Press.

Kumar, V. (1993) *Poverty and Inequality in the UK: The Effects on Children* London: NCB.

Labour Party (1996) *Early Excellence* London: Labour Party Publication.

Labov, W. (1972) *Sociolinguistic Patterns* Philadelphia: Pennsylvannia University Press.

Labov, W. (1981) Field methods used by the Project on Linguisitic Change and Variation in *Sociolinguist Working Paper 80* Austin Texas: South Western Educational Development Laboratory.

Lacan, J. (1977) *Ecrits: A Selection* London: Tavistock, (translated by A. Sheridan).

Lambert, J.F. (1996) *Des règles et du jeu.* Paper presented at the European Seminar of OMEP, UNESCO, Paris, 24–27 October 1996.

Lather, P. (1991) *Getting Smart: Feminist Research and Pedagogy within the Postmodern* New York: Routledge.

Le Page, R.B. and Tabouret-Keller, A. (1985) *Acts of Identity* Cambridge: Cambridge University Press.

Li Wei (1994) *Three generations, two Languages, one family* Clevedon: Multilingual Matters.

Lincoln, Y.S., and Guba, E.G. (1985) *Naturalistic Enquiry* Thousand Oaks, CA: Sage Publications.

Lubeck, S. (1986) *Sandbox Society* Hove: Falmer Press.

Maclean, M., Bryant, P. and Bradley, L. (1987) Rhymes, nursery rhymes and reading in early childhood *Merrill-Palmer Quarterly,* 33, pp.255–81.

Mallinson, V. (1980) *The Western European Idea in Education* Oxford: Pergamon.

Matthews, J. (1988) The young child's representation and drawing. In G.M. Blenkin and A. V. Kelly (Eds) *Early Childhood Education: A Developmental Curriculum* London: Paul Chapman Publishing.

Matthews, J. (1997) How children learn to draw the human figure: Studies from Singapore *European Early Childhood Education Research Journal* 5, 1, pp.29–58.

May-Bowles, J. (1998) The dissemination of research findings *British Educational Research Journal Newsletter* 63, p. 7.

McCallum, I. (1998) reported by C. Dean. 5000 pupils prove social class matters. *The Time Educational Supplement* 25 Spetember.

McGuire, J. and Richman, N. (1986) The prevalence of behaviour problems in three types of preschool groups *Journal of Child Psychology and Psychiatry*, 27, pp. 455–72.

McIntyre, D.I. (1980) Systematic observation of classroom activities *Educational Analysis* 2, 2, pp.3–30.

McKenzie, D., Mullooly, J., McFarland, Semradek, B. and McCamant, L. (1999) Changes in antipsychotic drug use following shifts in policy: a multilevel analysis *Research on Aging* March, 21, 2, pp.304–37.

McLean, S.V. (1991) *The Human Encounter: Teachers and Children Living Together in Preschools* London: Falmer Press.

McMillan, Margaret (1930) *The Nursery School.* Cited by E. Mellor (1950) *Education Through Experience in the Infant School Years* Oxford: Basil Blackwell.

Mehan, H. (1973) Assessing children's school performance. In H.P. Dreitzel (Ed.) *Recent Sociology. Vol. 5: Childhood and Socialisation* London: Collier Macmillan.

Miles, R. (1994) *The Children We Deserve* London: Harper Collins.

Mills, C. and Mills, D. (1998) *Dispatches: The Early Years* London: Channel 4 Television.

Milroy, L. (1980) *Language and Social Networks* Oxford: Basil Blackwell.

Milroy, L. (1987) *Observing and Analysing Natural Language* Oxford: Basil Blackwell.

Monbusho (1994) *Education in Japan: A Graphic Presentation* Tokyo: Japan.

Montessori, Maria (1936) *The Secret Childhood*. Cited by E. Mellor (1950) *Education Through Experience in the Infant School Years* Oxford: Basil Blackwell.

Morss, J. (1990) *The Biologising of Childhood: Developmental Psychology and the Darwinian Myth* Hove: Lawrence Erlbaum Associates.

Morss, J. (1996) *Growing Critical: Alternatives to Developmental Psychology* London: Routledge.

Mortimore, P., Sammons, P., Stoll, L., Lewis, D. and Ecob, R. (1988) *School Matters: The Junior Pears:* London: Open Books.

Moss, P. (1994) The early childhood league in Europe: problems and possibilities in cross-national comparisons of levels of provision *European Early Childhood Research Journal* 2, 2, pp.5–18.

Moss, P. (1996) Perspectives from Europe. In G. Pugh (Ed.) *Contemporary Issues in the Early Years* (2nd edition) London: Paul Chapman Publishing..

Moss, P. and Penn, H. (1996) *Transforming Nursery Education* London: Paul Chapman Press.

Moyles, J. and Suschitzky, W. (1997) *Jills of all Trades: Classroom Assistants in KS1 Classes* London: ATL.

Mugny, G., De Paolis, P. and Carugati, F. (1984) Social regulations in cognitive development. In W. Doise and A. Palmonori (Eds) *Social Interaction in Individual Development* Cambridge: Cambridge University Press.

Munn, P. (1994) The early development of literacy and numeracy skills *European Early Childhood Education Research Journal* 2, 1, pp.5–18.

Munn, P. (1995) The role of organized preschool learning environments in literacy and numeracy development *Research Papers in Education* 10, 2, pp.217–52.

Munn, P. and Schaffer, H.R. (1993) Literacy events in social interactive contexts *International Journal of Early Years Education* 1, 3, pp.61–80.

Murray, F. B. (1989) Explanations in education. In M.C. Reynolds (Ed.) *The Knowledge Base of the Beginning Teacher*. Oxford, Pergamon, pp.1–12.

Mussen P.H. (1989) Foreword in Vasta (Ed.) *Six Theories of Child Development: Revised Formulations and Current Issues* London: Jessica Kingsley.

Nagy, J. (1989) *Articulation of Preschool with Primary School in Hungary: An Alternative Entry Model* Hamburg, Germany: Institute of Education and UNESCO.

Nash, J. M. (1997) Fertile minds. *Time,* 10 February, pp.51–8.

Newson, J. and Newson, E. (1963) *Patterns of Infant Care in an Urban Community* Harmondsworth: Penguin.

Newson, J. and Newson, E. (1968) *Four Years Old in an Urban Community* Harmondsworth: Penguin.

NFER (1989) *Register of Educational Research in the UK 1987–1989. Volume 7.* Slough: NFER.

NFER (1991) *Register of Educational Research in the UK 1989–1991. Volume 8.* Slough: NFER.

NFER (1993) *Register of Educational Research in the UK 1991–1993. Volume 9.* Slough: NFER.

NFER (1995) *Register of Educational Research in the UK 1993–1995. Volume 10.* Slough: NFER.

NFER (1997) *Register of Educational research in the UK 1995–1997. Volume 11.* Slough: NFER.

Neill, S. StJ., Denham, E., Markus, T. A., Schaffer, H. R. (1977) Psychological influences of spatial design factors on nurseries. Research Report, University of Strathclyde, Departments of Psychology and Architecture.

Nunes, T. (1994) The relationship between childhood and society *Van Leer Foundation Newsletter* Spring 1994, pp.16–17.

Nutbrown, C. (Ed.) (1996a) *Children's Rights and Early Education* London: Paul Chapman.

Nutbrown, C. (Ed.) (1996b) *Respectful Educators, Capable Learners* London: Paul Chapman Press.

Nutbrown, C. and David, T. (1992) Key issues in early childhood education *Early Years* 12, 2, pp.18–21.

O'Brien, M. (1997) *Panorama* 3 February, London, BBC Television.

O'Brien, M., Alldred, P. and Jones, D. (1996) Children's constructions of family and kinship. In J. Brannen and M. O'Brien (Eds) *Children in Families: Research and Policy* London: Falmer Press.

O'Neill, J. (1994) *The Missing Child in Liberal Theory* London: University of Toronto Press.

O'Reilly, J. (1999) Revenge of the progressives. *The Sunday Times* 16 May, No.9, 116, p.19.

O'Toole, M. (1994) *The Language of Displayed Art* London: Leicester Press.

OECD (1995) *Educational Research and Development: Trends, Issues and Challenges* Paris: OECD.

OECD (1996) *Succesful Services for Our Children and Families at Risk* Paris: OECD.

OECD (forthcoming) *Country Note: The Netherlands* (Part of a survey of Early Childhood Education and Care in 12 OECD Countries) OECD: Paris.

OFSTED (1998) *The Quality of Education in Institutions Inspected Under The Nursery Education Funding Arrangements* London: OFSTED Publications.

OFSTED (1999) *The Quality of Nursery Education: Developments Since 1997–98 in the Private, Voluntary and Independent Sector*. London, OFSTED, p.3.

Osborn, A.F. (1981) Under fives in schools in England and Wales, 1971–1979 *Educational Research* 23, 2, pp.96–103.

Osborn A.F. and Milbank, J.E. (1987) *The Effects of Early Education* Oxford: Clarendon Press.

Parlett, M. and Hamilton, D. (1972) *Evaluation as Illumination: A New Approach to the Study of Innovative Programmes* Centre for Research in Educational Sociology. Paper No. 9. University of Edinburgh.

Parten, M.B. (1932) Social participation among preschool children *Journal of Abnormal Social Psychology* 27, pp.245–69.

Parten, M.B. (1933) Social play among preschool children *Journal of Abnormal Psychology* 28, pp.136–47.

Pascal, C. (1993) Capturing the quality of educational provision for young children: A story of developing professionals and developing methodology *European Early Childhood Education Research Journal* 1, 1, pp.69–80.

Penn, H. (1997) *Comparing Nurseries* London: Paul Chapman.

Pestalozzi (1826) *The Swan Song*. Cited by E. Mellor (1950) *Education through Experience in the Infant School Years* Oxford: Basil Blackwell.

Phoenix, A., Woollett, A. and Lloyd, E. (1991) *Motherhood: Meanings, Practices and Ideologies* London: Routledge.

Piaget, J. (1954) *The Construction of Reality in the Child* New York: Basic Books.

Plewis, I. and Veltman, M. (1996) Opportunity to learn maths at Key Stage One: Changes in curriculum coverage 1984–1993 *Research Papers in Education* 11, 2, pp.201–18.

Plomin, R. (1986) *Development, Genetics and Psychology* Hillsdale, NJ: Erlbaum.

Plomin, R. and Rowe, D.C. (1986) Genetic and environmental etiology of social behaviour in infancy *Development* 4, pp.15–62.

Pollard, A. with Filer, A. (1996) *The Social World of Children's Learning* London: Cassell.

Postman, N. (1985) *The Disappearance of Childhood* London: Comet/W.H. Allen.

Prais, S. (1997) *School-Readiness, Whole-Class Teaching and Pupils' Mathematical Attainments* London: National Institute of Economic and Social Research.

QCA (1998) *Standards at Key Stage 2: Report on the 1997 National Curriculum Assessment for 11-year-olds in English and Mathematics* London: QCA.

QCA (1999) *The Review of the Desirable Outcomes for Children's Learning on Entering Compulsory Education* London: QCA.

Qvortrup, J. (1990) A voice for children in statistical and social accounting. In A. James and A. Prout (Eds) *Constructing and Reconstructing Childhood* London: Falmer.

Qvortrup, J., Bardy, M., Sgritta, G. and Wintersberger, H. (1994) (Eds) *Childhood Matters* Vienna: Avebury – European Centre Vienna.

Raban, B. (1995) *Early Childhood Years: Problem or Resource* Inaugural Lecture, Melbourne University Australia, 27 July 1995 .

Raeikkoenen, K., Matthews, K., Flory, J. and Owens, J. (1999) Effects of hostility on ambulatory blood pressure and mood during daily living in healthy adults *Health Psychology* 18, 3 (May) p.228.

Ranson, S. (1996) The future of educational research: learning at the centre *British Educational Research Journal* 22, 5, 523–36.

Reading, R., Langford, I., Haynes, R. and Lovett, A. (1999) Accidents to preschool children: comparing family and neighbourhood risk factors *Social Science and Medicine* February, 48, 3, pp.321–30.

Reynolds, D. (1985) Ten years on: a decade of school effectiveness research reviewed. In D. Reynolds (Ed.) *Studying School Effectiveness* London: The Falmer Press.

Reynolds, D. (1996) *Worlds Apart: A Review of International Surveys of Educational Achievement Involving England* London: HMSO.

Reynolds, M.C. (1989) Students with special needs. In M.C. Reynolds (Ed.) *Knowledge Base for the Beginning Teacher* Oxford: Pergamon Press.

Richardson, K. (1995) *Child Development: Methodology Handbook* Milton Keynes: The Open University Press.

Robinson, P. (1997) *Literacy, Numeracy and Economic Performance* London: Centre for Economic Performance.

Robson, C. (1993) *Real World Research. A Resource for Social Scientists and Practitioner-Researchers* Oxford: Blackwell.

Romaniuck, H., Skinner, C. and Cooper, P. 'Modelling consumers' use of products *Journal of the Royal Statistical Society* A 162, 3, pp.407–22.

Rosenshine, B. and Furst, N.F. (1973) The use of direct observation to study teaching. In R.M.W. Traers (Ed.) *Second Handbook of Research on Teaching* New York: Rand McNally.

Royall, R. (1997) *Statistical Evidence: A Likelihood Paradigm* London: Chapman and Hall.

Ruddock, J. (1998) Educational research: the prospect for change... In J. Ruddock and D. McIntyre (Eds) *Challenges for Educational Research* London: Paul Chapman Publishing.

Ruddock, J. and McIntyre, D. (Eds) (1998) *Challenges for Educational Research* London: PCP.

Rutter, M. (1972) *Maternal Deprivation Re-Assessed* Harmondsworth: Penguin.

Rutter, M., Maughan, B., Mortimore, P. and Ouston, J. (1979) *Fifteen Thousand Hours: Secondary Schools and their Effects on Children* London: Open Books.

Safford, P.L. (Ed.) (1994) *Early Childhood Special Education* New York: Teachers' College Press.

Sameroff, A.J. and Fiese, B.H. (1990) Transactional regulation and early intervention. In S.J. Meisels and J.P. Shonkoff (Eds) *Handbook of Early Childhood Intervention* New York: Cambridge University Press.

Sammons, P., West, A. and Hind, A. (1997) Accounting for variation in pupil attainment at the end of Key Stage 1 *British Educational Research Journal* 23, 4, pp.489–512.

Sankoff, G. (1980) *The Social Life of Language* Philadelphia: University of Pennsylvania Press.

Saville-Troike, M. (1982) *The Ethnography of Communication* Oxford: Basil Blackwell.

SCAA (1996) *Baseline Assessment Scales* London: SCAA.

SCAA (1997) *Nursery Education: Desirable Outcomes for Children's Learning on Entering Compulsory Schooling* London, SCAA. .

Schaffer, H.R. (1990) *Making Decisions About Children* Oxford: Blackwell.

Schaffer, H.R. (1996) *Social Development* Oxford: Blackwell.

Schaffer, R. (1992) Joint involvement episodes as contexts for cognitive development. In R. McGurk (Ed.) *Childhood Social Development: Contemporary Perspectives* Hove: Lawrence Erlbaum.

Schon, D. (1983) *The Reflective Practitioner* London: Temple Smith.

Schon, D. (1987) *Educating the Reflective Practitioner* San Francisco: Jossey Bass.

Schratz, M. and Walker, R. (1995) *Research as Social Change* London: Routledge.

Schulman, L.S. (1986) Paradigms and research programs in the study of teaching: a contemporary perspective. In Wittrock, M.C. (Ed.) *Handbook of Research on Teaching* New York: Macmillan.

Schweinhart, L.J., Weikart, D.P. and Toderan, R. (1993) *High Quality Preschool Programs Found to Improve Adult Status* Ypsilante, Michigan: High/Scope Foundation.

Sharp, C. (1995) School entry and the impact of season of birth on attainment *Educational Research* 37, 3, pp.251–65.

Sharp, C. and Benefield, P. (1995) *Research into Season of Birth and School Achievement: A Selective Annotated Bibliography* Slough: NFER.

Sharp, C., Hutchison, D. and Whetton, C. (1994) How do season of birth and length of schooling affect children's attainment at Key Stage 1? *Educational Research* 36, 2, pp.107–21.

Shatz, C. (1992) The Developing Brain *Scientific American*, September, pp.61–7.

Shipman, Marten (1976) (Ed.) *The Organisation and Impact of Social Research: Six Original Case Studies in Education and Behavioural Science* London: Routledge and Kegan Paul.

Simons, H. (1995) The politics and ethics of educational research in England: contemporary issues *British Educational Research Journal* 21, 4, pp.435–49.

Skinner, B.F. (1974) *About Behaviourism* New York: Knopf.

Smilansky, S. (1968) *The Effects of Socio-Dramatic Play in Disadvantaged Preschool Children* New York: Wiley.

Smith, G. (1985) Language, ethnicity, employment, education and research: the struggle of the Sylheti-speaking people in London. In *Centre for Language Education/Linguistic Minorities Project Working Paper 13* London: University of London Institute of Education.

Smith, P.K. (1974) Ethological methods. In B.M. Foss (Ed.) *The New Perspectives in Child Development* Hardmondsworth: Penguin.

Smith, P.K. (1990) *Killing the Spirit* New York: Penguin.

Smith, P.K. and Connolly, K. (1972) Patterns of play and social interaction in preschool children. In N. Blurton Jones (Ed.) *Ethological Studies of Child Behaviour* Cambridge: Cambridge University Press.

Smith, P.K. and Connolly, K.J. (1980) *The Ecology of Preschool Behaviour* Cambridge: Cambridge University Press.

Smith, P.K. and Green, M. (1974) Aggressive behaviour in English nurseries and playgroups: Sex differences and response of adults *Child Development* 45, 211–14.

Spindler, G. (Ed.) (1982) *Doing the Ethnography of Schooling. Educational Anthropology in Action* London: Rinehart and Winston.

Stainton, R. and Evans, E. (1999) *Uncommon Entrance: The Report of an Evaluation of the 1998/99 Baseline Assessment Arrangements in England by the National Union of Teachers* London: NUT.

Steadman, C. (1982) *The Tidy House* London: Virago.

Steadman, C. (1988) The mother made conscious. In M. Woodhead and A. McGrath (Eds) *Family, School and Society* London: Hodder and Stoughton/Open University.

Stenhouse, L. (1975) *An Introduction to Curriculum Research and Development* London: Heinemann.

Stierer, B. (1990) Assessing children at the start of school: issues, dilemmas and current developments *The Curriculum Journal* 1, 2, pp.155–69.

Strand, S. (1997) Pupil progress during Key Stage 1: A value-added analysis of school effects *British Educational Research Journal* 23, 4, pp.471–88.

Strasser, B. (1967) A conceptual model of instruction *Journal of Teacher Education* 18, 1, pp.63–74.

Strauss, A. and Corbin, J. (1990) *Basics of Qualitative Research: Grounded Theory, Procedures and Techniques* Thousand Oaks, CA: Sage Publishing.

Stronach, I., Hustler, D. and Edwards, A. (1997) Editorial: Proliferating paradigms, proliferating editors? *British Educational Research Journal* 23, 2, pp.123–5.

Sure Start Unit (1998) Play, learning and childcare. Sure Start Stakeholders' Event Workshop, held on 19 November, Stakis Metropole Hotel, London.

Sylva, K. (1992) Conversations in the nursery: how they contribute to aspirations and plans *Language and Education* 6 (2, 3 and 4) pp.141–8.

Sylva, K. (1994) The impact of early learning on children's later development. In C. Ball (Ed.) *Start Right: The Importance of Early Learning* London: Royal Society of Arts.

Sylva, K. (1995) *Research as a Medieval Banquet: Barons, Troubadours and Minstrels* Paper presented at the RSA Start Right Conference, London, September 1995.

Sylva, K., Roy C., and Painter, M. (1980) *Childwatching at Playgroup and Nursery School* London: Grant McIntyre.

Sylva. K., Melhuish, E., Sammons, P. and Siraj-Blatchford, I. (1996) *Effective Provision of Preschool Education* London: Institute of Education, University of London.

Sylwander, L. (1996) Why we need an Ombudsman for children. In Council of Europe *The Child as Citizen*. Strasbourg: Council of Europe.

Taba, H. and Elzey, F.F. (1964) Teaching strategies and thought processes *Teachers College Record* 65, pp.524–34.

Tannen, D. (1990) *You Just Don't Understand: Women and Men in Conversation* London: Virago Press.

Taylor, P.H., Exon, G. and Holley, B. (1972) *A Study of Nursery Education* London: Evans/Methuen Educational.

Tharp, R.G. and Gallimore, R. (1988) *Rousing Minds to Life: Teaching, Learning and Schooling in Social Context* Cambridge: Cambridge University Press.

The Economist (1997) Education and the wealth of nations: Leader *The Economist* 29 March, pp.17–18 and pp.25–7.

The Times (1995) Editorial: Three kind mice. *The Times* 12 September.

Therborn, G. (1996) Child politics. *Childhood* 3, 1, pp.29–44.

Thompson, I. (1995) The role of counting in the idiosyncrataic mental calculation algorithms of young children *European Early Childhood Education Research Journal* 3, 1, pp.5–16.

Thompson, I. (1997) *Teaching and Learning Early Number.* Milton Keynes: Open University Press.

Thompson, L. (1993) Time well spent or *du temps perdu? European Early Childhood Education Research Journal* 1, 2, pp.39–50.

Thompson, L. (1994) Making friends: a social network analysis of peer relations in multilingual kindergarten. Paper presented at the Fourth European Early Childhood Education Conference, 1–3 September, Gothenburg, Sweden. Available on ERIC Document Reproduction Service, Washington, DC, USA. Reference No. ED 391 386, p.37.

Thompson, L. (1995) The Cleveland project: a study of bilingual children in a nursery *Journal of Multilingual and Multicultural Development* 3, 1 pp.5–16.

Thompson, L. (1996) School ties: a social network analysis of friendships within a multicultural kindergarten *European Early Childhood Education Research Journal* 4, 1, pp.49–69.

Thompson, L. (1999) *Young Bilingual Learners in Nursery School* Clevedon: Multilingual Matters

Times Educational Supplement (1998) Editorial: Not drowning by numbers: 20 March, p. 20.

Tizard, B. (1974a) *Early Childhood Education* Windsor: NFER.

Tizard, B. (1974b) *Pre-School Research in Great Britain: A Research Review* London: Social Science Research Council.

Tizard, B. (1990) Educational research and educational policy: ss there a link? The Ninth Vernon-Wall Lecture, The Educational Section Annual Conference of The British Psychological Society.

Tizard, B. and Hughes, M. (1984) *Young Children Learning, Talking and Thinking at Home and at School* London: Fontana.

Tizard, B., Blatchford, P., Burke, J., Farquahar, C. and Plewis, I. (1988) *Young Children at School in the Inner City* London: Lawrence Erlbaum.

Tizard, B., Carmichael, H.M. and Pinkerton, G. (1980) Four year olds talking to mothers and teachers. In L.A. Hersov and A.R. Nichol (Eds) *Language and Language Disorders in Childhood* Oxford: Pergamon Press.

Tolnay, S. and Crowder, K. (1999) Regional origin and family stability in Northern cities: the role of context *American Sociological Review* February, 64, 1, pp.97–112.

Tooley, J. (1998) *Educational Research: A Critique* London: OFSTED.

Tough, J. (1976) *Listening to Children Talking: A Guide to the Appraisal of Children's Use of Language* London: Ward Lock.

Trevarthen, C. (1992) An infant's motives for speaking and thinking in the culture. In A.H. Wold (Ed.) *The Dialogical Alternative* Oxford: Oxford University Press.

Trow, M. (1998) American perspectives on British higher education under Thatcher and Major *Oxford Review of Education* 24, 1, p.111–29.

Tschudin, V. (1994) *Ethics: Education and Research* Middlesex: Scutari Press.

Tunstall, P. and Gipps, C. (1996) Teacher feedback to young children in formative assessment: a typology *British Educational Research Journal* 22, 4, pp. 389–404.

Turner, I.F. (1977) Preschool Playgroups Research and Evaluation Project. Final Report submitted to the Government of Northern Ireland, Department of Health and Social Services. Department of Psychology, the Queens University, Belfast. Cited by D. Wood, L. McMahon and Y. Cranstoun (1980) *Working with Under Fives* London: Grant McIntyre.

Tymms, P. (1996) *Baseline assessment and value-added: A report to the School Curriculum and Assessment Authority* London: SCAA.

Tymms, P. (1997) Monitoring the progress of children during their first years at school: Current research in early childhood *OMEP Updates,* Summer, 90, pp.1–2.

Tymms, P. (1998) Starting school: a response to Chris Whetton, Caroline Sharp and Dougal Hutchison *Educational Research* 40, 1, pp.69–71.

Tymms, P. (1999) Baseline assessment, value-added and the prediction of reading *Journal of Research in Reading* 222, 1, pp.27–36.

Tymms, P., Merrell, C. and Henderson, B. (1997) The first year at school: a quantitative investigation of the attainment and progress of pupils *Educational Research and Evaluation* 3, 2, pp.101–18.

Tymms, P., Merrell, C. and Henderson, B. (1997) Baseline assessment and progress during the first three years at school *Educational Research and Evaluation.*3, 101– 108.

Tzouriadou, M., Barbas, G. and Bonti, E. (1999) The standardization of the Utrecht Early Mathematical Competence Test in Greece. Symposium contribution at ERLI 1999, Göteborg, Sweden.

UNICEF (1996) *The State of the World's Children 1995* New York: UNICEF.

United Nations (1989) *The Convention on the Rights of the Child* New York: UNICEF.

US National Academy of Science (1992) *Research and Education Reform* Washington DC, National Academy Press.

Usher, R. and Edwards, R. (1994) *Postmodernism and Education* London: Routlege.

Utting, D. (1995) *Family and Parenthood: Supporting Families, Preventing Breakdown* York: Joseph Rowntree Foundation.

van den Heuvel-Panhuizen, M. (1996) *Assessment and Realistic Mathematics Education* Utrecht: CD-β Press.

van den Oord, E. and Rispens, J. (1999) Differences between school classes in preschoolers' psychosocial adjustment: evidence or the importance of children's interpersonal relations *Journal of Child Psychology and Psychiatry and Allied Disciplines* 40, 3 pp. 417–30.

Van der Rijt, B. and Van Luit, J. (1998) Development of early numeracy in Europe. Paper at European Conference on Educational Research, Llubljana 17–20 September.

Van de Rijt, B. and Van Luit, J. (1999) Development of early numeracy in Europe. Paper from the Poster Symposium, EARLI Conference, University of Utrecht Gothenburg.

Van de Rijt, B., Van Luit, J. and Pennings, J. (1999) The Construction of the Utrecht Early Mathematical Competence Scales *Educational and Psychological Measurement* 59, pp. 289–309.

Vasta, R. (1993) *Six Theories of Child Development: Revised Formulations and Current Issues* London: Jessica Kingsley.

von Bertalanffy, L. (1968) *General Systems Theory* New York: George Braziller.

von Bertalanffy, L. (1978) *Perspectives on General Systems Theory* Cambridge: Harvard University Press.

Vygotsky, L.S. (1987) *Collected Works of L.S. Vygotsky: Vol. 1, Problems of General Psychology* (translated by N. Minick) New York: Plenum Press (Original work published 1982 in Russian).

Wade, B. and Moore, M. (1996) Home activities: the advent of literacy *European Early Childhood Education Research Journal*, 4, 2 pp. 63–76.

Walker, R. (1985) *Doing Research: A Handbook for Teachers* London: Methuen.

Watson, D. and Taylor, R. (1988) *Life Long Learning and the University: A Post-Dearing Agenda* London: The Falmer Press.

Wells, G. (1978) What makes for success in language development? In R. Campbell and P. Smith (Eds) *Advances in the Psychology of Language* New York: Plenum. Vol. 111, 4a, pp.449–69.

Wells, G. (1981a) Language at Home and School. Newsletter of *Child Development Society*, 30.

Wells, G. (1981b) *Learning Through Interaction: The Study of Language Development* Cambridge: Cambridge University Press.

Wells, G. (1985) *Language, Learning and Education* Windsor: NFER-Nelson.

Wertsch, J.V., Minick, N. and Flavio, J.A., (1984) The creation of joint contexts in problem-solving. In B. Rogoff and J. Lave (Eds) *Everyday Cognition: Its Development in Social Context* Cambridge, Mass: Harvard University Press.

West, A. and Varlaam, A. (1992) Educational provision for four-year-olds *Research Papers in Education* 6, 2l, pp.99–131.

Wheldall, K. and Merrett, F. (1984) *Positive Teaching: The Behavioural Approach* London: Paul Chapman.

Whitburn, J. (1996) Contrasting approaches to the acquisition of mathematical skills: Japan and England *Oxford Review of Education* 22, 4, pp.415–34.

Whiting, B. and Whiting, J. (1975) *Children of Six Cultures* Cambridge, MA: Harvard University Press.

Wilkinson, R.G. (1994) *Unfair Shares* London: Barnardos.

Wilson, R. (1998) *Special Educational Needs in the Early Years* London: Routledge.

Wood, D. J., Brunner, J.S. and Ross, G. (1976) The role of tutoring in problem-solving *Journal of Child Psychology and Psychiatry* 17, 2, pp. 89–100

Wood, D., McMahon, L., and Cranstoun, Y. (1980) *Working with Under Fives* London: Grant McIntyre.

Wragg, E. (1986) Editorial *Research Papers in Education* 1,1 p. 3.

Wragg, E., Oates, J. and Gump, P. (1976) *Classroom Interaction* (E201 Educational Studies Handbook: Personality and Learning) Milton Keynes: Open University Press.

Zeichner, K., Liston, D., Mahlios, M. and Gomez, M. (1987) The structure and goals of a student teaching program and the character and quality of supervisory discourse *Teaching and Teacher Education* 3, 4, pp. 349–62.

Index